Peace Entrepreneurs and Social Entrepreneurship

To my grandkids, Galia, Noah and Yuval with endless love and wishes for meaningful and insightful lives.
Amalya Oliver-Lumerman

To my beloved Yehuda, Jonathan and Mika, may you live in peace.
Tammar B. Zilber

To those who inspired it and will not read it. To those who inspired it and are not here with us. My grandparents: Fatima, Ahmad, Amina and Muhammad.
Haneen Sameer Magadlah

To my father, Leopold, and my grandmother, Rachel, who taught me about caring, responsibility and courage. I will always love and remember you.
Tammy Rubel-Lifschitz

To my kids, Avishag-Miryam, Ariel and Halleli-Naomi. As your grandfather, George Calif, used to bless you every Friday night: Depart from evil, and do good. Seek peace and pursue it.
Yosepha Tabib-Calif

Peace Entrepreneurs and Social Entrepreneurship

Life Stories from Israelis and Palestinians

Amalya Oliver-Lumerman
Professor of Organizational Sociology, Department of Sociology and Anthropology, Hebrew University of Jerusalem, Israel

Tammar B. Zilber
Professor of Organization Theory, Jerusalem School of Business, Hebrew University of Jerusalem, Israel

Haneen Sameer Magadlah
Faculty member, Department of Educational Studies, Al-Qasemi Academic College of Education, Baqa Algrbiah, Israel

Tammy Rubel-Lifschitz
Lecturer, Department of Sociology and Anthropology, Hebrew University of Jerusalem, Israel

Yosepha Tabib-Calif
Faculty member, Department of Educational Studies, David Yellin Academic College of Education, and teaching fellow, School of Education, Hebrew University of Jerusalem, Israel

 Edward Elgar
PUBLISHING

Cheltenham, UK • Northampton, MA, USA

Published by
Edward Elgar Publishing Limited
The Lypiatts
15 Lansdown Road
Cheltenham
Glos GL50 2JA
UK

Edward Elgar Publishing, Inc.
William Pratt House
9 Dewey Court
Northampton
Massachusetts 01060
USA

Paperback edition 2023

A catalogue record for this book
is available from the British Library

Library of Congress Control Number: 2021943596

This book is available electronically in the **Elgar**online
Business subject collection
http://dx.doi.org/10.4337/9781789906295

MIX
Paper | Supporting
responsible forestry
FSC
www.fsc.org   FSC® C013604

ISBN 978 1 78990 628 8 (cased)
ISBN 978 1 78990 629 5 (eBook)
ISBN 978 1 0353 1555 0 (paperback)

Printed and bound by CPI Group (UK) Ltd, Croydon, CR0 4YY

Contents

Contributors

AUTHORS

Amalya Oliver-Lumerman is in the Department of Sociology and Anthropology at the Hebrew University of Jerusalem, Israel.

Tammar B. Zilber is in the Jerusalem School of Business at the Hebrew University of Jerusalem, Israel.

Haneen Sameer Magadlah is in the Department of Educational Studies at the Al-Qasemi Academic College of Education, Israel.

Tammy Rubel-Lifschitz is in the Department of Sociology and Anthropology at the Hebrew University of Jerusalem, Israel.

Yosepha Tabib-Calif is in the Department of Educational Studies at David Yellin Academic College of Education and the School of Education at the Hebrew University of Jerusalem, Israel.

INTERVIEWERS

The following people contributed to this book by interviewing and doing the initial, technical editing of the life stories in this book. They were all research students in different disciplines at the Hebrew University, involved with the Hoffman Leadership and Responsibility Program:

Einat Walter

Lital Myers

Nechumi Yaffe

Roni Mikel Arieli

Shakked Lubotzky

Vered Zioni-Koren

Yoni Yahav

Introduction: peace entrepreneurship, life narratives, and the Israeli-Palestinian conflict

Amalya Oliver-Lumerman, Yosepha Tabib-Calif, Tammar B. Zilber, Tammy Rubel-Lifschitz, and Haneen Sameer Magadlah

Imagine a group of 30 doctoral students, fellows in the program dedicated to leadership and social responsibility, listening to two speakers – Hadassah Froman and Khaled Abu Awwad, a Jewish woman and a Palestinian man – who came to talk about themselves and their collaborative peace initiative. They shared their incredible life narratives with us, telling about painful events and endless struggles coupled with significant insights and discoveries. Together they founded ROOTS, "A unique network of local Palestinians and Israelis who have come to see each other as the partners we both need to make changes to end our conflict. Based on a mutual recognition of each People's connection to the Land, we are developing understanding and solidarity despite our ideological differences" (www.friendsofroots.net/about). We were moved and fascinated, quiet, and focused until they finished talking. This book originated in that meeting, as we felt motivated to share the voices and stories of these and other brave and unique people and their painful and inspiring journeys. This book presents the life stories of 11 peace entrepreneurs in their own voice. The events described in this book were analyzed as part of a personal, subjective construction of identity and meaning, rather than as an historical documentation of past events.

Despite the ongoing bitter conflict between Israel and the Palestinians, there are still those who believe in the possibility of peace and dedicate their lives to advance activities that may bring peace to the region. These people are a mystery to us. They are dedicated and committed and are fearless fighters for peace by initiating various peace-related ventures and activities. We titled them 'Peace entrepreneurs' because they all created peace-related ventures, at times alone and at times with others. Also, similar to business entrepreneurial ventures which face a low survival rate, peace entrepreneurial ventures also

1

struggle for survival. Their survival is dependent on resources, support, commitment of active members and issues of social legitimacy.

In this book, we approach 'peace entrepreneurs' as a sub-category of social entrepreneurs, and focus on peace entrepreneurs as people committed to establish a social venture with the aim of promoting peace activities in a context of extreme intergroup conflict. We use a life narrative approach to study peace entrepreneurs in the context of the Israeli-Palestinian conflict.

We start this chapter with a short review of the literature about entrepreneurship and social entrepreneurship and then discuss peace entrepreneurship. As this concept is sporadically used, we define the main parameters associated with it and the challenges we see in the effort to clarify its domain. After laying out the life story approach we used in our empirical study, we present the case we explored – the Israeli-Palestinian conflict, and how we approached and interviewed the impressive peace entrepreneurs whose stories we will share in the main part of the book.

THEORIES OF ENTREPRENEURSHIP

The literature on entrepreneurship is broad and diverse, yet there is little agreement on how entrepreneurship should be defined and what should be the main parameters to study it (Anderson and Starnawska, 2008).

To offer a short review of the literature, one may group the existing literature into four broad approaches. The first and early one is the trait approach (Low and MacMillan, 1988) that focuses on the individual-level study of the psychological traits of entrepreneurs. Studies refer to the psychological characteristics of entrepreneurs, such as a high need for achievement, risk-taking, or internal locus of control. These person-centric studies claimed, for example, that people with a greater preference for uncertainty chose to be entrepreneurs. However, only those personality traits that were related to the task of the entrepreneur were found to be associated with success (Rauch and Frese, 2007). Venkataraman (1997) claims that initial theories of entrepreneurship were dominated by the effort to explain entrepreneurship as resulting from the types of people engaged in entrepreneurial activity. This, he argues, ensued in overlooking the role of opportunities in entrepreneurship.

The second approach moves from the individual entrepreneur to the venture and focuses on studying successful strategies of new and existing business ventures. Gartner, in a highly cited paper (1988) titled "'Who is an entrepreneur?' is the wrong question," claims that entrepreneurship is the creation of an organization coupled with a set of additional parameters. He suggests a behavioral approach to entrepreneurship rather than the trait approach that was used in the past. Martin and Osberg (2007, p. 30), for example, highlight three main parameters of entrepreneur/venture behavior: a sense of opportunity, creative thinking, and determination to bring about something new.

The third approach to entrepreneurship is again on the venture level. It focuses on the formations of new entrepreneurial ventures, yet it details a broader range of features related to the entrepreneur and the venture. This is evident in another paper by Gartner (1990), in which he discusses the main characteristics of entrepreneurs and incorporates issues related to the formation of the entrepreneurial venture. According to his findings, entrepreneurship is positioned between the themes of entrepreneurs (e.g. individuals with a unique personality and abilities), innovation (e.g. the ability to do something new), organization creation (e.g. the behavior involving the creation of a new organization), creating value (e.g. entrepreneurship creating additional and new value) and uniqueness (e.g. it must involve uniqueness).

Finally, the fourth approach incorporates both the individual and the venture levels and highlights the impact of the environment on the entrepreneur and the venture. In this context, Shane and Venkataraman (2000, p. 218), in a highly cited and critical article, state that:

> Perhaps the largest obstacle in creating a conceptual framework for the entrepreneurship field has been its definition. To date, most researchers have defined the field solely in terms of who the entrepreneur is and what he or she does. The problem with this approach is that entrepreneurship involves the nexus of two phenomena: the presence of lucrative opportunities and the presence of enterprising individuals.

Thus, they argue that the field of entrepreneurship should be defined by both the individual entrepreneur and the opportunity he/she detects and operates on. The discovery of an opportunity is only a necessary condition for entrepreneurship, yet, not a sufficient one. Following the detection of an opportunity, a nascent entrepreneur needs to decide to exploit the detected opportunity.

This fourth approach takes a field perspective (Bruyat and Julien, 2001) and claims that the definition should incorporate the environmental conditions favorable to the entrepreneurial act. Bruyat and Julien (2001) argue that entrepreneurship should be examined as "the dialogic between individual and new value creation, within an ongoing process and within an environment that has specific characteristics" (2001, p. 165). In this approach, an entrepreneur is a person who has the capabilities of creating, learning, and influencing the environment in which he/she operates.

In sum, to understand entrepreneurship, it is crucial to learn about the interrelations between the entrepreneur, the entrepreneurial venture, and the environment over time (Bruyat and Julien, 2001). Also, we need to understand the nature of the opportunity (Shane and Venkataraman, 2000) explored and appropriated by the entrepreneur. Such entrepreneurial opportunities vary on several dimensions, and these affect their values. We adopt this comprehensive approach in this book, yet in our context, we do not focus on the economic gains and success of entrepreneurship, but rather on social ones.

SOCIAL ENTREPRENEURSHIP

Austin et al. (2006) distinguish between two types of entrepreneurship. The first type is 'commercial entrepreneurship,' and it represents the identification, evaluation, and exploitation of opportunities. These opportunities can generate profits. The second type is 'social entrepreneurship,' which refers to identifying, evaluating, and exploiting opportunities that result in social value. Peace entrepreneurship, the focus of this book, belongs to this second category.

Despite the fragmentation of the literature on social entrepreneurship (Dacin et al., 2010, 2011), we find parallels to the four perspectives in the general research on entrepreneurship. Research that focuses on the individual social entrepreneur suggests that social entrepreneurs are unique path-breakers (Galera and Borzaga, 2009) or value creators (Mair and Noboa, 2006). The second approach focuses on the entrepreneur's behavior and explores the motives, search processes for goals and activities, and the ethical challenges social entrepreneurs confront (Zahra et al., 2009). The third approach focuses on the venture formation as related to the intentions of the social entrepreneur (Certo and Miller, 2008; Mair and Noboa, 2006) and focuses on how the preferences of the social entrepreneur are transformed into the selection of opportunities and the establishment of the social enterprise.

Finally, the fourth approach integrates the entrepreneur, the venture, and the context – be it the field or environment where the social enterprise is established. Recent work on social entrepreneurship (e.g. Mair and Noboa, 2006; Mair and Marti, 2006) claims that the context – the ongoing relations between the social entrepreneur and the environment – shapes the formation of the social enterprise. In other words, social entrepreneurs are actors that react to the context within which they operate and in which they are embedded (Weerawardena and Mort, 2006). The context can range from a sense of grievance of a neglected or abused group that needs support and correction to the urge to form new interaction opportunities between balkanized sub-groups.

PEACE ENTREPRENEURSHIP

The concept of 'peace entrepreneurs' was used in the past with different foci. Forrer (2010), for example, refers to peace entrepreneurship through categorizing business practices "according to a continuum in reference to conflict zones. On one end of the continuum lies conflict sustaining practices ... The midway point is described as coping/survival practices ... At the other end of the continuum are conflict-reducing practices (e.g. peace entrepreneurship activities)" (p. 450). Thus, for Forrer, peace entrepreneurship ranges from conflict-sustaining to coping practices, and to conflict-reducing practices.

Another perspective is offered by Lehrs (2016, p. 381), who refers to "Private peace entrepreneurs" as private citizens who do not have an official authority yet initiate diplomatic meetings with official representatives from the two sides of the conflict to promote any form of resolution. Thus, this perspective focuses mainly on the conflict resolution aspect of peace entrepreneurship.

Subedi (2013) offers another definition. In his account, "A pro-peace entrepreneur ideally possesses resources, capacity, self-interest, willingness, and commitment to work for peace, therefore has significant potential to contribute to peacebuilding" (p. 193). This definition offers many degrees of freedom for characterizing peace-related entrepreneurial ventures.

In this book, we extend Subedi's definition, while taking a narrower approach, focusing the definition of peace entrepreneurship on conflict-reducing practices and aim for resolution. By peace entrepreneurs, we refer to a specific group of social entrepreneurs *who possess a willingness and commitment to operate in the peace and conflict resolution domain by establishing social ventures with the aim of facilitating or promoting peace-related activities and applying conflict resolution strategies and practices, all within a broader context of conflict*. Thus, our approach to peace entrepreneurship focuses on the individual entrepreneur, his/her peace-facilitating or promoting venture, and the environmental context of the conflict within which these efforts may create social value.

A triangle of relations – between the individual, organizational, and contextual aspects – constitutes the construct of peace entrepreneurship (Figure 0.1). We conceptualize the individual aspect as life narratives, including the main life events that lead to the commitment and the urge to become a 'peace entrepreneur.' The organizational element relates to the peace-related venture, with all the choices made to shape its form and activities, including the creative opportunity, the forms of exploitation, and the value creation of the venture. The context includes both the external, seemingly objective environment, and the way the entrepreneur perceives it. In doing so, we integrate insights offered by the theories of business entrepreneurship and social entrepreneurship discussed above. We refine the focus of the definition and future research to include both the entrepreneur's life narrative and the entrepreneurial venture, and their interrelations, grounded in context.

Despite the recent growing interest in social entrepreneurs, we have to date very little evidence on how their personal narratives are associated with their social entrepreneurial ventures. To fill this gap, we take a distinctly interpretive approach to social entrepreneurship (Packard, 2017), specifically one that focuses on the role of life narratives as identity (Ochs and Capps, 1996). Such

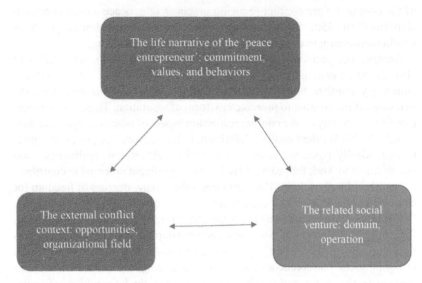

Figure 0.1   *The construct of peace entrepreneurship as composed of the*
               life narrative, the features of the peace-related social venture,
               and the internal and external context

a narrative[1] approach helps us shift the inquiry "from entrepreneurship as an
act to entrepreneurship as a journey" (McMullen and Dimov, 2013, p. 1481).
In other words, the entrepreneur's identity is associated with the entrepreneurial venture established through the opportunity chosen and the actions taken.

LIFE STORIES AND THE NARRATIVE APPROACH

To better understand how peace entrepreneurs come into being, how they
operate, and how they remain optimistic and active despite their conflict-laden
field of action, we use a narrative approach. We collected and analyzed life
stories of people who have devoted a significant part of their life to establishing social-oriented ventures to promote peace between the Israelis and the
Palestinians. In the following section, we present the primary principles of our
narrative approach.

First, traditional approaches view identity as fixed and static. A narrative
perspective is different as it relates to identity as continually changing. Identity
is the ongoing stories people tell about themselves and others, by which narrators construct the essence of 'who they are.' Narrators are active agents in
shaping their identity. People do not have a single, absolute version of their life

story, but different and even contradictory versions, expressing the multiple aspects of their identity (Ochs and Capps, 1996).

Second, according to a narrative approach, identity stories are not based on objective reality but are social constructions (Lieblich et al., 1995). As an interpretive being, the narrator narrates her life story out of a desire to produce for herself, as well as for others, an internally and temporally coherent story (Bruner, 1987, 1990). The stories told by the narrator do not represent historical truth but rather a narrative one. In that sense, the life story is not an accurate reflection of objective reality, but the product of selection and choice (Spector-Mersel, 2011). The narrator chooses what, when, and how to narrate his story, what to bring to the forefront of the story, what to leave behind the scenes, where to begin the story, and where to conclude it. According to this view, the narrator has the freedom to create and organize the events of her life, including choices that the narrator is not necessarily aware of. Therefore, the way she tells her life story is not a coincidental collection of events, but rather an articulation of the meaning her reality has for her (Bruner, 1986).

This focus on narrative construction integrates nicely with a process-as-narrative perspective within the study of social entrepreneurs (Van de Ven and Engleman, 2004, p. 345). Specifically, it integrates with Morgeson et al. (2015), who focus on life events as significant roadblocks in social entrepreneurs' development. According to Morgeson et al. (2015), significant life events are encounters between 'entities' including individuals (for example, parents, siblings, friends, teachers, etc.) and organizations or social groups (for example, school, funding agencies, social circle based on ethnic, religious, ideological denominators). Such events have a discrete nature that is different from stable flow or regular, repeating routines. They are bounded in space and time, and they grasp the attention of the focal person. When accounting for their lives – to others or themselves – narrators choose which events and sub-stories to include in their life story (Spector-Mersel, 2011). These are significant building blocks of life experiences, and they play an important role in affecting memories, thoughts, expectations, and motivations. Those events and sub-stories included in the narrated life story are deemed important enough and serve as focal points for sense-making (Morgeson et al., 2015) – the story itself. As such, they may offer insights regarding the 'critical incidents' that shaped the entrepreneur and his or her activity (Cope and Watts, 2000).

Third, the narrated stories are created through dialogue between the narrator/s and the audience (as temporary and changing roles). The changing meanings the narrator gives her identities should also be understood through the context in which the story is told: to whom the story is told, in which context, who else listens to it, etc.

Fourth, the personal story is not a product of the narrator's individual reflections and constructions alone. Like any other individual story, the life story is

always grounded in collective memory, interpretive schemes, cultural reper-
toires, and shared metanarratives (Lieblich et al., 1995; Lomsky-Feder, 2004;
Lomsky-Feder and Sasson-Levy, 2016; Zilber et al., 2008). Every personal
life story also echoes the stories of members of the same group that are related
to the social standing and status of the individual within it (Tuval-Mashiach
and Spector-Mersel, 2010). Without these social contexts, the story itself is
meaningless.

USING LIFE STORIES TO EXPLORE PEACE ENTREPRENEURSHIP

In the context of entrepreneurship, life narratives make sense of the entrepreneur's life (Downing, 2005). They link aspects of people's interactions that are
significant in the formation and development of the entrepreneurial experience.
Despite the growing application of the life story methodology to study social
entrepreneurship in recent years, the literature is still somewhat limited. Some
studies have used this approach to better understand entrepreneurs' motives,
inspirations, challenges, and difficulties through their own perspective. For
example, Christopoulos and Vogl (2015), Germak and Robinson (2014), and
Yitshaki and Kropp (2016a) used life story methodology to inquire into social
entrepreneurs' motivations, opportunity recognition, and prosocial activities
that are shaped by their life experiences. Yitshaki and Kropp (2016b) explore
the role of passion and identity in social entrepreneurs' life stories compared
to high-tech entrepreneurs.

The literature in the specific context of peace initiatives is even more limited.
Some extra-academic initiatives have tried to connect peace entrepreneurship
and life stories. One is justvision.org, where you can find in-depth interviews
with Israeli and Palestinian peace activists. The organization also produces
films that document nonviolent struggles by entrepreneurs and attempts to
promote peace. Another project is called *Sixty Years, Sixty Voices*, edited by
Patricia Smith Melton (2008). It offers short interviews with Palestinian and
Israeli women, focusing on the gender lens. These projects and others try to
give voice and face to peace activists, highlighting the complexity of life in
a conflict zone, on both sides of the conflict, even though the power relations
between them are asymmetric. The present book continues this approach by
offering a more in-depth look into the lives of peace entrepreneurs, tracing the
inspirations that motivate people to act in such a challenging field.

To conclude this section, our main interest is in understanding what makes
a peace entrepreneur. We will identify the significant events that constitute
peace entrepreneurs' life stories and use them as focal points to exploring
the individual- and venture-level stories constructed around them. On the
individual level, we will aim to understand how peace entrepreneurs describe

the early stages in their life where they decide to commit to peace-related activities. How do these decisions evolve, and who are the significant others in their journey? How do they react to various challenges? What are the rewards and feedback that encourage them to continue operating? We will also explore how the individual-level stories connect to the venture-level stories. Finally, we will also explore what role peace entrepreneurs ascribe to the environment and their interrelations with it.

NARRATIVES OF THE ISRAELI-PALESTINIAN CONFLICT

The Israeli-Palestinian conflict is an ongoing struggle over a small piece of land that both peoples inhabit. Describing and analyzing this intractable conflict is a sensitive and explosive endeavor, as almost every seemingly historical 'fact,' let alone its interpretation, is disputed as part of the conflict itself. The two peoples hold very different – in fact, quite similar yet opposite – narratives of the historical claims for the land, and the roots of the conflict over it, while each side assigns the other nation as the villain and itself as a victim (Adwan et al., 2016; Assmann, 2018; Bar-On and Adwan, 2009; Kacowicz, 2005). Thus, it is almost impossible to offer a balanced account that escapes a judgmental or biased perspective.

The different national narratives are echoed in academic research as well. The specific paradigm chosen to organize this land's history and politics determines which national story is eventually heard. In this short introduction, we follow a critical paradigm (e.g. Kimmerling, 1983; Kimmerling and Migdal, 2003) that is relatively more open to encompass both sides. It also fits well with our inclusive life-story methodology, as it allows us to capture various 'voices' of activists from the field. Thus, it offers a more complicated and nuanced depiction of the conflict, away from the dichotomous narratives that dominate the public discourse on both sides.

Clearly, even with our inclusive approach, all choices involved in describing the Israeli and the Palestinian narratives are loaded with symbolic and political meanings and implications. For example, this is true concerning the conflict's historical roots (e.g. Morris, 2001). Some set the origins of the conflict at the establishment of the State of Israel in 1948. Here we have two opposing narratives. This founding event marks a great victory and achievement for the Jewish people, having an independent state after many generations in exile. Yet, it is termed by the Palestinians as the 'al-Nakba,' meaning catastrophe or disaster, as it involved the displacement of many of the Palestinian people who inhabited the land and fled – or were forced to leave – to neighboring Arab countries (Abu-Lughod and Sa' di, 2007).

Some will set the starting date of the conflict earlier, with the Zionist movement, its early nation-building efforts in Europe, and the gradual return to (or, in the Palestinian version: migration) and settlement of Jews in Eretz Israel/ Palestine during the late nineteenth century. Yet others will attribute much importance to the 1967 war (or the Six Day war as termed by the Israeli Jews). During this war, Israel occupied, or freed (again – alternative narratives), the West Bank, East Jerusalem, and the Gaza Strip, as well as the Sinai Desert (later returned or given back by Israel to Egypt as part of a peace agreement in 1979) and the Golan Heights. During the 1967 war, many more Palestinians fled or were forced to leave their homes.

Alongside the disputed timeline, the scope of the geopolitical background and context needed to understand the conflict is also disputed (e.g. Owen, 2013). Some see its roots as part of power struggles between colonial forces, which used this Middle Eastern land as part of their 'resources' in their dealings. Others situate it in the broader relations between various Arab countries, some of which directly border Israel (Egypt, Jordan, and Syria) and others further away yet very influential (e.g. Iran, Iraq, and Saudi Arabia).

The very definition of 'Palestinians' or 'Palestinian Arabs' is also contested and political (Rabinowitz, 2001). It may refer to those who reside in the Gaza Strip and the West Bank, territories occupied by Israel during the 1967 war, who have no citizenship rights in Israel and may live under the Palestinian authority rule. Some use the same label to include some or all Arabs who live within the territories of Israel. The latter group are Israeli citizens and are characterized as Arab-Israelis or Palestinian-Israelis or 1948 Arabs.

Even material aspects of the conflict are controversial. Material issues such as how big is the land and how many people populate it are disputed. Indeed, the spatial and demographic counters of the conflict are hard to grasp (Ben-Ze'ev and Yvroux, 2018). Cartographic and population figures are also a political endeavor (Leuenberger and Schnell, 2020; Wallach, 2011). Still, the most common counts (according to the Israeli Central Bureau of Statistics, 2018 and the Palestinian Central Bureau of Statistics, 2018) is that Israel rules 22,145 km² (8550 square miles; including Jerusalem, the Golam Heights, and parts of the West Bank). In this space live 8.7 million Israelis (25 percent of them are Muslim-Arabs, Christian-Arabs, or Druze). The Palestinian Authority rules over 5655 km² (2183 square miles) and 2.9 million people in the West Bank. The Gaza Strip, formally under Palestinian Authority rule, is de facto ruled by one of the Palestinian factions, Hamas. It is estimated that in the space of 365 km² (141 square miles) live some 1.9 million people.

The conflict between Israelis and Palestinians involves civilians directly on both sides. Each community lives according to an 'ethos of conflict' (Bar-Tal, 2007).

> [The conflict] occupies a central position in public discourse and the public agenda, supplies information and experiences that compel society members to construct an adaptable worldview, is a determinative factor in the selection of lines of behaviors, continuously shapes the lives of the involved societies, and imprints upon every aspect of individual and collective life. (Halperin, 2014, p. 69)

The similar structure of the two peoples' narratives stems from the fact they are engaged in competition over scarce resources. Both assume that one party's presence prevents the very existence of the other and that coexistence is impossible (Maoz, 2000). During the long struggle between Israelis and Palestinians, both sides have suffered tremendous losses in human lives, injuries, destruction, and economic resources. Still, these narratives exist within an asymmetric power relation. Within Israel, the Jewish majority (some 75 percent of the population) is in control of most material and political resources and determines the country's national character (Abu-Nimer, 1999; Rabinowitz and Abu-Baker, 2005). The unequal relationship between Arabs and Jews living in Israel, all Israeli citizens, is reflected in many dimensions, among them in education (Feniger et al., 2015; Golan-Agnon, 2006), health (Saabneh, 2016) and healthcare (Baron-Epel et al., 2007), economic status (Semyonov and Lewin-Epstein, 2011), work experiences (Shoshana, 2016), language use and teaching (Or and Shohamy, 2016), and stereotypical depictions (Bar-Tal, 1996). There is also a significantly asymmetrical relationship between the State of Israel and the Palestinians living in the West Bank and the Gaza Strip territories. Israel continues to occupy lands heavily inhabited by the Palestinians and settle Jews in these disputed territories.

Given all the national, religious, social, cultural, political, and psychological dimensions of the conflict, Israelis and Palestinians are caught up within an intractable conflict (Bar-Tal, 2007; Kriesberg, 1993). One aspect of the conflict between the two peoples is the harsh and fierce disagreements within each society regarding the desired solution. Political, religious, and social divisions within the Israeli and the Palestinian people complicate even negotiating a deal between the two nations.

Yet, history teaches that even such conflict, involving collective identities and grounded within power relations, can be resolved (Kriesberg, 1993). Such resolutions require efforts on both the political level and on the collective and individual socio-psychological levels (Bar-Tal, 2000a). Indeed, throughout the conflict, there were various attempts at reconciliation and peacemaking. On the governmental, formal diplomacy level, there were numerous initiatives to bring the two nations together, spearheaded by the United Nations, United States, and European countries. All such attempts failed eventually in striking the final deal and bringing real peace, most recently, the Oslo Accords between Israel and the Palestinian Liberation Organization (1993), and the negotiations at Camp David (2000) and Taba (2001) (Kacowicz, 2005; Salinas and Abu Rabi, 2009).

There are two possible solutions on the table – a 'two-state' and a 'one-state' solution. According to the two-state solution, Israel will return to its pre-1967 borders, and the rest of the land will be an independent Palestinian State. Within this framework, still open to further negotiations, are the fate of Jerusalem and some heavily populated Israeli settlements. Other solutions, such as the 'One State' or 'A Land for All,'[2] on the other hand, call for both people to live under one integrated government in all the land. In the meanwhile, and along the many years of the conflict, international financial aid supports the Palestinians in the West Bank and Gaza (e.g. Brynen, 2000).

Beyond the formal peace negotiations, there were also bottom-up peace initiatives. Within both Israeli and Palestinian societies, there have been many grass-roots attempts to bring the people together (Hallward, 2011; Kuriansky, 2007), chiefly through political movements (Hermann, 2009; Svirsky, 2012), Jewish-Arab encounters, and the Peace Education Movement (track two diplomacy) (Bekerman, 2018; Kahanoff, 2016; Maoz, 2011). Yet these attempts are also fraught with ambivalence and conflict, both on the individual and at the social movement levels (Rosenwasser, 1995; Thiessen and Darweish, 2018), and so far have not brought large-scale change. Recent studies in both nations expose the deep suspicion, distrust, and fears both peoples have towards each other (Halperin, 2014, 2016). There seems to be a general sense of pessimism about the future of the conflict (Leshem, 2017). Despite this pessimism, there are activists who are still committed to the conflict resolution process.

WHO ARE WE? OUR STORY

This book grew out of the Hoffman Leadership and Responsibility Program at the Hebrew University of Jerusalem. The Hoffman Program was started more than a decade ago by Amalya Oliver with a generous donation from the Hoffman family. The program's goal was to support doctoral students with excellent academic achievements committed to social responsibility issues and volunteering in social projects. This is the second book by the Hoffman Program to be published. The first, *Social Leaders in Israel* (2013), edited by Amalya Oliver, Tammar Zilber, and Avner de-Shalit, focused on the life stories of social leaders. The current book, on peace entrepreneurs, is, to a large extent, its continuation. The inspiration for the present book was a Hoffman event featuring Hadassah Froman and Khaled Abu Awwad (as described at the beginning of this chapter). Both Hadassah and Khaled – later interviewed for this book – spoke with great sensitivity and complexity about their social entrepreneurial collaborative venture, Roots-Shorashim-Judur, which aims at promoting peace through education and Jewish-Palestinian joint activities. Following their touching address, we felt the urge to develop the concept of peace entrepreneurs through empirical research, and this book came to be.

Amalya Oliver-Lumerman and Tammar Zilber invited Haneen Magadlah, Tammy Rubel-Lifschitz and Yosepha Tabib-Calif, all graduates of the Hebrew University who were past fellows in the Hoffman Program, to form a dedicated team to coordinate the interviews, review and edit them in Hebrew, receive consent from the interviewees, and then review and edit the translated version. We are in debt to many fellows of the Hebrew University that teamed with us for this project. They volunteered their time to join us in interviewing and in the initial editing of the transcribed interviews: Roni Mikel Arieli, Vered Zioni-Koren, Einat Walter, Nechumi Yaffe, Yoni Yahav, Shakked Lubotzky, and Lital Myers. Baruch Gefen translated the interviews from Hebrew to English. We thank Baruch for his dedication to this project and his sensitive and careful work of translation. Bekriah Mawasi translated from Arabic to English and we thank her deeply. Idit Chen assisted with the initial coordination of the tasks and the team members and we thank her. Audry Leinoff did a great job in preparing the stories for translation and compiling the glossary terms. Lital Myers offered most valuable advice and help throughout the entire process resulting in this book by joining the planning, interviewing, and managing the complex coordination between all the people and resources involved. We all benefited from her commitment, high professionalism, and kind spirit. We thank all these people from the bottom of our hearts. Finally, we thank Yifat Maoz from the Swiss Center for Conflict Resolution and Vered Vinizky-Seroussi, from the Harry S. Truman Research Institute at the Hebrew University, for the generous financial support for our project. We also thank our dear and special friends Hanoch Gutfreund and Roi Bear, who coordinated the Hoffman Program together with Amalya Oliver-Lumerman.

We present here the steps we took after our initial agreements to work together on this book. Our initial decision was that the book should come out in English, so the peace entrepreneurs' important voices will be shared with a broader audience than the Hebrew- or Arabic-speaking one. We also decided to follow a life narrative approach.

First, we contacted Hoffman fellows and alumni, inviting them to take part in the interviewing. Within a short time, a group of researchers was assembled. In a shared email, we explained the book's concept, and asked each partici-pant to suggest two names of relevant peace entrepreneurs who may serve as interviewees. We met in the Hebrew University for a day-long workshop on the methodology of life story interviews. We decided on a series of structured questions for the interviewees (as elaborated below). Subsequently, each participant chose to interview one entrepreneur. Each peace entrepreneur was interviewed by one researcher or jointly by two researchers. Most of the interviews were held in the interviewees' homes and lasted, on average, about three hours. All interviews were conducted during 2018, some in two sessions.

The book includes the stories of 11 peace entrepreneurs – men and women, Palestinians and Israelis, of diverse social backgrounds, ages and geographic locations, and various political persuasions. Our interviewees have each established and led a project for promoting the peace that involved a significant investment of time and energy and played a significant role in their lives. In that, we have sought to distinguish between them and social activists for whom peace is important and who act to promote it, but for whom it is only part of their overall activities for social justice. For the interviewees in this book, the peace project or venture is the core of their social activism. We are aware that we chose only some of the peace entrepreneurs active in the social and political spheres. Our choices do not reflect any evaluation of the quality or importance of the entrepreneurial projects. Due to the depth we intended for, and space limitations, we had to choose, and we wish we could have interviewed and given voice to many more peace entrepreneurs.

As a general rule, we asked our interviewees to tell us their personal story and the story of the peace initiative they were involved in. More specifically, we asked the interviewees to divide their life course into distinct periods and provide a title for each. In the interview, we asked them to describe the various periods relating to formative events and significant others and explain the titles they have given them. As part of their life story, the interviewees were also asked to describe their peace project. We asked what led them to act for peace, what inspired and motivated them, what difficulties they encountered, and what achievements they made.

The interviews took place in Hebrew or Arabic and then were translated into English. We intended to interview the Israelis in Hebrew and the Palestinians in Arabic. A few of the Palestinian interviewees preferred to be interviewed in Hebrew, since they had made public appearances in Hebrew and thus were comfortable expressing their ideas in Hebrew. Others were interviewed in Arabic by Haneen Magadlah.

In presenting the stories in this book, we applied the following principles. First, the interviewees' life stories are presented with their full names. In many interview-based studies, the interviewees are anonymized, with selected details of their background concealed to prevent them from being identified and protect their privacy. Yet, all our interviewees are known figures in their communities and were happy to openly share their stories. They all knowingly agreed to take part in the book. Second, as the stories are directed at a broad audience, we bring them in their entirety, presented as rich personal stories rather than organizing them into analytical themes, as standard in article-length narrative research. Most importantly, and in line with our narrative approach, we treated each life story as a subjective construction of past events. We therefore focused on their meaning for the peace entrepreneur that narrated them, and did not check for evidence of their accuracy, or even for their actual occurrence. Thus, the events described in this book are offered and analyzed as part of a personal, subjective construction of identity and meaning, rather than as an historical documentation.

Finally, the stories have been edited. After the interviews were transcribed, each interviewer went over the text for technical editing – to make sure there were no mistakes and added information about people, places, or organizations mentioned. Subsequently, two authors performed in-depth editing on each interview, turning them from dialogues to monologues. While we tried to stay faithful to the stories' content, we took the liberty of ordering them temporally. As required, we moved specific passages to appear in the 'correct' location along the temporal sequence, even if told previously or afterward. Each interviewee was asked to approve the final, edited version of the interview in its original language (Hebrew or Arabic). Only then the interviews were translated into English.

Translation brings about many challenges (Venuti, 2004). It took us a long while to find proper translators. After the translation into English, two of the authors went over each text and carefully examined whether it was clear and precise. This was not a simple matter as it is not always easy to capture the whole meaning and context of each expression, especially with the rich, emotionally laden, and culturally grounded life stories we gathered.

We present the stories in an alphabetic order of the interviewees' first name. We opted with this formalistic order system since we wanted to avoid any ordering agenda. In our view, each story is unique and insightful and making an ordering choice by gender, ethnicity, or content would have been wrong. While the stories are presented in their entirety, and with no interpretative comments, we did analyze the similarities and differences between them. In this analysis, presented in the book's final chapter, we seek to offer some closure and depict the main insights from the narratives.

As the stories are embedded in the Israeli-Palestinian conflict, they include many references to people, places, and events that non-Israeli or non-Palestinian readers may not recognize. Thus, we offer a glossary at the end of the book (terms in the glossary appear in *Italics* in the text). Each of the terms in the glossary has many different political constructions and connotations. The definitions we offer are meant to provide prompt clarifications that will allow readers to keep on reading. For a deeper understanding, we advise the readers to inquire about these terms further. To avoid biases, we consulted public websites, including Wikipedia, in English, Hebrew, and Arabic.

Working on this project was exciting, but also challenging for all of us. The stories we collected are rich, inspiring, and often very sad. As we engaged with them – as interviewers, authors, throughout the analysis and writing – they brought about appreciation, gratitude, and dismay, sadness, anger, and frustration. Following our life narrative methodological approach, we were always aware that these stories are constructions. We knew that what counts is the narrative – rather than historical – truth of the stories. Still, engaging with the stories was emotionally demanding. Our teamwork and strong collaboration and support helped us cope with the challenges the stories brought about. Throughout the process, we remember that dealing with the stories is much easier than dealing with the reality of conflict from which they stem.

Given the futile peace projects, pessimistic sentiments, and the dominance of fear over hope (Bar-Tal, 2000b), the unshaken optimism and untiring efforts of the peace entrepreneurs at the center of this book are even more impressive. We were all moved by their motivation and determination, and impressed by their optimism and continuous struggle for peace. We dedicate the book to them with deep appreciation.

NOTES

1. We use the terms 'story' and 'narrative' interchangeably, notwithstanding some differential definitions and uses in literary theory and other disciplines.
2. www.alandforall.org/english. The life story of one of the founders of this initiative, Eliaz Cohen, will be presented later in the book.

1. Jewish–Arabic collaboration through education

Amin Khalaf
Interviewed by Vered Zioni-Koren

Ever since I can remember, I wanted to be a teacher. The idea of inculcating knowledge – and more importantly, values – leading and shaping the next generation has always fascinated me. I first heard of Amin Khalaf and his vision of bilingual education in Israel while studying for my MA at the Seymour Fox School of Education of the Hebrew University of Jerusalem. I was glad I had this opportunity to interview Amin because I strongly believe that our society has the ability to work towards coexistence and that education can reshape thinking patterns and change realities.

I met a young idealist who was merely looking for an educational institution for his children that would reflect his wife's and his approach to education. When he failed to find one, he decided he'd establish it! Amin's charisma was captivating and inspiring. While his eyes shone with uncompromising passion, his face and manner of speech gave away hard feelings of sobering up, disappointment, helplessness, and questions about the ideology and values that Israel is headed towards at the onset of the 2020s.

WHY DO THEY HAVE AND WE DON'T?

Generally speaking, I consider myself a social entrepreneur. What is that? It is a person who looks around him, sees reality, and thinks of ways to improve it, to make the world more just and life better for everyone – myself as well as others. This characterizes the way I do things. It is a positive thing that I like about myself, and hope it will remain like that for the rest of my life.

It all started at the home in which I grew up, the small-village atmosphere. I was born in the village of Muqeible in the *Jezreel Valley* and I believe my family context was important. I am the son of a second marriage, my mom's only son, and, after two girls, the youngest child in our family. As a result, I had a lot of freedom to think, observe, deliberate, and decide. I had no dominant role model as a child. I was free. At home, I had older half-brothers, and some of them were socially active. They used to argue and debate, so I heard all about political values and the struggle for equal rights at home. That encouraged me.

I had many experiences as a child, but I hardly remember them. My sister used to make my lunch for school. One morning, I could not find her. I searched all over until I saw her crying behind the door. When I asked what had happened, she told me she was crying because the Egyptian president *Gamal Abdel Nasser* had died. We had his picture at home. In 1973, Egypt and Israel were at war known as the *Yom Kippur War*, *Ramadan War*, or the *October War*. We were scared, and it was hard for us to understand what was going on. People's cars were taken, we had to turn off the lights at our homes, things like that. We did not speak with the adults, heard nothing, asked nothing, and had no answers. We had to figure it all out ourselves.

When I turned 13, it was a very significant time for me – early adolescence and the identity-forming years. Being raised in a village, I was lucky, but also unlucky. Our village had no electric power before I was 10. People my age don't always remember, but ours was a deserted and neglected village with no infrastructure. At 13, in seventh grade, I loved to stand on a hill in the village and look north. They were finishing the construction of a new Jewish village named Magen Shaul, and I remember watching it: There were roads, a basketball court, a nice swimming pool. Then I started forming the identity question: Why do they have, and we don't?

So, I started looking for answers and a better understanding. It did not make me feel hatred or alienated; just the opposite: I wanted what people on the Jewish side had. I never really hated anyone. I could get angry or feel disappointed, but not hatred. I wanted to change things. If something is not good, I try to change it.

DISCOVERING MY LEADERSHIP SKILLS

At 13, I discovered my leadership qualities. My village used to mark Israeli Independence Day, and it was every child's dream to lead the Scouts in the march and carry the national flag on that day. That privilege was usually assigned to the best pupil, and I aimed at that too. Yet, something went wrong. Frankly, without any preparation, I don't remember talking about this to my friends, brothers, or other family members. Ahead of Independence Day, our teacher came to class and said: "We need to decorate this classroom for Independence Day." This is not the first time that I tell this story, and I still don't understand how I summoned the courage to stand up and say: "We don't want to." Even today, I say, wow! Where did that courage come from? I felt that it was the Independence Day of the State of Israel, not ours – second-rate citizens and members of the Palestinian nation. My refusal swept the entire class. I am sure it was mixed with fear. I don't remember what happened next exactly, but the teacher said that those who don't want to decorate may play in the yard, so we got up and went out – all of us, except for two girls who stayed behind to help the teacher. I remember feeling happy that it happened, but also wondered: What the hell happened here?

I was a good, nice, and likable boy, a good pupil too. I am not a rebel even today. I believe everyone in school was surprised. I was the leader of the Scouts at school that year, and we won the first prize in the annual Mount Tabor Walk of the *National Scouts Movement*. That was some achievement for a small and low-income village such as ours. The prize was a hike, but because I rebelled on Independence Day, they told me I could not go. They took the leadership position from me and gave it to another kid who was my best friend and cousin. They tried to drive a wedge between us. Those were hard days for me, and I don't remember that I had explicit support at home. Of course, they supported me, but they never said things like: "You are in the right direction," or "Do this and that," so I also experienced worries and uncertainty.

FROM THE VILLAGE TO THE BIG WORLD

I graduated from grammar school and was accepted to a good high school in *Nazareth*, which made me proud. It was a dream come true for me. Initially, I wanted to study at ORT Afula, a vocational high school, and learn a profession, but I was told that was impossible. Then I read in a youth magazine that 99 percent of the students of that Nazareth school earned matriculation certificates. It sounded good, so I said: *Yalla*, let's go there. I listened to my mother who, when she was still alive, always said: "Education, education, education, that's the only way to get ahead in life and out of the poverty and remoteness cycle." Over the year, two main voices guided my life. The first was being an active member of the *Israeli Communist Party (*Rakah*)*, which could block the access to good things in this country. The second was my mom's voice, saying: "Study hard and be a good boy." It's important for me to keep a balance between these two voices in my life.

I stayed in the village and commuted to Nazareth every day. We used to get off the bus at the entrance to Nazareth and walk up to school. Nobody does that today. In the evenings I'd return to my village, but I was incredibly frustrated because of that then. I wanted to live in the big city, join the school volleyball team, catch a movie, do things with other kids – but I couldn't. After school, I had to run to catch the bus because there was no other transportation home. I mean, there were buses from Nazareth to Afula, but none from Afula to the village. If I missed that bus, I was simply stuck. I am not sure that today's kids can understand this because the world has changed. Our parents had no cars or mobile phones. Today, kids can call their parents to pick them up. It is a different world.

The Nazareth school was good. It had a well-known headmaster, and he had a good effect on us. My world expanded. One of the most important things that happened and had a significant impact on me took place when I was in tenth grade of high school. There was an attempt to assassinate *West Bank* notables *Bassam Shakaa* and *Karim Khalaf.* Explosives were planted in their cars and Shakaa lost both his legs. That morning, our school devoted two hours to discuss the event. I went home that day, fearing that the Education Ministry would close down our schools. These were my fears. I mean, it is OK for Jewish schools to have the kids discuss current affairs, but we were not allowed to talk about such things. In seventh grade, still in the village, our headmaster spent an entire semester of civic lessons explaining that there is no Palestinian nation. We heard him but lacked the power or the knowledge to respond, which made us angry. In Nazareth, things were different. We went to school the next day, and it was open, so I gathered that we could discuss political issues, and no disaster would strike.

When I was in tenth grade, I discovered that we were entitled to a transportation refund from the Ministry of Education. But there was no one to arrange that. A year later, I went to the ministry headquarters in Jerusalem and started looking for the person who should give me a refund. This is nothing like the world of kids today. Then, we had the desire to seek justice. That Nazareth high school gave me something.

Then I went to university, which was quite a change, from a small village to Jerusalem. The world expanded further. The Hebrew University opened new worlds for me. I took courses in Arabic language and literature, and Islamic and Middle Eastern studies. There, I could study and discuss the history of the Israeli-Arab conflict and hear the Palestinian narrative.

Living in Jerusalem was great fun. Arab students surrounded me, and there was political activity, to which I dedicated hours. I was very active, and it sharpened my worldview. With all the debates among the Arab students and between the Jews and us, I became politically aware. We lived actively, studied, and thought. In my junior year, we staged a protest rally outside the Prime Minister's Residence, yelling and chanting slogans. I was afraid someone would come out and attack us, but this is a democratic country, and demonstrations are allowed. You can chant slogans, and nothing will happen to you. I felt I had a lot of latitude. In those years, I understood what the State of Israel was, what the Palestinian problem was, and what equal rights were. I met the leaders of the Arab population, and it gave me a lot of strength and knowledge.

At 26, I was active on the Jewish-Arab issue, but mainly with Arab students. I was also a journalist. Then the first *intifada* started, and things became more difficult. Later, I took a group facilitator's course at *Neve Shalom*, or *Wahat al-Salam* in Arabic, where I learned how to facilitate Jewish-Arab dialogue meetings. I also met my wife there. We're both educators. After the course, I served as a grammar school teacher at Neve Shalom. It is an extraordinary school that gave me plenty of knowledge relevant to things I did later, and I became involved in education. For me, the two great things that happened during that period were that I became increasingly involved in Jewish-Arab dialogue meetings, and I started instructing teachers at the School for Peace and then worked with *Peace Child YMCA Israel*.

"I BELIEVED IT COULD BE DONE": HOW THE BILINGUAL SCHOOL IN JERUSALEM WAS ESTABLISHED

After graduating from university, we stayed in Jerusalem and had a son. When he was two years old, we sent him to the *YMCA kindergarten* in the city center. His class comprised half Jewish and half Arab children, so they named it Gan Shalom – the Peace Kindergarten. I then started wondering where we'd send him to school. In those years, I was a class teacher in Jerusalem, in the high school of *Beit Safafa* and the *Givat Gonen* elementary school, so I was familiar with Jerusalem's school system. I became angry once I learned that schools in the western, Jewish part of the city prepare their students for the matriculation certificate, while schools in the eastern, Palestinian part do not. I also knew Arab children who went to Jewish schools on the western side, and I realized that this arrangement does not work well! I became convinced that I made the right decision not to go to ORT Afula for my high school studies. The two populations are very different, so it is not easy socially when you are different and have a hard time fitting in. We realized that sending our son to the *Givat Gonen* school on the western, Jewish side of Jerusalem would be complicated. Still, sending him to some East Jerusalem, Palestinian school would be problematic too. What do we do then? We decided to find a school where children prepare for *matriculation exams* in Arabic – which did not exist then. We started thinking about doing something even more meaningful in the education system. Then, someone introduced me to Lee Gordon, who had graduated from the *Mandel School for Educational Leadership*, and was thinking about establishing a joint Jewish-Arab kindergarten – and wow! We hit it off right away.

And so it started. All of these things together – finding an educational facility for our son, the YMCA kindergarten, my experience at Neve Shalom, and the desire to do something meaningful and promote Arab-Jewish collaboration in the State of Israel – helped me connect so well with Lee Gordon, who brought the idea of starting a joint kindergarten. Naturally, I had my own ideas. I was thinking of starting a class of Arab pupils in a Jewish school. Lee wanted a kindergarten, and I wanted a class, and we got together and got things rolling. First, together with several other people, we formed an association that we named 'Learning to Live Together' to open a kindergarten similar to the one at the YMCA. Then we established 'Hand in Hand,' a bilingual center designed to promote bilingual education in schools. Lee came from his world, and I came with my experience, and we started a dialogue and connected. We wrote down our vision, a page and a half, and were going to change the world. One of the things that we had in common and helped us was daring to jump in with lots of questions. It was all semi-voluntary, but we had a beautiful idea written on a piece of paper: To promote a joint civil society for Jews and Arabs in Israel through education. That is, establishing shared educational frameworks.

I was really excited, believed in it, felt it was possible. I spent a whole year in the Neve Shalom school, so I could answer many questions. Also, I have a lot of experience in education and I am a group facilitator. I can explain how teaching in two languages can be done. That helped us. The Hand in Hand Center for Jewish-Arab Education in Israel, our association, was a huge success story. After only 18 months of activity, we have established two schools in the north of Israel and Jerusalem.

The reason for the latter is apparent. I needed a kindergarten for my son. But why the Northern District? Because the director there loved our idea and said: Go ahead, find partners, and I am with you. So we started, and Lee obtained a list of Education Department managers in the Ministry of Education's Northern District. We began arranging meetings and traveling north while working on the Jerusalem project.

The first positive answer from the Jewish side came from the Misgav Regional Council in the Northam District, and we started a school there with partners we found in the region. I needed to understand how to connect the dots because Hand in Hand was a complicated project. For example, to form the steering committee in the Galilee, we had to find people from the Education Ministry, the Misgav Regional Council, Sakhnin, public figures, and parents. Finding partners is one of my strengths. When people asked me how I do that, I used to say that I use my 'gut feeling' – but now I think it is accumulated experience. It is like going back to my childhood and asking, why did your classmates follow you? Or, how do you make people believe in you? It just happens. I believe that accumulating experience is the road to leadership.

At the time, Meir Krauss, head of the Education Directorate of the Jerusalem Municipality, sent us messages saying this was not the right time to promote our ideas in Jerusalem. This was the mayor's stand. We might have given up anywhere else, but not in Jerusalem. I mean, I needed an educational institution for my son! So we established a small local framework in the *Experimental*

School in Jerusalem. If I remember correctly, the entire YMCA class joined the Experimental School with nine Arab and three Jewish pupils. But we had all kinds of problems at the Experimental School. The hardest thing was their resistance to change. Things ran smoothly in the first year, but I guess it is not simple to change systems. For example, we wanted the pupils to study 20 minutes in Hebrew and 20 minutes in Arabic in each lesson, but the Experimental School said this was too much. In the second year, when another YMCA class came, they said they would let in only those who meet the Experimental School's criteria. A world war broke out, parents were disappointed, but I also felt that we could not disappoint our Jewish partners. That started real problems.

That same year, Lee Gordon left for the United States, and Haim Erlich, the Experimental School headmaster, left his position and became my partner. We encountered more and more problems: Members of the school steering committee started arguing, and racist remarks were made. I remember how the parents had a meeting to decide if they wanted us or not. It was one of the most racist encounters I had ever attended. Harsh words were spoken against the Arab parents, and many left the meeting in tears. They kicked us out, saying: "We don't want you anymore." That experience still shakes me today. I was humiliated, but I had to shut up and not talk too much about this, not rock the entire project. I never prepare notes when I speak publicly, but I had things written down in that meeting. We did not talk much, and there were things that I wanted to say – but couldn't: "How can you kick us out like that? Why do you humiliate us?" The fantasy of making the Experimental School a sort of 'mini Israel' had failed. What were we thinking? Did we really believe that if 20 percent of the students were Arabs, that would change things at the state level?

That year, we devoted our efforts to the establishment of an independent school in Jerusalem. *Yossi Sarid* was education minister and *Ehud Olmert* was the mayor of Jerusalem. We worked very hard, and Olmert told us: I am with you 100 percent. Indeed, over the years, Olmert was the most important political figure for us. He truly supported us. The Municipality gave us a small building with two classrooms next to Denmark School in the *Katamon* neighborhood. Our most challenging class comprised the Experimental School graduates because when we left there, none of the Jewish students came with us. We were able to attract no one. The graduates were second graders; the first grade was steady, and we managed to establish a kindergarten – so we had three classes. They gave us a room, but there was no yard for the kids. Then, I invited Mayor Olmert for a visit, and he came with a large entourage. He looked around and said: "Where is the yard for these children?" The next day, they broke down a wall and made a passage for us to the yard. Later, we kept expanding at the expense of the adjacent Denmark School, which was very difficult because we had to fight for every classroom. After the idea started succeeding, the *Jerusalem Fund* stepped in and, thanks to contacts with the Municipality, gave us a piece of land. We raised some money and built the school. My three children attended it; two graduated, and my daughter is going to the eleventh grade next year.

We tried to do the same in *Haifa*, but it did not work. In *Jaffa* we had a kindergarten for one year before it shut down. Next, we established a partnership with an association in the Wadi Ara area and opened our third school in *Kafr Qara*. Several years later, partnering with an association from *Beersheba*, we established a kindergarten and then an elementary school there, but it failed. Today, we have four educational institutions: in Jerusalem, Misgav, Kafr Qara, and Beersheba. Only in Jerusalem did we develop it into a high school, but we tried all over the country.

That was very meaningful – the most significant – time in my life. We established schools believing that we were creating a model for an egalitarian Jewish-Arab partnership. We believed that we could teach everyone about living together in the State of Israel in terms of language, culture, and nationality. In those years, I honestly thought we were changing the world. Today, of course, my view is far more critical, and I have some questions, but things were very good and significant at the time.

EQUALITY IN LANGUAGE, CULTURE, AND NARRATIVE: THE HAND IN HAND WORLDVIEW

The basic concept of Hand in Hand is that children get to grow together – which none of us had experienced – maintaining equality on three levels: two languages, two cultures, and two narratives. I focus on equality because it is clear that we need it if we want to make peace. Both sides need to gain. At Hand in Hand, we don't use the word coexistence too often and speak more of civilians' partnerships and equality. When I established Hand in Hand, I had this fantasy that leadership that would change reality would emerge from it. I envisioned that every person that wants to learn how to become a leader would learn from our experience.

To establish a meaningful and equal Jewish-Arab partnership in our school, we decided on three practical pillars that reflected the three cycles: language, culture, and narrative. The first pillar is the bilingual concept: we wanted children who grow in the Hand in Hand system to speak both Hebrew and Arabic, and each pupil should choose the language he or she prefers. Languages reflect the balance of power in society. If we want to change it and promote equality, Jews need to know how to speak Arabic. The second pillar is culture, which means celebrating each other's holidays. The third pillar comprises narratives – making room for the national stories of both sides. Also, equality is expressed on the administrative level – we have two teachers in each class and two headmasters for every school.

One of the things I tried, to no avail, was to convince the Ministry of Education to reward bilingual teachers. If we believe that bilingualism – speaking both Hebrew and Arabic – is an advantage for teachers, and if the system rewards bilingual personnel, it would have a significant impact on the power relations between the languages and the people. If every bilingual teacher in Hand in Hand had been paid 10 percent extra, bilingualism would have had a real value. I hoped we could encourage the Jewish teachers to learn Arabic and collect the reward. If it was a very significant reward, not 10 percent but even an extra 20 percent to their wages, they might have even learned to master Arabic and used it daily. We tried to get the Ministry of Education to approve our dual teaching method – a Hebrew-speaking and an Arab-speaking teacher for each class. Even the *Dovrat Committee* (the National Task Force for the Advancement of Education in Israel) recommended that additional budgets for Hand in Hand be considered. I promoted this agenda, but it was hard, and we failed in rewarding bilingual teachers. I wanted to continue this struggle against the Ministry of Education, produce position papers on bilingualism and multiculturalism, and establish a learning center. Still, forces from within and without the organization held me back.

In my ideal world, we have to work to make Arabs speak perfect Arabic and have Jews speak some Arabic, but beyond that I wish to write a position paper addressed to the government, explaining how the State of Israel should manage language. It is clear that Israel cannot be entirely bilingual, nor can I insist that 80 percent of the Jews here speak both languages, but the reality is a far cry from all that. Another dream of mine, of which I wrote or did nothing, is the need to have bilingual education in towns where Arabs are above a certain population percentage. I mean, it is inconceivable that government officials in Arab towns do not speak both languages. For example, you cannot appoint a National Insurance director who is not bilingual in Nazareth. If government tenders made that requirement, it would make learning Arabic more critical and give its speakers an advantage.

BETWEEN EDUCATION AND IDEOLOGY

I was raised on the belief that Arabs in the State of Israel should be equal. I believed that through the experience gained at Hand in Hand, we would have the specifics of how that equality would look and, even before it came, how Israel should exist as an egalitarian state. When we started with Hand in Hand, we talked about Israel's nature – whether it is Jewish and Zionist, or a *state of all of its citizens*. I believe we should be addressing this issue because we need to create answers. These are neither academic nor political issues. We tried to figure out the solutions based on experience accumulated at Hand in Hand. When people ask me what was the most formidable challenge, I say: Human resources. The most challenging task was selecting directors for our schools, considering both ideological and educational aspects. I focused more on the ideological side. It may have been a mistake. I don't know. It mattered to me that we chose principals who were more committed to the association's ideology and less education-oriented. I may have been wrong.

I wanted the school to make social statements on issues such as *Land Day*, for example. If the Arab sector calls a general strike on that day, should our Arab teachers strike too? I thought they should, but most of the teachers did not. That initiated a debate on how schools bring populations together. The Arab parents told us that they wanted a place for their children to study well so they could go to university and be with educated people. The Jewish parents disapproved of the Arab teachers' strike, feeling it was against them – a very complicated thing. We had to conduct many discussions when most of our Jewish and Arab partners were against these discussions – they just wanted a school. It is not simple to manage a Jewish-Arab partnership. When we discussed Land Day, for example, the Jewish parents argued that Arabs stress the importance of land while Jews emphasize the value of human lives. The explanation is that each side focuses on what it lacks. The Palestinians don't have a state, and they worry that their remaining land might be seized, so they care about land, which is not to say that human lives don't matter. The Jews, on the other hand, have a state and land, so it is easier for them to talk about humanism. I believe it reflects some hidden racism that is hard to explain and not simple to clarify.

Succeeding with children requires great investment in their parents. Children go home to their parents and the parents decide where children of those ages study, so parents are part of the change. In the beginning, some parents were worried about the effect of the encounter with the other side's culture on the children's identity. Early on, when Jewish children entered a 'mosque' that we built inside one of the classrooms to mark the month of *Ramadan*, some parents felt it was the end of the world! Why? Some issues were religious and cultural, but also national. We wanted to mark the Palestinian *Nakba* Day and learn about Land Day, but the Jewish parents were worried, so we had to discuss it with them because parents are part of the change. I know that the parents created some of the difficulties in the Bilingual School. We invested quite a lot in this, and it helped, but when parents were bilingual, we had better chances of succeeding. Even today, I can speak of small things we failed in. For example, we wish that we had taken the symbolic step of buying trilingual computer keyboards for the families. The children were already learning two languages, so I wanted them to have trilingual keyboards at home like those they had in school.

External reality sometimes makes things hard too. We started in 1998 and until 2000, we were on the rise. After the *October 2000 events* we had to maintain what we had, and we could not dream and fantasize as we had done beforehand. I used to believe that Hand in Hand should be a beacon that lights the way for everyone, but after the Second Intifada (aka, the Al-Aqsa Intifada) I started viewing our schools as a rare flower that needed protection. Our optimism began to change in many respects when things deteriorated after 2000. There was great hope for real peace in the region before that, but 2000 was a year of crisis. We started thinking: What is the point of forming such partnerships when there are occupation and war? How do military service and school involvement combine? Many sensitive questions that address the complexities of complexities. Not simple at all. I don't have the answers to these questions. I just don't know.

NEVER GIVE UP

Can social change be promoted through education? I am still deliberating and have no answer for this question. It remains open. If the answer is negative, then the investment we made was wasted; if it is positive, we need to introduce the necessary changes and continuously develop our critical views. It runs even deeper than that. My high school had a very positive impact on me, and I believe that there are good Jewish schools that make a difference. Still, when it comes to the issue of Jewish-Arab partnerships, there is an interesting and fascinating question that has not yet really been examined: Do both sides genuinely gain from it?

I quit as Hand in Hand chairman after 14 years on the post. I felt I'd exhausted it. I wanted to grow with Hand in Hand and expand our influence and reach beyond the school, but the board and our donors were against it. Some argued that our only mission was to establish schools. Still, I believed we should go further, formulate and disseminate our knowhow and truly impact larger populations and policymakers. I've always encountered resistance from the partnership's Executive Committee and mainly from our Jewish donors. That naturally added up to all kinds of grievances and problems in the organization and the school. Still, the most important thing for me was that I felt I had done all I could. On my part, I made the school dream come true and established four educational institutions that cover this country from north to south. That's the image I had in my head.

I am at peace with my decision still. I remember how, during the Second Intifada, people in my village – only some 4 km from *Jenin* – would sit on their porches, watching the Jenin refugee camp and seeing the chaos that went on there, the pain and the rage. When I returned to my village, people asked me: "So, do you still believe in what you do?" and I said: "Yes, I do." That was my answer, even when I encountered difficulties. For example, my entire family resides in the West Bank. When my Uncle Amin passed, we wanted to attend the funeral. At the crossing, we felt very humiliated. I wanted to tell the soldier there: "Do you know what I do?!" but I choked and said nothing. That's hard!

To connect the present moment with the day I was 13 and refused to celebrate Israel's Independence Day, something inside me says: Never give up! It is hard for me to live in the State of Israel even today, but I do whatever I can. I believe that most people are busy with what's suitable for them and for their families, and less with what happens around them. That's legitimate. I am the kind of person who worries about the greater good and those things around us. I want to change the world, make it a better place, more just and egalitarian. That's how I was, that's how I am, and that gives me strength. I still want to make some changes, even today. I want to help the East Jerusalem residents learn Hebrew. I want to promote sustainability issues and impact on the world as a whole. So, to endure and not retract into your bubble, you must be an optimist. At the time, I used to say that I dream of 10 such schools in Israel. Today, I believe that six–seven schools constitute quite a fitting dream. I still wonder if I could go back and turn Hand in Hand into a lab to create a model for an egalitarian State of Israel. It would not be not easy, but it is possible.

Today, I have a critical view of things. I think about what can be done or promoted, which is why I speak of thoughts and questions. The most important thing is that I am not losing hope, still believe in what I've done so far, and want to keep doing it. I keep trying.

2. No one can conquer you because when you are free inside, you live in peace

Bassam Aramin
Interviewed by Yoni Yahav

I first met Bassam a decade ago at his office in the border town of Al-Ram. I was a freshman student taking his first steps in Palestinian-Israeli activism. He was the Palestinian coordinator of Combatants for Peace, an Israeli and Palestinian joint initiative started by former fighters from both sides. Bassam entered the grim cold room and immediately, all eyes, Israeli and Palestinian, were on him. His figure, thin and unimposing, was enough to silence the constant hum of conversation. I did not know his story then. It was less than a year after his terrible loss. But even his short, thoughtful sentences, his quiet almost whisper of a voice, and the respect in which he addressed the people around him was enough to hint at what imbued him with such an aura of leadership. It was only later – when I learned bits and pieces of his background and after watching him trot (impeded by his recognizable limp) through stone-strewn hills to join long marches and demonstrations, or sensitively diffuse complicated situations which could have easily ended in violence – that I understood why people kept using terms like 'noble' or 'brave' around him. Terms that Bassam himself would quickly brush off. Yet as I met Bassam again for the sake of this interview, I sensed that the effect on his surroundings was noticeable. Whether in his office enveloped by his supporters or crossing the checkpoint through a packed crowd of Palestinian workers on his way to my apartment in Jerusalem, his words and conduct were strongly animated by the qualities of humility and the self-confidence of moral persuasion. Listening to him speak, and indeed just observing him address friends and foes with his all-too human sense of respect and conviction, was to tap into the unconventional that everything 'was going to be OK after all.'

I was born in 1968, in a cave near the Dead Sea, close to *Hebron*, to a family with 16 siblings. My life in the desert was perfect. Children don't think in terms of Jews, Arabs, or Muslims. You know nothing about all that. When I was four, we saw a helicopter landing on a nearby hill. My mother, aunt, and cousin watched it. I just saw something coming out of the sky. I'll never forget that. Soldiers emerged from the helicopter and walked towards the ravine, climbing right at us. I was so scared that I could not even look at them. They called on my cousin and talked to him. I believed then that he was a grown-up, but he was really four or five years older than me. My mother said: "These are Jews." And I asked: "What Jews?" and then I heard the sound of a gunshot – they slapped him across the face. Terrified, I crawled under my mom's garments as my aunt started cursing and yelling at them, and my mother said: "Shut up! They'll kill us all."

After that, I forgot the word 'Jews' until, when I was 11 or 12, we moved to Se'ir Village outside Hebron, where I started seeing foreign soldiers who did not look like us and spoke a foreign language. Those were Jewish soldiers, I was told, which sent me right back to the soldiers who came out of the sky and descended from the chopper. All I knew about them was that I should fear them because they could shoot me. It is tough to grow under a foreign government, particularly when you don't understand, and when you ask others who don't understand, you get no real answers. For example, I asked my father (who died in 1995): "Who are they?" "Jews," he said. "And what do they want?" "They want to dominate the Arabs." "Why?" He did not know.

When I was a teenager, Israeli soldiers, who we called the Jewish soldiers, went crazy when they saw a Palestinian flag. They shot it, burned it, or chopped the stick it was tied to. As children, we were very amused, watching them go mad like that. Indeed, when I was 13, in 1982, four of my friends and I formed a local fighting group. It did not have a name. We started writing graffiti on the walls, slogans such as "Freedom To Palestine." I did not even know what we were saying there, but we knew they knew what it was and that it drove them crazy. We also wrote "No To Zionists." What are Zionists? It is a curse. It is the worst thing you can say to them. To me it meant nothing. We would hang Palestinian flags on trees outside our school and then wait for the army to show up, and were disappointed when they did not. As children, we would wait for them to appear and go crazy, so we had some action in the village. You are just dragged into that. This is your life. You mostly fear your parents. I used to fear my father, though he never touched me; I was more afraid of my big brother.

I limp, so they always told me that I should educate myself because some kids throw stones and other kids write. It may have influenced my future. I badly wanted to be involved like the other kids, hurl stones – and if I had a gun, even shoot them. But my friends did not want me to partake in such activities because I was limping and that put them at risk. Because they threw stones and ran, the soldiers might grab me, so it was best if I did not come with them. That's why I never got to shoot or harm anyone even when I was defined as a terrorist or warrior. My most violent act was lifting a Palestinian flag. It went on like this for years. Attending demonstrations, I heard the name Hitler. Who was Hitler? I asked because the soldiers went mad when they heard that name. Who is he? They told me that he killed 6 million Jews. Wow! In my childish mind, Hitler was a great giant who killed 6 million. Still, they said, that's a lie.

That was on my mind until I turned 16 and a friend found some military equipment in a cave. There was a very serious *Kalashnikov (AK-47)*, two hand grenades, and more stuff that was probably left behind in *1967*, from the war with the Jordanians. We did not know how to use that and did not touch those things at first. In 1984, two of my friends later hurled the two hand grenades at army jeeps in the village. They exploded, but no one was hurt because they did not know how to use them. We were arrested a year later and I was sent to prison for seven years. In jail, you consider yourself a hero, a warrior. The veteran inmates welcomed us respectfully, proud of this new generation that carried on the struggle against the enemy and the occupation. But I wondered: Why must I spend seven years in prison? What kind of warrior am I? True, I raised a flag and was part of a squad, but personally, I did nothing.

I was 17 then. Now, in prison, every organization has its system, and I belonged to the *Palestinian Liberation Organization (PLO)*, but I was an innocent child and did not even know what PLO meant. My friends may have known more, but I did not even know what the PLO, *Fatah*, or the *Popular Front for the Liberation of Palestine (PFLP)* even were. Still, I learned a lesson in jail that I would never forget: If you know your enemy, you can defeat or kill him; but if you just hate him, you are killing yourself. Honestly, if you hate someone all the time, it will only give you a heart attack. Hatred hurts no one but the hater. I seized the opportunities I had in prison and started learning Hebrew so that I could master the enemy's language and know how to kill him, destroy him, defeat him.

I needed to understand the aggression and cruelty of the Jewish soldiers who came to our village, and why they shot at you when you threw a stone. Now, that's unbelievable: A child throws a stone, and immediately they place the entire village under a three-day curfew, gather all males aged 15 to 60 on the football pitch, and question them until they catch the offender. As children, we used to say that the soldiers were cowards, terrified of a Palestinian stone. Also, you didn't understand the cruelty of their reaction because you couldn't compare a stone to a curfew. So, we believed they were scared, and they imposed curfews on us.

SEVEN YEARS BEHIND BARS

In my first year in prison I watched *Schindler's List* – a film about the *Holocaust*. It was entirely accidental for me. Only later did I realize it was screened on Holocaust Remembrance Day. At the time, I did not know what the Holocaust or a memorial day were, but I understood it involved Hitler and the Jews. A few minutes into the film, I started crying. It was very hard, particularly with my background. I was not familiar with or an expert on such brutality. I felt ashamed watching those naked people on the screen. Where did they come from? Where did the hatred come from? They did not just shoot them, but humiliated them first. Why? I kept telling myself that this was just a movie with actors, but could not believe that this had happened, that there were people in our world who did such things. I just wanted to know more about that crime. Did it really happen? Was this just a movie, or did this really take place, and why?

In prison, wardens and inmates did not talk to each other, and the guards were banned from talking to us. Usually, when you guard a group of criminals and murderers, you don't treat them with respect because they are criminals and have no honor. One day, a guard who was just as tough as any noticed that I was a limping and silent man who could be nice, so he wanted to understand what I was doing in prison because I was not the terrorist type. We started arguing and I said: "You are a terrorist, not I. We are freedom fighters who resist the occupation." He said: "No! you are illegal settlers and occupiers, and you kill Jews." I said: "Are you crazy? We are settlers?! You are settlers and criminals." "Read history," he said, "because this is how they teach you to hate the Jews. We came here to liberate the Land of Israel, and even though we let you live and make a living, you murder us. Why do you kill us?"

I realized then that he truly believed we were the settlers, so I said: "Maybe we are settlers. Come on, convince me." And he replied: "And if you are convinced?" "I would declare before the entire prison that I will stop fighting. That's it. I will say I was wrong," I said. "Do you have the courage to do that?" he asked. I said: "Yes, I do." I was motivated by my desire to find ways of convincing him, defeating him. He asked: "Are you a nation?" and I said: "Yes, we are the Palestinian nation." "Where did you come from, then?" He asked. "I don't know," I said. "We've been here for the past 2,000 years." "How long?" He asked again. "A lot," said I. "Since when?" He asked. "I don't know," I replied, "but 2,000 years is a sacred history." He encouraged me to learn about myself, who I was, what a Palestinian was, where we came from, and also about what Jews were, who was an Israeli, what was Zionism – so that I could argue with him better. I realized that if you knew more, you behaved differently, knew how to be good with yourself, believed yourself and what you knew, believed in your narrative. Without it, you saw nothing else.

So I started educating myself. Like an excellent student, I began writing down specific questions for me to ask him the next time we spoke so I could convince him. We became good friends in just a few months and I started waiting for him to come on duty. He told me that he was telling his children and wife about me. We truly became personal friends and I felt like I won and convinced him that I was neither a terrorist nor a warrior or a murderer, that I was a child who became a warrior because the occupation turned me into one. He said he was willing to live in peace and have two states for two nations. At the time, it was a massive victory because then he started treating other prisoners with respect. He realized that the Youths Wing, designated for prisoners aged 12 to 19, mostly comprised children under 16. That was before the First *Intifada*. On October 1, 1987, we were 120 prisoners in the Youths Wing. Whenever they took us for a walk in the yard, they would sound a siren and send us right back to our rooms. We believed they did that on purpose, deliberately keeping us from walking in the yard. It became a known routine: an alarm would sound, we were sent back to our rooms, and often let out a few minutes later. That day was different. We saw soldiers we had never seen before, where usually there were only prison guards or police officers. They stood in two lines across from our cells – very scary big guys with veiled faces – and all we could hear was them beating and someone crying and yelling, and you understood nothing. I was in the last cell. Suddenly the door opened and some 10 such soldiers came in. They undressed us humiliatingly, threw us in the corridor where I had to walk and be hit from both sides, and none missed, until we reached the yard. I looked ahead of me and saw everyone there, naked, and they were being beaten as the soldiers screamed and smiled, acting like machines. Suddenly I remembered the movie I had watched a few months before and saw myself in the same situation, the fact that we were all naked was the most humiliating thing. I then strongly identified with the weak in the movie, Jews in that case, and remembered I was outraged that they did not resist or at least yell. I know there was not much they could do, but they could at least scream in the face of the murderer who was about to shoot them. So I started yelling and cursed them in Arabic and English, and they kept beating just the same. Me yelling was nothing special, but it made me feel strong. At the end of the corridor, six soldiers grabbed me and two others, shoved us aside, and started beating the living hell out of us. The man who commanded over that force became a general later. He broke his silence over the past two and a half years and started talking about the occupation and how hard it was to oppress another nation. Then, he was head of the force and slapped me, which brought back memories of my cousin and how I had heard him being slapped around by soldiers when I was four or five. That slap sounded to me like an explosion in my ear.

Suddenly someone came and covered my body with his, lying on top of me. That was my friend guard. He yelled at the soldiers to get away. They talked in Hebrew and I did not get everything they said, but I heard him say that he knew me, and that I had leg and heart problems. "He will die, and that will be your responsibility," he told them. I felt he was trying to make me play dead so they would spare me. Then he grabbed me and just shoved me into a small room and closed the door. They kept exchanging screams, but he told them: "No one will touch him." He was willing to die for me. It was all over in a few minutes, and later he took me back to my cell and apologized.

In prison, you can't go to sleep thinking everything will be all right because they can break into your cell at 03:00 for a shakedown. And even if you have nothing, they will search your room just to intimidate you, to stop you from sleeping well, to make you regret being human and wish you were a beast so they would not detain you. It is paradoxical because it makes you stronger. You become determined to go on with your armed struggle against this heinous criminal enemy. It was as if they aimed at destroying our humanity, wanting us to live like animals and think of nothing but revenge. I, however, did not want to think only of revenge. *Jibril Rajoub* taught me as much. He said that if I only think of killing and taking revenge, even if that's my enemy, I become an animal with no positive intentions to create something. If killing is all that you desire, you are a beast. The other thing I learned is that there is no 'I' – you don't think about your own pain, but only about Palestine, the Palestinian nation, its liberty. Mentally, that greatly helps to survive the rough prison life.

MENTAL STABILIZATION: THINKING LIKE A FATHER, NOT AS A BOY

I was released from prison in 1992 after spending 55 days in detention, several months in *Ramallah* during the trial, and almost seven years at the Hebron Police Jail. Free again, I still believed that armed struggle was the only way to fight against that nation: the soldiers, and the settlers who were even scarier. Settlers are very hard and violent. It is very easy to justify acts against soldiers because you see them only in this context, as if they have no family or parents. The settlers are very rough and violent, so it is easy to justify harming them. We never viewed Jews as humans. Before I was released, peace talks were held in Madrid where the PLO delegation was subject to the Jordanians and the Palestinians were unhappy. A year later, the *Oslo Accords* were signed. Personally, after seven years in prison, all you want to do is have a good time, but you are always scared. That is, you are at home and see a jeep 5 km away, and immediately you start thinking they are coming to detain you. So you move away from the house and think: I have done nothing, even before I did nothing. Fear lives with you 24 hours a day. When the Oslo Accords were signed in 1993, it was like a dream come true, with *Yasser Arafat* and *Yitzhak Rabin* together. So I started wondering: Why did I have to spend seven years in prison?! If only they had made the agreement and shook hands earlier, they could have spared me the humiliation. And why did all those people die? Then I thought that if they had not, we would not have achieved that result. They always said that there was no solution to this conflict and only violence would win, and suddenly we could live without fearing death or prison.

A TURNING POINT

Everyone has a turning point in life. Mine came when I watched television in 1994 and saw Palestinian youths who surrounded Israeli military jeeps before they left *Jenin*, which was handed over to the *Palestinian National Authority*'s (PA) control. The Palestinian youth threw flowers at the soldiers as if to say: "You just go in peace and leave us alone. We're waiting for the Palestinian police." And I thought: What a crazy nation we are. Just a moment ago, we wanted to shoot them, and now we bid them farewell. I decided then that I did not want my son to be a hero like me and spend seven years in prison. I didn't want him ever to hurl rocks at anyone. Now that we had peace, I could educate him and explain things, which did not happen to me when I was a child. That's what I thought then.

I married a Palestinian woman from Sheikh Jarrah in Jerusalem and I came from Hebron. On our wedding day, I was supposed to come and pick her up from Jerusalem in my car. But there was a curfew, so I waited for her at a road-block outside Jerusalem. Her family brought her there. After spending several months in the village, I started working for the Palestinian National Archives at the PA Ministry of Information. That was a good period, seeing Israelis all over at peace. We drove to *Tiberias* and *Haifa*, we went everywhere, even to the beach.

After the age of 25, I was getting older and starting to think like a father, not as an 18 year old who thought he could just grab a knife, kill 6 million Jews, and leave without a hitch. Now, I had responsibilities. I was not a coward, but I started reconsidering things. It is normal. I started planning my son's life. I got married in 1993, and a year later had a son named Arab. It is very hard and you are always afraid. It is only natural. You start wondering what will happen to him when he grows up. I wanted to live far from even the main village street so that if demonstrations were staged and gas canisters were fired at us, my son would be somewhere else. I considered buying him a gas mask, though there was nothing to buy. So you calculate and you're scared.

I discovered that Palestinians and Jews have been trying to annihilate each other and failing for the past 100 years, and we're both still here. Some 600,000 Jews established the State of Israel with some 250,000 million Arabs in countries around them, and the Jews are still here. Despite everything we have done, Israel is strong and supported by America and the West, and we are very weak. Nevertheless, Israel is not yet safe and Palestine is not yet liberated, and you raise children that will either die or go to prison.

I started being active in my society. In Israel you can say: I don't take an active role, I don't care about the Jewish nation, Israelis, or Zionism. I want to raise my children and study, and get involved in nothing else. In Palestine, you cannot be uninvolved. You have to be involved, particularly after you spend seven years in prison. I have a right to speak and do something. I paid that price not because I had a personal or family issue, but because my nation is at odds with the Jewish nation. I care about the Palestinian nation, which is why I engaged in activities with former prisoners, my friends. I know thousands of former prisoners who I met while in prison. I felt that we were headed for peace and it was time to educate people in peace and nonviolence. We could stage a nonviolent struggle. Millions could go out to the streets, but without violence. We used to talk about this freely with the most extreme individuals: If you want to fight, nonviolence is the way to go. They said, we have tried that for the past 100 years. And we said, and what's the result?

Between 2000 and 2002, the Second Intifada peak years, I lived in *Anata*, near the Shu'afat refugee camp just outside Jerusalem. We breathed tear gas that reached our home from the roadblock every day. Some of my friends and I had the courage to openly say that suicide terrorists do not serve our cause. Terror attacks were a strategic mistake of Palestinian diplomacy because they significantly weakened the Israeli peace camp at the time. Many Palestinians were against those attacks that politically attained the most destructive results. In 2003, the media started reporting about Israelis who refused to serve in the Israeli Defense Force. Palestinians are amazed and curious when they hear of an Israeli soldier who is against occupation and oppression. When the Israeli movements of *Breaking the Silence*, *Courage to Refuse*, and the '*pilots' letter*' appeared on the scene, I very much wanted to meet the people and understand how they realized we have a right to a state of our own. Did they understand that another nation lives here, or did they fear that the Palestinians might kill them?

FORMING THE COMBATANTS FOR PEACE MOVEMENT

In 2005, the first meeting of four Palestinians and seven former Israeli officers and soldiers was held at the Everest Hotel in *Beit Jala*. It was a hard meeting for all of us. That was the first meeting between the people who wanted to kill our people and us, who did everything we could to annihilate them. Real enemies, meeting face to face. Palestinians who knew me from before could not believe this because in prison I was quite an extremist and everyone knew my views. "What? You talk to Israelis? You?" they asked, and I said: "Yes." "We don't believe you," they said, "even army veterans?" "Yes," I said.

After that first meeting, we decided we'd hold another. I took down the names of Israelis, former soldiers one and all. It was quite frightening. I mean, they were real soldiers, not like me who was a child when I did the things I'd been tried for. I Googled them and found they were real people: *Yonatan Shapira*, *Zohar Shapira*, and *Yehuda Shaul*. I told them I could introduce them to Palestinian society as "former war criminals who now acknowledge your right to freedom and a state." They had a similar idea of introducing us to Israeli society by saying: "These are former terrorists who now speak of peace and nonviolence. We brought them here." So I was their passport to their people and they were my passport to my people. That's what we thought in the beginning, and it really was good.

After a year of such meetings, we established the Combatants for Peace Movement, with some 300 members in the first year. We started addressing audiences on both sides, spreading the message that war does not serve any side. We said that the Israeli soldiers do not improve Israel's security because they create more enemies on the Palestinian side; and that Palestinian terrorists do not serve Palestinian interests, but only create more hatred among the Israelis. There is no military solution for this conflict, so we must fight together against the common enemy, against the continuation of the occupation that leads to cruelty, retaliation, and terrorism. It was a dream, but we were ready. Every one of us has his own story, but we all share a desire to live normally, peacefully, and morally – on both sides. Worrying for their side, each serves the other side as well. Violence will never make your enemy cross over. I found myself studying those people, how they look at us at the army barriers, feeling they should learn why we hate them. Back then, in 2005, I already had six children. We started the meetings early that year, but could not even decide on the name of our movement. It took a year of discussions before we agreed on Combatants for Peace.

The movement's opening declaration took place on June 10, 2006. I remember we went to the Palestinian President Abbas (also known as *Abu Mazen*) and invited him to the declaration so that he could see that we – Israelis and Palestinians, former soldiers and prisoners – are now fighting for peace together. He was amazed and said: "Well done! I hope you will make peace." And we said: "God forbid. You wait for us to make peace? We are young. You need to make peace; we want to enjoy peace." So he said: "*Inshallah* [God willing]. You should tell the Israeli soldiers that they determine how things will be: If the Israeli soldiers treat Palestinians with respect, they will be respected back." We invited former prisoners, social activists, and political activists from the PLO and the PFLP. The local council head wanted to hold the meeting in Anata as a way of showing respect to me and another three former warriors and prisoners from the village. The Palestinian prisoners are the warriors of the Palestinian nation, and the Palestinian society greatly respects and believes in us. Some 300 Israelis and 200 Palestinians attended the first declaration. On that day, there was some tear gas, just a little, and the Israelis asked: Why are they doing this? Well, they fire tear gas because whenever there is a gathering, there is also fear. Two years later, we held a ceremony in *Tulkarm* to mark the thirty-sixth anniversary of the occupation, and some 8,000 people attended.

THE DEATH OF MY DAUGHTER ABIR

On January 16, 2007, an Israeli soldier aged 18 and a half shot and killed my third daughter Abir just outside her school in Anata. He had no reason to shoot her, but unfortunately he did. She was leaving school with her sister and two more girls at 9:30 AM, after completing her exams, and crossed the street to buy some candy when a Border Police jeep drove by. A single shot was fired from the jeep's back window – a rubber bullet that hit her in the head from some 50–60 feet. She fell and died two days later at the Hadassah Medical Center in Ein Kerem, Jerusalem.

More than 30 Israeli families and members of Combatants for Peace arrived two hours later and spent the next two days in the hospital with me until Abir passed away. I remember reporters asking me: "Now what?" and I said: "I have no doubt that we want no revenge, but I want justice. Should the worse happen and Abir dies, I'd make them launch an inquiry, though I am certain they will eventually close the case for lack of evidence." Abir passed two days later and indeed, on the third day, they started an inquiry. It took them three whole days, but the fact they did was a historic achievement. It was truly unbelievable.

After four and a half years, the Supreme Court stated that though it is a mother's right to know who killed her daughter, it has been four and a half years and they closed the case for lack of evidence. It is because of cases like this that the Palestinians feel we will never see an Israeli soldier on trial for killing a Palestinian. Many people say it has been like that since *1948*. The case of *Al-Azaria* was an exception. It was so because everything was photographed and there were Jewish witnesses, and even he was released on parole after ten months. Personally, I had no doubt. It was clear to me that I did not seek revenge. During the two years before Abir died, I worked with former murderers – soldiers who share my activities with Combatants for Peace. I am their best friend though it may well be that they fired at Palestinians during their military service. On a personal level, I am at peace because nothing could ever bring my daughter back to me, but I've always said that I want to know why. Why?! I would never accept the soldier's explanation because nothing could ever justify murdering my girl, but I need an explanation: Why did you do that? What were you thinking? Abir was only 10.5 years old. Idan Meir, who was with me in Combatants for Peace, wrote a play about Abir titled "Don't Look Hangdog around Here" that played at the Cameri Theater of Tel Aviv. In the play, two soldiers challenge each other to shoot the girl with the long hair in the head. A game. We have 14 eyewitnesses, but they are all Palestinians, which means they do me no good.

For me, life split in 2007 – there's all that happened before and after that year; as in before the *Nakba* and after it, or before and after the Holocaust. Personally, my thoughts are to promote peace and be a peace activist. In the past, there were incidents when I had to address some group and said I was tired and that they should send someone else. Now, I don't allow myself to miss a single opportunity. I hate traveling, but have since traveled some 200 times, given hundreds of lectures, five–six a day sometimes. I don't know where I get the energy for it. I decided I am doing this for Abir, and that the whole world should talk about her and what happened to her because she was a Palestinian girl. And not because whoever killed her was an Israeli or a Palestinian, but because he was never put on trial. Someone shot and killed my girl and I want him to stand trial, regardless of the struggle. She was neither a fighter nor a hero.

YOU ARE NO LESS A VICTIM THAN YOUR VICTIM

I met the man who shot my daughter three years later in a Jerusalem court-house. Then, I tried to get into his head. I realized that he did not see my wife or me, nor did he take us into consideration. That was my opportunity to talk to him – "Why don't you admit? Are you scared? You did not kill a Jew. You killed an Arab. You should be proud of it. You may even be promoted" – but he was not allowed to answer me. I told him the truth: "I want you to know that you are neither a hero nor a warrior. You did not kill a terrorist or some radical fighter. You killed an innocent girl aged 10. Now, if you think it is OK to kill another girl or Arab, enjoy your crime. I do not seek revenge because I don't take revenge from victims, and you are a victim. You are no less a victim than your victim." I watched him as I spoke and saw he could not believe he was hearing a terrorist, a Palestinian. So I told him: "Whenever you want, whenever you feel like it, if you'd be willing to ask for my forgiveness, I will forgive you. I am not doing this for you. It is for me. You don't know how much I love my daughter. I have five more children and I want to raise them differently. I do not want them to think about you or be your victims when you are a victim yourself."

I met him two months later, and he was a different man. I believe in our roots. That's life. We are humans, and though we are sometimes very cruel and murder another human, we can always go back to our roots. He became religious, grew a beard, and donned a yarmulke. He was a child of 18 from *Kiryat Shmona*, it was his first tour of the territories, and he wanted to give his country something more, but killed this girl. He must have discovered that he really killed a girl who had a father and a mother with a heart and tears. I don't envy him.

When I saw him for the second time, in court, he could not look at me, and I could see he was sorry. I hoped we could meet before the trial ended and that he would come to me and say: "I am sorry. I killed your daughter, and I beg for your forgiveness." Abir was not a head of state or one of his kind in the world, but she was my child, and he does not know what he did to me. I wanted him to understand what she meant to me, and then I could tell him: "Go. You are free. I forgive you." He was not willing. They told me it would be wrong to do that during the trial because it would be as if we were trying to influence and pressure him, which was not healthy. Through a middleman, I learned that he was filled with remorse, having understood that he had killed a 10-year-old girl, a normal girl whose parents are peace activists. I felt that was my revenge. I could very easily grab and kill him, but what would I gain from his death? Even if he would be in prison for a million years, what would I gain from this? Your pain remains your pain. If, however, he realized he had made a mistake, understood that killing children was wrong, and asked for my forgiveness, that would be my revenge.

After the trial, we were in the process of arranging a meeting. I was ready. When they asked me what I wanted from him, I said I wanted to ask him "Why?" and that if he asked for forgiveness, I wanted to forgive him. He was not willing to meet. It was not easy for him. The military system said it was not them and they were not accountable, so if he suddenly stated: "Yes, I killed her, firing by mistake," he feared they might throw him in jail and he would suffer. I believe that he will be ready one day and will come. That is on a personal level.

ABIR TELLS ME: "RISE, DON'T FORGET ME"

On a more general level, you kind of develop a new vision. We learn every day that there is no difference between Palestinians and Israelis. We have the same fears and expectations, and we hate each other because we want peace. Israelis are becoming more extreme – electing *Benjamin Netanyahu*, *Avigdor Lieberman*, and *Naftali Bennett* – because they want peace. They want a strong leader to end the struggle, kill all Palestinians, drive them out to the sea or to other Arab countries – anything for a solution. The Palestinians elected *Hamas* for the very same reason: They, too, want to end the conflict by destroying Israel. I, however, discovered that the majority really want normal peace without killing or expelling anyone, but they have no voice or courage because that option is scary.

I believe that peace activists in Israel have a harder time than their Palestinian counterparts. These days, it is very hard to speak of peace in Israel. You'd be persecuted if you did, God forbid. I can also understand the Palestinians who attack me because I seek a solution as Israelis attack their own peace activists. It is very difficult. All these years, I have never been threatened really. They may say I am a 'Jew lover,' but no one has ever accused me of treason. I am known as a peace activist who operates within Palestinian society and works with moral people on the other side who want peace and act against the occupation also for their own society. I believe that people like me have no right to keep quiet. I have no right not to speak because I have no fear because the worst has already happened to me, so what do you fear more?! I believe this is the only way to defend the Palestinian nation, or at least my own children. I have five, and I want to protect them this way. That's what motivates me personally to remain active 24 hours a day and never rest.

Now, not everything you know about your enemy is the enemy. I realized that I must develop, learn about the Jews, and learn to distinguish between Jews and Israelis. I studied the background of the Palestinian-Israeli conflict and, with insights I gained from it, I am seeking the most effective way to fight the conflict. I must change my reality from bad to better, which is what has been motivating me 24 hours a day because I live under the same conditions for 24 hours a day. You evolve and make partnerships with the other side, and you have a family and want them to grow normally. The situation is not normal, so I am very active personally, trying to change reality for my children and myself. When everyone works for their family, a global peace movement can be formed. That is my goal. When I speak with Palestinians, I say: "Don't worry about me. Do it for yourselves, for your children. Don't worry about the Israelis. They have been the chosen people for the past 3,000 years. They can look after themselves and you should worry about yourselves. When I raise and educate my children in Jericho like that, and an Israeli in Eilat raises his children like that – we help each other."

It is difficult sometimes. I use the respect I earned as a former prisoner to propagate my vision and message within my society. I argue that I work for them, not for the Israelis, and it is working. I remind them that we have a right to struggle, regardless of whether they name us murderers or terrorists. The problem is that terrorist activity does not serve us – not because it harms or hurts Israelis, but because it destroys us, and we don't want that. What's wrong with harnessing Israelis to the cause without hurting them? When you explain things normally, they are accepted. You have to stand up and state your arguments, and people will respect you.

One of our problems is the peace industry. Just like the war industry, where some people make a living selling weapons, there are people who sell peace, giving nonviolence workshops, for example. This has turned into an industry. For me, however, it is something else, a way of life. We are all humans and our message is truly universal. For example, I so strongly identified with Smadar Elhanan, daughter of my 'brother' *Rami Elhanan*, so much so that, while addressing an audience, I said: "On 16 January, 2007, an Israeli soldier shot and killed my daughter 'Smadar,'" instead of saying 'Abir.'

We can use our pain differently, not only for revenge, and revenge is not only killing someone. There are other ways to take revenge. I looked at the face of the soldier who killed my daughter, that victim, and said: "I forgive you, but it is not for you." I felt then I had my revenge. If he came to me someday, got down on his knees, and asked for my forgiveness, I would have my revenge: I would forgive him but show no pity. I mean, forgiving is a form of revenge, but it is a personal thing of how you look at yourself.

This insight is a kind of path, and if you have supporters, it is great. The most important thing is keeping yourself out of danger. I speak English and Hebrew on television, at schools, with the president, with Hamas, with the settlers. If they like it, *Ahalan and Sahalan*, fine; if not, this is the path I follow without trying to convince them. The truth is that everyone I speak with accepts that because it is very hard to oppose messages of peace, equality, and security for all. This is very hard to resist.

Our vision was based on a Nelson Mandela saying: "To make peace with an enemy, you must work with that enemy," then he becomes your partner. We said right from the start that we are partners – not brothers or friends. Partners do not need to love each other. We are all partners. We are the combatants on both sides and we have our dignity. It was harder on the Israeli side, but we took slow, healthy steps. Sometimes we took a step back, but we never ceased – and it worked.

My daughter Abir is my motivation. First I wrote: "Your killer will die and you will outlive him because no one will remember him and you will be remembered by the whole world." It is Abir that keeps telling me: "Rise! Don't forget me! I have five more siblings. Look after them at least." It is very hard for me to explain why I did not watch over her. It was my fault, perhaps. Maybe I should have kept her at home and not let her out, but that is irrational. At the same time, the enemy gives you strength. When you cross a roadblock and he wants to shoot you, hold up your arms and then, if you speak for two minutes, he could hug you and say, "I wish the whole world were like you," and then feel sorry and start crying. This gives me the power to go on. When I discover that even very cruel people are mere humans, it gives me the strength to keep speaking with such dedication. You are free of your victim mentality because you have no enemies to hate or conquer. When no one can defeat you because you are free inside, you live in peace. My faith helps me, too. I am religious. Before I go to sleep at night, I forgive the whole world. Then, everyone is aligned and there are no differences between Jews, Christians, Muslims, Palestinians, and people in general.

I DON'T PLAY A ROLE – THAT IS MY LIFE

I think that when you believe in a cause and strive to attain it, it becomes part of your life. I don't play a role. That is my life. I keep traveling around the world. Today, I work as a spokesman for the Parents Circle Families Forum (PCFF) on the Palestinian side and in charge of international relations. Also, I guide narrative groups on both sides and instruct new speakers in telling their personal story at the forum. Working with bereaved families is very hard because each has its own tragic story and I know today how strong you must be so as not to be affected by the current situation. This is not easy at all. I believe there is a goal and that we'll eventually have a peace agreement, though we don't know when and how much blood will have to be spilled before it happens. I will not change my mind because I know that. Therefore, it is essential not to get carried away by violence or even despair. The goal and the task are very hard, but I keep my spirits up and believe that it will happen in the end.

Currently, the situation is tough, dark, and not just politically. In reality, every day brings us closer to peace. Every day I hear of more wrongs and tragedies caused by the occupation, but every day I also see an Israeli or a Palestinian joining Combatants for Peace, and that keeps me balanced. I am always happy to see gatherings of young people whose meetings and communication are not obvious, who come from nothing but hatred and fear, spending time together on our summer camps, and cry in the end because they hate to separate. It gives me hope to see that young men and women don't hate each other the way our fathers and grandfathers did. Our parents lived through the Nakba and the Holocaust and just needed to survive. Today, we start thinking: Why do we kill each other? What could be wrong if a Palestinian boy met an Israeli girl? Society is more open and despite the old hatred, new generations are more open.

We do manage to get individuals on both sides to get together, but we are totally cut off from each other as nations. There is total closure between the two nations. Politically, this is also very difficult because not only Israelis and Palestinians are involved in this conflict. You have the Americans, the Iranians, and other parties with vested interests in the conflict – some want to solve it, others want to exacerbate it. So I believe there will be peace, only I can't say when.

I believe that the Palestinians must be taught about the Holocaust. From their point of view, the Jews have been using the Holocaust to explain the occupation, which is why the Palestinians don't believe in and deny the Holocaust. I remember, for example, what happened with my prison inmates who were willing to talk about peace, but never about the Holocaust. They'd say: "Do you believe their lies? That's what has been killing us. This lie turned us into refugees." They even asked: "Do you have Jewish roots? What's wrong with you?" That's how it started, but eventually they were willing to hear me because I had things to say about the Holocaust and why we deny it. I then realized that it is important to educate about the Holocaust, not as a personal issue, but as a fact. On the Palestinian side, this is my mission – not for the Jews, but for my nation, for my side to be familiar with the enemy's past and history. We need to see how Jews accept their history, and how you find that Jews are very simple people. My mission was to truly understand that, first for myself and my children, and then for my society. That changed me and helped me, so I want to help them.

I don't believe there is absolute evil. That's the difference between humans and animals. Some people are murderers, but no one was born a murderer and the environment always has an impact. If you place even the most moderate person in a room with violent people, he would want to defend himself and will become violent. A moderate man might get into a fight for half a minute, during which he might kill and become a murderer. Things are more complicated with the police and the army, whose role is to kill. I am certain that not all Nazi soldiers were killers. I am sure some of them helped and hid Jews. That they were just human and could not understand why that race had to be eliminated. So there is no absolute evil in humans. I don't believe there is.

I chose to study the Holocaust and attended the University of Bradford, England, in 2010–2011. Studies were very difficult because I went there for a year when it takes two years to earn a degree, and everything was in English, which is my third language, but you understand nothing with their British accent. Still, I earned my master's degree. You know, when you earn an academic degree and you work for the Palestinian Authority, you report that and get a promotion and a salary raise. I, however, have been keeping my MA certificate in my suitcase, never filed it with the Palestinian Authority, and no one ever saw it. I studied for myself, to learn about the Holocaust. Later, I also visited several concentration camps.

When I was in Weimar, Germany, I went to see the Buchenwald Concentration Camp. Entering it, I saw a lovely park with trees and a small zoo. It turned out that Nazi officers would bring their children there to play outside, and then they would enter the camp and kill 500 people. I needed to understand how such people could get up in the morning, kiss their wives, hug their children or cry if they were ill – an ordinary human being who is also a killing machine.

How did these things combine? Was it in their blood, or did the role and the environment have an impact? This is very hard to understand, particularly when you are a normative person. I can imagine that if I were born a German and lived under Hitler, God forbid, I'd be proud to be German, join the army, and conquer the world for Hitler. We would all feel national pride and not be ashamed of ourselves. In the process, I learned something that is always useful: Always try to see yourself on the other side of situations, imagine yourself as both a killer and as a victim, and try to understand the other side. It helped me to realize that while there is a struggle between good and bad, often things are not good or bad, black or white, but there are things you cannot control. In life, one needs to be wise, not get carried away, and try hard not to be violent or become a killer.

Personally, this approach helped me with my family. With my son, who was 13 when Abir was murdered, I was already in a very different place. Two years before the murder, I worked with Combatants for Peace 24/7. That is, I worked with those sworn enemies, with the same soldiers who had murdered and killed, imposed curfews, detained us, and demolished our homes. Then I discovered the humanity and noble soul of the enemy, who was no longer my personal enemy but became my partner. He told me how he grew up and I understood him. Even that boy who killed Abir, I know him. He came from Kiriat Shmona, a place of missiles and fear, and grew up in bomb shelters. In his mind, he always needs to be on the safe side. He probably came from a normative family that did not teach him to hate Arabs, but he was in the army, which is very hard. The first time he entered Anata was a mistake. At first, the army said: "We were not there," but eventually, the commander of the Jerusalem security fence said: "These were my soldiers who mistakenly entered the village on their own accord." I demanded that he told me the truth. I told him many things: "Why are you ashamed? After all, what did you kill? You just shot an Arab. So what? It is not a crime." One of my Israeli friends from Combatants for Peace tried to help me imagine what went on in his head when he shot a girl for no reason. He related: "We went to catch a terrorist, besieged the house and started throwing stun grenades in, so they all came out. Suddenly I saw a seven-year-old girl running from the house toward the soldiers. In that moment, I was afraid she was carrying explosives and might harm my men," he said. "I did not believe I was doing that then." And he was an officer with *Sayeret Matkal*, one of the most known special forces in the Israeli army, and an educated man. His own acts shocked him and, remembering he had just had a baby girl, in that moment, he refused to continue the *army service*. So I can only imagine what the boy who shot Abir was thinking, and I tried to convey that feeling and understanding to my son when he wanted to avenge Abir.

I told my son: "They will shoot you for throwing a stone. They just shoot and you die, and your stone might not even hit their jeep. Is your life worth just a stone?" Then I showed him a film about the Holocaust and I remember that he cried and I did too. He told me he wanted to understand why they were killing the Jews. They must have done something wrong. The Jews are bad, but why did it happen to them? This started a conversation about Nazis and Jews, and about the boy who murdered Abir, and about the Palestinians.

There is no absolute justice. No such thing. I learned that from an Israeli judge who presided over the High Court of Justice when it considered our petition regarding Abir's death. She said she did not doubt that an Israeli soldier indeed killed Abir Aramin, but that does not belong in the media or the court. She said that in this particular case, the Army did everything it could to inquire and find the truth, so I did not have a case, and there are no documents or testimonies. She said courts are not there to make justice, but to separate people. What does justice mean when my child is dead? Would it be justice if they paid me $100 million, or put the soldier behind bars for a million years? Or sentenced him to death? I only want my daughter back, and nothing could replace a human life. So I said from the start that getting my daughter back would be just, but there is no absolute justice. There is, however, relative justice. I mean, when a person helps society and people thank him and reward him; or when a person commits a crime, and they jail him. There is no justice when criminals go unpunished. A person who does something wrong should punish himself if we want to protect justice and society – not for me; for that person.

Abir did not die for Palestine. She was not a warrior. She was killed by mistake, but deliberately, and I want her murderer to stand trial for social justice, to keep society normative. Not for the Palestinians, but for the Israelis – no more and no less. Now, this helped me because I promised my son that the soldier would face trial, and he said: "You're dreaming." "No way," I answered. "He will face trial. He may not be convicted as he should be because the Army follows other laws, but he will stand trial!" They compensated me, and I was willing to give that money away just to see him in court, so that I could show my son that it happened. They say that absolute justice exists only in heaven.

The Palestinians had all of Palestine and now they have only 20 percent of the land. They still have documents proving their ownership of land and they remember the names of their villages that they did not own 3,000 years ago, but recently. Is that justice? No, it is not. Is it just to let us return to their lands and homes? That is not justice either. I lost my home, it has since been destroyed. My return to that same house would require the demolition of so many floors of the building that stands there now and would be unjust to the people who currently live there. Many Jewish refugees who arrived in Israel were given houses as a way of doing them justice, but that turned me into a refugee. When you do justice to some while unjustly treating others, that's not justice. The least that could happen is for the parties to assume responsibility for recent-past deeds: The British for their promise, the Israelis for their occupation, and the Palestinians for killing children and civilians as part of their struggle. We should all acknowledge the wrongs we inflict upon each other. That is reconciliation, which produces comprehensive justice. The rules do not say that if you killed my daughter, you apologize and I forgive you, and bye-bye. Both nations are offenders, both are bereaved, both are victims. I believe there will be something on a general level, which is the politicians' role. When a peace accord is attained, we start talking about reconciliation and turn it into a two-way process. It will happen in the end.

Yes, I was a prisoner. Prisoners are not victims but brave warriors. We volunteered. It is not like the Israeli Army where you are obliged to serve. No! Here, I volunteer because I am a very sensitive person who cannot accept our oppression and enslavement by another nation, other people. That's how it begins. When I speak with young men in the villages and discuss violence and nonviolence, many of them say they have never heard of the latter. They are far from that narrative. If an army jeep drove by and you did not hurl a stone at it, you are ashamed. You only want to throw a stone. Why? Because that's the way it is in the village. When my son was 14, two years ago, he told me: "Come on, Dad. All the kids throw stones." "Did anyone tell you to do that?" I asked. "Not really, Dad," he said. I told him: "You watch the funerals and hear the little children in the procession chant, 'Ho *Shahid* (martyr), be calm.' It is a social thing." He told me: "I may not throw stones because I am the son of Bassam Aramin," but I never told him not to. I try to educate him because I want him to understand why throwing stones is wrong. I said: "Suppose you have a stone and you hurl it, what will that achieve? Say we start a Palestinian state tomorrow and we need a justice minister. Who shall we choose," I asked him, "the one who killed the most Jews?" "No," he said. "We will choose a lawyer." "Great," I said. "And who do we elect as education minister: the man who hurled more than 1,000 stones?" "No," he said. "We will elect a teacher or principal." "Yes," I said. "That's how you build a state." I said: "Well done and congratulate the struggle of those who hurled stones, but they cannot serve as doctors later because physicians do no not need a Kalashnikov." "I never thought like that," my son replied. "Good," I said. "Now imagine you go out to throw a stone and there is someone there who studies Hebrew, Arabic, and English, and wants to be a physician or an engineer. You throw that stone, liberate here and you destroy there, and he liberates there and builds here." I want to protect him because he is my son, but I want him to feel that I too am a national patriot. That's how I address the young, and if I manage to change the way they think, it is an achievement. My son, for example, understood that making peace is a way to retaliate Abir's blood.

THE FIRST PALESTINIAN WHO FORGAVE HIS DAUGHTER'S MURDERER FOR RECONCILIATION BETWEEN THE TWO NATIONS

Sometimes, others have a hard time accepting my way. A friend of mine once read in the paper that I was willing to be the first Palestinian who forgave his daughter's murderer for the sake of reconciliation between the two nations. He yelled at me angrily: "Did you say that? How could you? Have you no shame?" And I said: "Hush now. Take it easy ... Why should I be ashamed? Come, read it again: I am willing to be the first to forgive my daughter's murderer. See? I said 'my daughter' – not *your* children. What is mine is mine and does not belong to the Palestinian nation." And he said: "You know what? I am truly sorry. I read this and went mad." "Why are you mad?" I asked him. "You should be proud of me, of my humanity. Why are you angry? My daughter was not a member of the *Al-Aqsa Martyrs' Brigades*. She was an ordinary girl. Now, if I got out and killed even five soldiers, what would that accomplish? How would that solve my problem? It would stay with me to the day I die. Nothing could be done about it," I said. He understood my thinking, though I am not sure he accepted my view. "What if it happened to me?" he wondered. "God forbid," I replied. "Don't even think about this. It would have been different if it had happened to you. You don't know how you'd react, but I did not think I'd act this way either."

Several days ago, in Luxemburg, I appeared with Rami Elhanan. A girl in the audience asked: "How would you respond if they killed another child of yours?" I've never been asked that before. Rami looked at me, but I only said: "Next question, please," and could not answer. After the meeting, she came to see us, crying, and said she was sorry for asking this question. I hugged her and said: "I am sorry. I can't say if your question was smart or silly, good or bad, but I could not answer it. That is all. I never meant to offend you and I'm truly sorry." People sometimes ask me if I would have joined Combatants for Peace if Abir had not been murdered. I don't know. Perhaps not. When she died, however, I was already involved with Combatants for Peace and could very easily reach the PCFF – which is a victims' forum while Combatants comprises the warriors who created these victims – so it was an easy transition for me.

I HAVE DONE EVERYTHING TO BRING PEACE, BUT I AM NOT AN ENTREPRENEUR

I did not initiate or start anything new. I am a part of a whole. I always say that I want to be able to look at myself, at my son or my grandson, and say

I did everything I could to give them a better life and attain peace. I never rest, nor can I afford to be pleased with myself and my working methods, but I am certainly not an entrepreneur.

Practically, it all starts and ends with education. That's it. I say, if you have love, you give it; if you have none, it is because you were raised in a tough manner and that is your life. The next generation that grows in the Palestinian towns has never met Israelis. They see the other side as enemies on television, sometimes not even as soldiers. Just imagine: Ever since the Israeli disengagement from the *Gaza Strip* in 2006, we have not seen a single Israeli soldier there. I try to think like a Gazan. The level of hatred is very high, but just as it is dark and hard now, if a Palestinian and Israeli initiative should emerge, they would connect within 15 minutes. I tour the world and bring together Palestinians who live in Gaza with Israelis who served there as soldiers. As soon as they start talking about accepting each other, the Israelis sympathize and the Palestinians understand. From the worst places, an encounter forms.

It is very difficult to educate for love in the current situation. I don't believe there is absolute evil, but fear followed by suspicion and hatred is in human nature. Love is the normal thing, but then someone makes us fear and then hate. People think: You are different, so you want to kill me, conquer me, take my money, dominate my water, food, and landscapes. That's how hostility and hatred begin. Still, we have a lot in common. Jews, Christians, and Muslims are members of faiths who all pray to the same God. That is why education is so important. We, the Palestinians, need to start learning Hebrew and study the Israeli narrative, which we believe is a lie. We need to know what they say and understand how they live with their history, how they grow up, what they think about us, and how they view our history. The Israelis, too, need to study about us. Imagine what would happen if all of the Palestinians learned what went on in the Holocaust, while all the Israelis became acquainted with the Palestinian Nakba of *1948*. That would change the way each side perceives the other.

My duty is not to dwell on the past because it is over and gone, with the good and the bad in it. It is my job to look forward and say that reconciliation is possible. When I traveled to England, I saw Indian security guards. India was under British occupation, but that ended and now Indian natives may relocate to England, receive citizenship, and join British society. In the United States, I see Muslim and even Pakistani security officers in airports, and I wonder: Could I ever be a security officer in an Israeli airport? Possibly! For this to happen, we need to educate both nations to see the other side as human beings and defend the humanity of the other side. That is the first step.

3. Peace, a mission for generations

Eliaz Cohen
Interviewed by Lital Myers and Amalya Oliver-Lumerman

Eliaz Cohen is a poet, literary editor, and social worker. He is a religious settler who works for peace and coexistence with his neighbors. His main initiative is called A Land for All – Two States, One Homeland. It outlines a way for the Israeli and Palestinian nations to attain peace and reconciliation in their shared motherland. In the summer of 2012, Eliaz and several leading Israeli and Palestinian partners started holding meetings all over Israel to forge the initiative A Land for All – Two States, One Homeland that was revealed in 2015. He also took part in other initiatives that promoted peace in this land and brought Jews and Palestinians closer.

Eliaz Cohen is viewed as a leader of the renaissance of young and religious poets in Israel, and has published five poetry books. He is a co-editor of *Mashiv HaRuach* – a periodical of Jewish-Israeli poetry – and supervises creative writing classes and offers different literature courses through the Ministry of Education in Israel.

We met Eliaz twice. Once in his house at the settlement *Kibbutz Kfar Etzion* where, on a chilly September day, we spent four hours sitting in the living room of his peaceful home and, with only birdsong in the background, listened to Eliaz tell his story as a poet does. He talked about the projects he has been involved with since childhood. He explained how his life experiences formed his identity, why he sympathizes with his neighbors, and all about his work for peace in this land. We were saddened to learn that while we held that interview, Ari Fuld was stabbed to death in a terror attack at the *Gush Etzion Junction*, less than 1 km from where we were, in the southern *West Bank*.

We did not cover everything we wanted the first time, so we met again a few months later. We spent two hours in the Harman Science Library on the Edmond Safra Campus of the Hebrew University of Jerusalem, listening to him detail his various peace initiatives.

IT STARTED BEFORE I WAS BORN

It started before I was born. In 1956, my uncle, Eliezer Feldman, fell in the *Sinai War*. He was my maternal grandparents' firstborn son. They named him Eliezer after Moses' second son, and I was named after him. Being my parents' eldest, I very often think about their expectations of me that came with the name. He was a bright boy who wanted to be a doctor, and died in a heroic but stupid battle. I was raised into that, bearing his name. It is a burden that I have been carrying since childhood and a void that stayed with the family. That void expanded over the years because you see his friends grow old, mature, and evolve, while we keep watching that space he left behind. It is on my emotional mind when I think about the critical aspects of war and peace, justifying acts by the other side or sacrifices the Jewish-Israeli side made, and sympathizing with the other side.

My father worked as an economist for El Al, the Israeli airline, so we flew abroad a lot. Shortly after Israel and Egypt signed the *Egypt-Israel Peace Treaty*, we flew to Cairo. I remember discussions at home before the trip, where Mom expressed her reservations. She was a very broad-minded woman, a clinical social worker whose heart was open to everyone, and suddenly we saw her becoming uptight, refusing to forgive the Egyptians who, in her mind, had killed her big brother. We went without her and it was fascinating, but my uncle's death still makes an impact.

In recent years, I was one of the founders and promoters of the *Roots-Shorashim-Judur* Initiative and of a Palestinian initiative called *Taghyeer* (Change), that speaks about forming a Palestinian national identity based on the non-violent resistance theory and is led by, among others, Ali and Khalid (two brothers who also lead the Roots-Shorashim-Judur Project). They had an idea about forming a reconciliation garden, so we built it together – settlers, Palestinians, and youth groups that we have there. Wonderful things are happening in very many circles. Sometimes they initiate and we join them, sometimes we move forward and they join us, and sometimes we work together. We have a deep and attentive partnership that was made out of listening to what everyone needs from their partners. Our center is located some 200 m from the Gush Etzion Junction. *Ali Abu Awwad* wrote a letter about this reconciliation garden to his brother Yousef, who was killed by Israeli Defense Forces (IDF) soldiers at the beginning of the second Palestinian uprising (aka, the Al-Aqsa *Intifada*); and I wrote to my grandfather, Grandpa Hezko – Eliezer's father. My grandparents died when they were still very young, and clearly there is this bereavement shockwave. They were very optimistic and strong people. They were involved in the establishment of *Yad LaBanim*, dedicated their energies to other bereaved families, and were also very active socially. Still, their tragedy must have been killing them on the inside all the while. Recently, I went back to family albums and found a picture of Grandma that I've never seen before. She had it taken with an auntie from America with a portrait of my uncle, the living-dead, in the background. In that picture, probably taken shortly after Eliezer was killed, Grandma looks like she is terminally ill – withered, listless, forcing a smile – but I remember her very much alive and carrying the entire family on her shoulders.

I write to Eliezer and often correspond with him in my poems. So Ali wrote to his brother Yousef and I wrote to Grandpa about my uncle, and we both placed our letters in glass boxes. We believed there should be texts there in both Arabic and in Hebrew. Such glass boxes were planted in the terrace, which makes people curious to read them. I wrote to Grandpa Hezko and to my yet unborn grandchild, showing empathy for the price they paid in the context of the Israeli-Arab conflict, and how we were in that never-ending bloody cycle and could not find our way out. In my letter, I wrote: "Finding a place and a picture of the future is a never-ending commitment." I can imagine my grandkids' generation living their present in what I picture as my future.

My dad's side of the family relates more to *Revisionist Zionism*, and it is also more liberal, and even a little secular. Grandpa removed his *yarmulke* while still in Poland. He served as one of *Ze'ev Jabotinsky*'s secretaries and toured Europe with him, urging Jews to make *Aliyah* and warning them about the Holocaust to come. *Ze'ev Jabotinsky* foresaw it years before it happened. Grandpa met Grandma and they came to Israel, where he was a commander of a Betar training company. They lived here as a mixed couple – he was secular, and she was religious – which was quite rare in the 1930s and 1940s before the State of Israel was established. When his grandchildren were born, he donned the *yarmulke* back, so I knew him as a religious grandfather. He had this knitted *yarmulke* and prayed, and studied the Torah. I remember that when *Menachem Begin* made the peace accord with Egypt, Grandpa wrote to him and scolded him for abandoning the Greater Israel values. My father absorbed that spirit even earlier and joined the Land of Israel Movement, which was formed right after the *Six Day War in 1967*.

Promoting the idea of Greater Israel, that movement comprised thinkers and philosophers such as *Natan Alterman, Uri Zvi Greenberg*, and *S.Y. Agnon*. It was a significant movement, and my father was one of the younger people that joined it. While the writers and philosophers were mainly addressing the minds, he tried to turn their ideas into real acts on the ground several years before *Gush Emunim* was established. In 1969–1970, my father promoted the first attempts to establish small settlements. He and others located Jewish-owned plots and set up two small groups designated for settlements in Nablus and Battir. They tried to get *Knesset* members and representatives affiliated with the *Labor Movement in Israel*, who were then in power, to lobby for them. So in 1969–1970 they had a supporting lobby comprising people from the *National Religious Party*, *Herut Party* (future Likud), who were leaning to the right, and even some from the Labor Party, who were leaning to the left. That movement broke apart eventually. My parents got married in the summer of 1970. When the Gush Emunim settlement movement was established in 1974, my father joined it even though he did not really belong to those guys and did not attend their schools and *yeshivas*. He gained his doctorate in economics from the Technion.

PIONEERS: MOVING FROM THE CITY OF PETAH TIKVA TO THE 'VIRGINAL' SAMARIA HILLS

I was born in the winter of 1972 and one of my first memories is from the *Yom Kippur War*, when just Mom and I were in Petah Tikva because Dad was in the army. I remember that Dad was absent, holding Mom's hand and running scared to the bomb shelter, and the sound of sirens. That period – the entire time we lived in Petah Tikva, before settling in *Elkana* – is like prehistory for me. My history started when I was seven years old. My memories are clear, but there is this dividing line between my early childhood in Petah Tikva and Elkana, which was new, pioneering, with more nature. Petah Tikva was a city in central Israel, while Elkana was a settlement on the virginal hills of Samaria. I remember feeling attracted to, curious about, and a bit afraid of the Palestinians who were our neighbors. There was an illusion of coexistence.

My family – already with three children – moved from a nice bourgeois apartment in Petah Tikva to a 48 m² concrete prefab box in Elkana. Whenever we go back and recall that, we say those were the best years for our family. Then, my little brother joined us and my parents said: "This is our home; it is small but nice and furnished." My childhood was dipped in pathos. Everything was "first." "The first Jewish settlement here after 2,000 years." We inaugurated a basketball court, so it was "the first basketball court since …" The road they built was the "first road." These things sink in and create an *esprit de corps* and local pride. When you live in a city, everything is taken for granted. You don't see a road or anything built before your very eyes. Living in Elkana was exciting: The settlement was growing and expanding; the synagogue moved from a temporary structure to a large one; the library moved from a small room to a large hall.

Then, a real settlement was built. They built relatively large houses because there were large families of at least six children each, and so we got stuck with large homes. Today, some people of my parents' generation are going back to their original communities in the heart of the country or moving to Jerusalem. Those who settled in Elkana in the early years paid the price in terms of their living conditions. They consciously opted for less, giving up on convenience, accessibility, workplaces. Being the eldest before we moved to Elkana, I remember conversations that I picked up during Sabbath dinners at my grandparents' in Petah Tikva. "Why do you need that?" they asked, not referring to ideology or danger, but – Why give up on your good life in Petah Tikva and move to some barren hill with nothing on it? Why this adventure?

As a child, I felt like a pioneer and that the whole world was looking up at us. We had lots of visitors. I remember not only American politicians, but also movie stars who came to see settlers' children, as we stood and sang for them. We were a show for them, poster boys, objects of admiration. We used to talk to them and showed them the view of Israel's entire Coastal Plain, explaining how important it is that we're there. It filled us with pride, which turned into hubris at some point. Of course, there was an opposition. I remember *Peace Now* people demonstrating in Elkana on Saturdays. The grown-ups used to debrief us, telling us not to shout or curse, but present them with flowers and candy. I wish we could have that sort of dialogue today.

THE FRACTION LINE: THE FIRST TERROR ATTACK

We felt like we were reliving the acts of the Second and Third *Aliyah*. They dried swamps, while we conquered hills. Our parents took the initiative and decided that our curriculum should include lessons in Arabic and Arab folk-lore so that we learned a little about our neighbors' culture. They brought *Ali Yichya*, no less – a teacher of Arabic language and Arab culture who, along with several others, later established Ulpan Akiva in *Netanya*, for which they won the *Israel Prize*. He came to us and taught Arabic to the young settlers' children. For us, it was an extraordinary experience because he was a charming and warm person, and he too experienced it as crossing a line. Years later, he told me that when they invited him, he was not sure he should accept or decline. After all, the people who invited him were busy with an enterprise he could not relate to, and he was taking a risk via-à-vis the Israeli-Palestinians, for whom that was a line that should not be crossed. Still, he said his life's mission was teaching languages, using Arabic and Hebrew as a bridge for reconciliation. "How could I not do it with you?" he said. "Actually, it is an opportunity."

That lasted three years, from 1978 to 1981. It was important for everyone who thought that since we moved to this region, we need to study it, get to know it, get closer. I remember it ended one Saturday night, after a car of an Elkana family that was coming back from a visit at the heart of the country was hit by a hand grenade that was thrown at it from a Palestinian village. That was the first terror attack. The car was damaged and a few people were injured, but no one was killed, thank God. That was a fraction line and anxiety followed, and the first price we paid was that Ali stopped coming to Elkana. Why?

Because. Our instinct said there is an enemy, and he represented that enemy, its language and culture, and we did not want that. None of that was openly declared or spoken, but the cutoff was very sharp. Then, fear sneaked in and they erected fences and increased guard duty. I used to join Dad then, feeling like a little man who, together with his father, guarded the Samarian hills. Dad was given an Uzi and I got to hold the handle.

In routine times, the settlement defended itself, and again there was the connection between budding masculinity and fear, where every guard duty was an adventure. I remember that, at some point, after our shift ended, we'd play basketball and barbeque hot dogs, and this atmosphere was created. There was no awareness of a Palestinian nationality yet, only we all honestly wondered: "We came here positively, so why don't you accept us? Please, do." That, more or less, was the attitude. The grown-ups had no developed political concepts either.

As far as I was concerned, my formative years started when Israel and Egypt signed a peace treaty, and we were coming upon April 1982, the *Yamit* evacuation date, Passover. A bunch of families left Elkana and moved to Yamit to support the settlers there. We had several waves like that, and we went to visit them on holidays and, being part of the anti-disengagement movement, attended rallies. They even staged a hunger strike – the longest ever on the Jewish side: 52 days – so for us, the children of the settlement, that was a time of solidarity with the Yamit settlers. It was all about Greater Israel that we believed in, and every house had this sticker that read "The Land of Israel Belongs to the Nation of Israel." That was part of the DNA of anyone who was raised by members of the National Religious Movement and still is – religiously, politically, you name it. We had that ownership awareness that was totally indisputable. Peace was not yet the bad word as it is viewed now by many National Religious Zionists and by Israeli society as a whole, but the question of the price was always there. So, fine: peace for peace, or perhaps territories for peace – all those questions came up and started sharpening my political views and stands. I remember being most ambivalent because suddenly we were making peace with the Egyptians, those who killed my uncle Eliezer, those who fought against us, who were the no. 1 enemy of the State of Israel and had the biggest army. Clearly, we were happy about peace, but then there was the question of price: How much will it cost us?

In those years, I was a very political child. In 1982, I was 10, in fourth or fifth grade, and a member of the editorial board of the school's newspaper, which addressed political issues too. That year, *Operation Peace for the Galilee* (the first War of Lebanon) broke out, and I remember writing an editorial justifying it.

WITH A GOOD RHETORICAL ABILITY, A NOT SO BAD THEATRICAL ABILITY, AND A DEVELOPED JUSTICE FEELING

The First *Intifada* started in 1987. By then, I had spent little time at home because I went to a yeshiva, a religious high school, which means sleeping in dorms and going home only once a fortnight – which is quite crazy. After all, it means leaving your settlement, family, and home at 16. I joined Rabbi Neriya's *Kfar HaRoeh Yeshiva* in the *Hefer Valley*. It is an excellent yeshiva, with religious and high school studies of the highest quality, which mattered to me then. Even when I was in kindergarten and grammar school, I could not be rebellious or mischievous, or do wrong things that children do, such as teasing others. That worked against me too. They used to call me Justice-Warrior Eliaz. It came out of me at a very early age, so when something else came out, they said: "Eliaz? You are a justice warrior. We did not expect *that* from you." They used to give me a sort of shaming.

At some point, I thought of really becoming Justice-Warrior Eliaz and dreamt of being a public defender for the state, protecting those who could not pay for their defense. I knew I had a fine rhetoric skill, not-bad theatrics, and a developed sense of justice, so I thought of studying law, but it is tough to enroll with a law school. The television carried all kinds of series about lawyers and courts, so it was clear to me that I was not going to make money, which did not interest me much, and I did not care about defending evil people, I wanted to be a good lawyer who helped those who needed it the most. I started looking for a strong high school that would make it easier for me to be accepted in university. I had this calculated path and I knew I wanted to join the IDF's Academic Reserve [a program for high school graduates who defer the draft and attend university before their military service]. Still, when I graduated high school, I had a change of heart. I told myself that I don't have to decide now, and that if I wanted to be a lawyer or public defender, I would be, but now – before joining the IDF – I want to do things I might not be able to do later. So even though I came from a very open-minded home that was even anti-rabbinical, I decided to join the *Or Etzion Yeshiva*.

After I checked several yeshivas, looking for the strongest and most total experience, I found a very diversified school there in terms of rabbis, views, and a variety of approaches to the Torah, but also to studies and to life, as well as a strong student commitment without 'school police.' I knew I was not going to be this glorious warrior, which helped me choose Or Etzion because it was the only *hesder* yeshiva where you study for two years before joining the army. I studied there for some 18 months, and it was a real heaven. All the while, I remembered Dad's warning from childhood: Choose what you take.

I saw some guys changing before my eyes and turning into blind followers of this or that rabbi. That never worked for me, certainly not with the resistance I brought from home. My parents were terribly worried when I chose the yeshiva and dropped the academic reserve. They could not understand what was happening to me, but I kept telling them: "Don't worry. I am not going to change on you." My parents worried that I was becoming a *Hardal* (a *Zionist Ultra-Orthodox*) right before their eyes, but I told them it was not that, and then I joined the army. I realized quite fast that I would not bloom there. I felt I was going to fall in battle. The story of my Uncle Eliezer weighed me down before the draft. I walked around the house, bidding the rooms farewell. It was hard and very emotionally charged.

In the army, I decided to break away from my *hesder* buddies and joined a regular fighting unit. I did that with two other guys – just us out of 30 yeshiva students. I faced some serious challenges during that period, but it saved me really because the majority of those 30 were sent to serve in the territories, which was horrible. Even though they came equipped with a high moral standard, they were mentally burned out that year. They were assigned to operational activities in the territories for a whole year – not just a few weeks or months – which they spent at the *Dheisheh Refugee Camp*. It was a disaster. Halfway through that year, I was assigned to their unit for two weeks, and it was awful. That was in 1991–1992, the final phase of the First *Intifada*, and we were right at the friction points in the territories.

WHEN QUESTIONS BECOME MORE SPECIFIC

I started regretting not taking a commanders' course because, as an ordinary soldier, you can make minimal impact. You could minimize damage, but as a commander you have a little more power to make a difference. Anyway, I felt the army's entire mission in the territories was very wrong. Our main task was chasing children – teenagers, at best – who threw stones. It was a game of cat and mouse, and it was pointless. You must chase a bunch of kids, and you can't really catch a child; and even if you do, then what? Do you arrest an 11 year old, or 13? Serious moral issues emerged there.

As part of our mission, we fought against nationalistic and patriotic symbols of Palestinian awakening. We had to remove nationalist graffiti they painted on walls and other places, and take off *Palestinian Liberation Organization (PLO)* flags they'd hoisted. I remember that our questions became more specific: How can we even fight this? What is the point of all this? Will we ever win this way? It happened suddenly, and we were not ready for this. We believed that if we broke some arms and legs, as *Yitzhak Rabin* said, we'd succeed in subduing them. Clearly, it was not working, and I found myself facing my commanders and refusing orders more than once. I saw wrongs being committed in front of my eyes, so I cared less for the political questions, or about winning. If I were certain that our path was just, I'd perhaps be motivated to do things that felt immoral to me but for me the main difficulty was the issue of morality.

I remember patrolling the *Hebron* alleyways, feeling frustrated about failing to capture stone-throwers who kept laughing at us, humiliating us. We reached this wide alley and saw a nationalist slogan, in Arabic, with PLO flags, drawn on a wall. We could see that one of my company commanders was looking for a victim and found an old Palestinian who was just sitting in his garden. That officer, a Sephardi who spoke some military Arabic – horrible Arabic, really – and had some Arabic from home, started a conversation with the old man that went like this: "Who wrote this?" "I don't know," the Palestinian said. "Not me." So the officer said: "Good. So now you get out there and wipe it off." Forcing them to remove slogans or flags themselves was a thing. We wanted to humiliate them, make them go on a limb. The old man said: "What?" and showed him his walking cane, explaining that he was old and sick. The officer walked up to him and kicked his chair from under him. At that point, I leaped at the officer, pushed him aside, and took my rage out on him; and I am not a big or strong guy. I yelled at him: "You will do no such thing! We're soldiers!" At that point, of course, the entire family of the old man came out – young children, his daughters – the whole thing turned into chaos, and I shoved my commander. He flew away and then got up and walked towards me with murder in his eyes, and sprayed me with curses I'll never forget, including: "You leftist settler a**hole." He did not know how to define me, and the adjectives just got mixed up. One of our company commanders arrived at the site of the event, pulled me aside, and said: "Eliaz, I understand what you did here politically, but we cannot act like that. We must not argue in front of them, certainly not to insult a commander," but I was so agitated that I did not care at all.

When I completed my military tour, the *Oslo Accords* had just been signed – September 1993; it is the twenty-fifth anniversary right now – and I went back to my yeshiva, which had turned into a serious ideological stronghold of right-wing, religious Zionism under *Rabbi Drukman*. Then, I was right at the heart of the Greater Israel ethos, settlements, worrying for the state and Zionism and the future. We believed Oslo was threatening all of that – the nation's settlement enterprise and Zionism in general. So I joined the Oslo opposition and we marked the boundaries of our struggle – only democratic means, blocking the road at the most, and not confronting the security forces. Rabbi Zvi Yehuda HaCohen Kook, the *Gush Emunim* spiritual leader (and teacher of Rabbi Drukman), drew the boundaries of the Gush Emunim struggle clearly, naming the three no's: no physical violence, no verbal violence, and not even violence of the heart – that is, not even hatred or negative emotions. Struggling for the Land of Israel, we must be completely pure. Do not violate these instructions because then, the whole thing would not be worth it. That was the instruction we received from Rabbi Drukman: "If you find yourself beginning to develop negative emotions toward the state, the police officers, and the soldiers, this entire business becomes blasphemous and is not worth it." We have to be conscious and sensitive to our environment. We must make people aware, as if we lose in the public sphere, we would do damage and introduce hatred, and so we will lose the entire campaign. It would be like scoring an own goal. We were very attentive and knew it was not easy to conduct a struggle like that – democratically and gently.

I looked around me and saw police on foot or horseback, and special patrol unit officers in black uniforms, beating the hell out of rabbis, pregnant women, and totally non-violent demonstrators, men and women. I'd never even imagined such things. At the same time, more and more territories were given to what was then the PLO (and would be the Palestinian Authority), and more and more terror attacks were perpetrated all over Israel. We started losing friends, both settlers and residents of 'smaller Israel.' I remember myself getting really charged.

At some point, we went to hang flags on the *Ramat Aviv* street where Yitzhak Rabin lived. People told us: "They won't let you hang signs against Yitzhak Rabin, Oslo, or the government on Yitzhak Rabin's very street." Then, we said: "We want him to break down." No one talked about murder, God forbid. Absolutely not. They did say, however, that Yitzhak Rabin has this history, that he cannot hold it together when times get rough. As it were, we knew he was ambivalent about the whole Oslo affair, upset by the terror attacks, and suspicious of *Yasser Arafat*. It was all public knowledge then. We wanted to hang signs outside his windows that counted the dead and call them "victims of peace," or hang pictures of those victims, or of blown-up buses – things that would drive him crazy until at some point he would say, "I cannot take this anymore," as Menachem Begin did before he stepped down.

My story approaches the eve of Yitzhak Rabin's murder – which was an Archimedean point. Before that well-cited demonstrations with incitements and provocations were staged, and I remember partaking in a rally at *Zion Square* in Jerusalem. That was a very stormy period. We were struggling over the Gush Etzion hills, trying to 'establish facts' by capturing yet another hill and other state-owned plots that were slated for settlement but had not been settled yet. When I saw the violence at the demonstrations, I felt I could not stand it. It really made me sick – to my mind and stomach – and I decided I would not go back there anymore. I was going to get married and build a home, which we did in Kfar Etzion – a very modest 50 m^2 apartment.

REALISTIC UTOPIA

Years later, all of that made me involved in and promote two projects. One suggested a political vision, a new horizon for the Israeli-Palestinian conflict. We named it *Two States, One Homeland* – which is more or less the model. The core of that vision is *A Land for All*, which is the name of our movement, except that some people read Land as State (we don't). We are not for a single state, but speak of the two-state solution and believe that our model is actually the only solution that would be durable and start a reconciliation process, not mutual mistrust. We speak of two states in a single confederative model – that is, with shared institutions. The movement's model is Together and Separately. That is, there is an Israeli movement, a Palestinian movement, and a shared and coordinated movement with a common tongue. Other movements don't really deal with a political solution, but rather focus on human rights, citizens' rights, attaining economic and social equality, etc. All of those values are found in our movement as well, but we focus on proposing a political vision and here the *Peace Index* is to me the most important yardstick. I am also involved in the local Roots-Shorashim-Judur initiative, which is a physical center we established on Palestinian lands owned by the Abu-Awwad family of peace activists.

The A Land for All initiative started with many people on both sides at the same time. On our side, it involved people who underwent personal processes, like me and my other partners from the left, right, and center, and from the post-Zionist left, who gathered in large numbers in 2009–2010 and created a think tank, a forum named *Eretz Yoshveyha* (Land of Its Inhabitants). It was created by *Yehuda Shenhav*, who invited his doctorate students and others, including myself, to that forum. It was just the right place and time. Other than me, on the settlers' side were *Uri Elitzur*, a Gush Emunim founder, *Yoav Sorek*, an intellectual from the younger generation, and Emily Amrusi Hollander, a young journalist and writer; and several younger members and social activists of both sides. It is a forum where ideas are raised, not a movement, only a forum of meetings without touring the ground.

We felt it was time to think about a new paradigm for the conflict, not only the reality. We had to examine different dimensions – geographic, demographic, affiliations, identities. It was an excellent infrastructure for the initiative that evolved later as it translated our thinking process into political-diplomatic ideas. At the same time, without our knowledge, a Palestinian forum was created. It was associated with ideas that originated in *Fatah* and PLO, such as a single secular state in the entire region – which for them was Palestine, of course, but also contained the Jews as a minority with rights or demographically equal.

Some of our Palestinian partners spent years in Israeli prisons, which served as a melting pot for the Palestinian society. Many Israelis are not aware of that, but prisons are where they learn Hebrew, take university classes, and learn how to get organized. It is like our military service, but it is more than that because they spend more years there. In prison, they learn tools of non-violent protests such as hunger strikes, and undergo a kind of transformation. Most Israelis think that prison is a school for terrorism, but what happens eventually is the very opposite. It also brings generations together, as they have opportunities to talk among themselves. On the Palestinian side, when they celebrate or mourn, generations sit separately and don't speak with each other. It is not like in our Sabbath dinners, and thus such cross-generational interactions are rare in political forums or movements.

Then the *Eretz Yoshveyha* forum dissolved and some members, primarily *Meron Rapoport* and I, wanted to present a realistic political vision. We knew we did not want to be yet another initiative, a movement of Israelis talking among themselves, which happens quite often. We wanted to be a serious peace movement that presented a solution, with partners on the other side. Clearly, we needed our ideas and model to be shared. You cannot just imagine things without sharing with your future partners. You cannot draft an agreement signed by the United States president and the European Union (EU), and only then show it to the Palestinians. You have to have a process.

We held some initial trial meetings between Rapoport and *Awni al-Mashni* to test the waters. They were group coordinators. In the meantime, we tried to translate our vision into action among ourselves. We called it "the return of practical utopia" – namely, we do not shy away from speaking about a utopia because it is realistic. This could perhaps explain the large number of thinkers in our movement – we have philosophers, writers, and poets. We won't be able to resolve this conflict without some creative thinking because it is too complicated, too deep, and involves identity issues. This conflict is not only national, territorial, or religious. It comprises numerous layers that have been loaded on it over the past 100 years.

With that in mind, we came to our first joint meeting at *Beit Jala* – a location that Israelis and Palestinians can access. It was very exciting, I remember. It was during the month of *Ramadan*, and it was our opportunity to 'test' just how religious our partners were. We sat around a large table and it looked like a negotiation conference, and though we knew we didn't want to use that language, we did not yet have our own language, concepts, or definitions. In the first meeting, we spoke English, Arabic, and Hebrew, and tried to make the last two more present. Rapoport and Al-Mashni were the opening speakers, which was a bit unbalanced because we had fewer ties to the Israeli government. In comparison, they had more ties to the Palestinian government. They both belong to more or less the same generation, certainly the generation of *Abu Mazen*'s successors.

The key question was: Is there a partner? When we meet people from the other side, we realize they are our mirror image: they too feel that there is no partner, they also feel suspicion, mistrust, and of course they too are trauma-tized. Except that on their side there is despair, while our side is indifferent – which roughly reflects the things each of the two societies had experienced.

In his opening speech, Awni told us that, as a Palestinian, he knew the Israelis felt a deep connection with every place in this country, and then he named Nablus, Hebron, Al-Quds (Jerusalem), Beit El, and Shilo. You cannot imagine how I felt when I heard Awni say enthusiastically: "This is your history!" and with the same enthusiasm he went on: "Now, just as I know and acknowledge that, I want you to acknowledge that Palestine for me is not just *Jenin*, Hebron, and Jerusalem, but also *Haifa, Jaffa*, and *Acre*. Palestine is the land between the River Jordan and the Mediterranean Sea. You need to understand and acknowledge that. I acknowledge that this entire land is your homeland in terms of your identity, experience, and connection, and you need to acknowledge that it is mine, too."

We badly wanted to hear these words. We already knew that was their experience. It did not scare us. Israelis have these scare stories: They want to throw us into the ocean. This, however, is the truth, and those who don't know that are terribly far from the Palestinian view of things. If you don't speak to Palestinians and hear them a little, you don't understand. This is not propaganda, but very basic identity. Very many Palestinians between the Sea and the River Jordan – certainly the *Palestinian diaspora* – have an identity as refugees or refugees' children, and that will remain for as long as that story is not settled, acknowledged by us. In that moment, it became clear to me that we had a strong partner who understood things that I failed to convince the majority of Israelis about, and that we needed to respect the deep affiliation both nations felt with the entire country.

Some of our partners, who were members of Palestinian negotiating teams in the Oslo Accords and so on, insisted that we try to formulate 'agreements' and not 'accords.' The difference between the two is that accords are attained through a language of negotiations. This is the language of power balances, a language that Israel knows and that, regrettably, the Palestinians have been using since the *Madrid Conference* of 1991 to this day. It will not produce peace. It may produce accords, signed papers, but peace and reconciliation cannot emerge from it. This also helped us, the Israelis, be more precise about the common tongue we have been forming. Since then, we were holding marathon meetings every other Thursday, and not only in Beit Jala. Most of the meetings took place in Al-Bireh and *Ramallah*, and we asked for no one's permission to attend. For us, this meant that whenever we went there, we violated the regional commander's decree forbidding Israelis from entering the Palestinian territories, which was the civil cost we were willing to pay for future generations. The central nucleus has remained since the first meeting and more are joining us. Eventually, we reached an agreement on 11 fundamental principles from which the initiative would evolve into specifics, through the collaboration of both nations, and economic, security, and other experts from the two societies.

In early 2014, we were joined by *IPCRI* and *Gershon Baskin*, its founder and chief executive officer. They have access to Israeli and Palestinian researchers, some of whom are associated with us, so they suggested we form four research groups – dealing with security, refugees, borders, and the boundaries of social-economic policies. These groups have been working for some four months now and are partly funded. So far, everything has been done by volunteers. We were a little worried about IPCRI because every organization has its agenda, and they are closely identified with the two-state solution. Now, we're no strangers to the two-state concept and the realization that each nation has a right to self-definition – that is a basic, moral, and judicially right – and the reciprocal interest of both nations, but we believe that these rights should be realized in a shared, confederative space, not based on the separation concept that the Oslo Accords created.

The research groups issued papers that were published in a book that we did not fully endorse. The process was not fully professional, nor did it keep our language all the way, but it had some important advantages. We expanded the pool of experts beyond those who were spearheading the movement, which provided us with additional perspectives and more room to sound our ideas. The book was launched in 2014, on the symbolic date of *November 29*. They were more interested in making a splash in the local and international media, and impress the EU ambassador and Fatah members who showed up. The book was launched in East Jerusalem's Ambassador Hotel, and they had this big celebration. For us, it was the first opportunity to place our idea on the table in front of the Israeli and world media. There was some tension over 'who is the groom and who is the bride.' Still, it was important for us because it was the first time that we had appeared in public, beyond the few conversations we had had with journalists and policymakers.

Thus the big question arose: What do we want to be when we grow up? Do we want to be a movement or an initiative? This is a fundamental question. I was among those who advocated the movement format. I believe that we should not present a done deal, as was the case with the *Geneva Initiative*, with 120 pages, including footnotes – take it or leave it. We want to be a movement because, among other things, our ideas are based on intuitions, feelings, and affiliations. So we said: Let's start parallel processes, excite the masses with a new idea, see how they accept it, and ask for feedback with question and answer sessions, ideas, and mass sharing. So, as a movement, we made an effort on the ground level, and for the next two years, each of us attended numerous house meetings, speaking to 18 or 30 or even 50 people crowded in a living room, hungry for new ideas. It was very exciting. All in all, we, a group of 20–30 activists, organized some 450 such meetings. It was a crazy effort, and everyone volunteered, not even asking for travel expenses.

Those meetings were held all over Israel, with every sector. We mainly focused on population groups that so far were outside the so-called 'peace conversations' – settlers, the ultra-Orthodox, Sephardim, and young people, some of whom were indifferent. We all invested plenty of time in that, and it was so moving, and open to questions and answers. We saw glimmers of hope in many eyes, but also heard of fear of changing the status quo because Israelis live under the illusion that everything is fine and under control. Sometimes, we 'crossed the line' and went to see Palestinian students in universities, or senior officials, meeting people all over the West Bank – in *Bethlehem, Tulkarm*, Ramallah – cooperating with sister movements such as *Combatants for Peace* or the *Bereaved Families Forum – Parents Circle*. We found them all wanting to hear, curious, and hungry for some new ideas.

Then, the incident with the three *kidnapped boys* occurred, and things began to deteriorate in the *Gaza Strip*. Everyone who still believed in 'conflict management' took a serious blow. We were very pleased about it. I mean, it was tragic and awful, but on the theoretical level of ideas we saw this as an incredible opportunity. The Palestinians kidnapped three Jewish boys, and nearly turned the entire Middle East upside down. So people realized that, in practice, the conflict was managing us, not the other way around. And that the conflict should not be contained, but rather resolved. That was the message we tried to deliver in those house meetings, which continued but were very hard to organize at that time. Harsh remarks were exchanged on the streets and on social media, and everything became very difficult. So we decided to hold fewer house meetings because many of us were in the reserves anyway. It was a horrible summer. Still, we in the movement continued our internal meetings and insisted on clarifying things further, feeling each other's pulse as friends, humans, and partners. By then we shared a common language and everyone felt responsible for the brotherhood that we'd forged and was dear and important to us all.

In times like this, the leadership and military forces – those who eventually manage this conflict – are completely devoted to the balance-of-power concept. We felt it would not end before our movement did something truly massive. We started talking about working from the middle up – that is, we chose a new strategy of talking to mid-level policymakers and have been following it since 2015–2016.

Today, people on the ground already know us. We have held some 150 more meetings since 2015, even though the movement was losing steam. It looked like we were going backward, from a movement to an initiative. That is the easiest thing that peace movements can do – close themselves up in some room, formulate ideas, feel good with each other, and turn into yet another organization in the so-called 'peace industry' (forgive the expression) and actually die like this. Since 2008, I have been personally in touch with people at the relatively secondary echelons such as consular or ambassadorial aides. They have come to talk to me in my village after hearing some of my ideas. I find it very funny that a poet tossed some ideas around, and they all flock to Kfar Etzion – delegations from the United States, the EU, and Far Eastern embassies – saying it was vital for them to hear me out. They told me that they knew already in 2008 that the two-state solution would never happen and that they were looking for the next thing, which was amazing. It means that the world is waking up, but we in Israel don't have a clue. In May 2016, the movement sent a delegation to the EU. We knew that our ideas were popular with them and we were invited, but this time our message got across better than we'd expected.

We keep working as a functional movement in terms of ideas: self-definition by each of the two nations, cooperation, and a confederation, living together and separately, and we are an Israeli movement, a Palestinian movement, and one we share; we're a movement and an initiative. Speaking to policymakers on both sides, we work our way from the mid-level up, covering every aspect, which is terribly sensitive. We've known for years that the political echelons cannot be trusted, that no one talks about content, only about covers. So we decided to publish our slightly expanded ideas in a brochure. We have an excellent website with more material than just the 11 principles. We speak there about the movement and the process and have question and answer pages summing up our various meetings and conferences.

THE ROAD TO REDEMPTION

I am thrilled with our project and believe it is the road to redemption. If I could change anything, I'd bring in more settlers because they are far less spoiled. Sorry for saying that. I know what happens on our side in times of crisis – sometimes you don't succeed, but for me, there is no such thing as failure. I've learned that if you must hit your head against the wall, and you do it again and again, the wall will break. That was the ideology of the Second Aliyah and, if you will, of the settlers too. Our administrators in A Land for All are an amazing group of people who worked on the ground against human rights violations more than I did. To me, they are brothers and sisters. On the other hand, they are associated with the academia, so they can suddenly take a six month sabbatical or go to conferences abroad, so they are not always here and when things get rough, forgive me for saying, they break down.

At some point, the movement became an institution: We established a registered association and have a comptroller, an auditing committee, and members. We work in an orderly fashion. We would love to bring in more people, but I have not yet found people who are excited enough about this.

Since I joined this movement, while already named 'the settlers' poet' and taking part in the religious artists' creation of Mashiv HaRuach, I have been known as a reputed second-generation settler whose father established the settlement movement before Gush Emunim was even founded. At the same time, individual members of the settler sector are suspicious of me. I am not a great Gush Emunim fan. As a child, I grew within the Gush Emunim movement. Still, I am very critical of the fact that this enterprise is blind to the Palestinians, and indeed of the exclusive approach on which I was raised: "The Land of Israel Belongs to the Nation of Israel," or the other way around. It was a shift from the ownership approach to the intimate belonging approach, and that's the revolution I underwent thanks to, among others, *Rabbi Froman* and thanks to personal moves I made and questions I posed and still raise in my community. Some have treated me as a deserter, traitor, abandoner. It pops up now and then, certainly in extreme Facebook posts: "You love the Arabs more than you love us." At the same time, there are many religious Zionists and settlers, mainly the younger generation, who want to be part of the new vision of peace. That is, as groups of settlers spread to the very extreme ends of the hills, a 'leftist' alternative has emerged from within that same community.

There are waves of media exposure. In our movement, our Palestinian partners and we have become the media presenters of the 'confederation' concept. We had significant exposure in 2016, but we don't really have a budget. We receive some money from the Rockefeller Foundation, we take money out of our own pockets, and we collect a symbolic membership fee. We did reach two private religious-Zionist donors who were willing to trust and invest in us. Incidentally, this created a buzz in our secretariat as people wondered: "What is going on here? Why are they the only people who give us their trust and money?" I am not talking about millions. There were two donations of 100,000 shekels each.

The Palestinian side has a problem with the *Palestinian National Authority*, which bans association from dealing in politics and policymaking. They must focus on education, social welfare, and culture. I guess people dealing in politics threaten the establishment. We have been speaking to private Palestinian donors, but we're not there yet, and they don't want to get into trouble.

Do I feel like a peace entrepreneur? Absolutely! I think this is the whole story, really. Generally, in life, I consider myself a cultural entrepreneur. I use my intuition, creativity, social ties, rhetorical skills, and everything else I have to formulate ideas, determine the target, and take it as far and as deep as I can. I was raised in a community with a mission and I am not ashamed of it. Some of my poetry is also a kind of internal engine. When I try to express a collective voice, I am driven by sincere sympathy, and when I meet partners from the two nations, it takes me higher, focusing me.

Naturally, questions are being asked, and we don't have all the answers, not even I, but I am sure this is the way to go. I've grown up and realized that this is a mission for generations to come – not one, but many. I am optimistic, very optimistic given all that is happening, including the bad things that I am confident will not last forever. At some point, the hunger for change will bring about change, or we will all sober up, which might be painful and I don't yearn for it. I hope it will happen more naturally and more gradually.

People are afraid of change. This fear is universal, but sometimes we need to raise the question of the price we pay, our lack of control or ability to manage things here. That too is part of the sobering-up process, and it is not simple. It is also the process I undergo inside and I share with many others. A Palestinian partner once told me: "You will never forgive us for the fatal mistake we made at the November *1947* UN vote when we said 'No,' and after you danced all night, the Arab countries started a war against you." He then dropped a bomb: "You think we are worse than the Nazis." We said, "No, of course not!" but he said: "Yes, you do. You've forgiven the Nazis. You've forgiven the Germans after the *Holocaust* and made the Reparations Agreement and all that. Us, you don't forget and don't forgive." He said further: "It is time you Israelis let go of that and stop constantly arguing over who said yes and who said no." After all, he said, with our permit issuance policy, we decide how much bread a Palestinian can bring home, how much water will flow through the pipes, how much electricity we provide. We control the Palestinian Authority's president whom we call chairman. We, with our permits, decide where the president of Palestine can travel.

We in our movement discuss all this, and the moral, conscientious, social, and economic price we pay for that and for reality, which is terrible and must be fixed. We say that it is time to discuss 'the profits of peace' and not just 'the price of peace.' We want the conversation topics to cover more than only the Israeli-Palestinian conflict. Our addition to this is a voice that comes from various directions, but is more pronounced and politically defined: We call for spatial integration. We are not here to build yet another crusaders' fort or Jewish ghetto – which seems to have been the primary strategy of the State of Israel in recent years. We talk about taking down the walls and integrating locally, and the promise of our solution is opening up to the Orient.

4. A Jewish radical

Gershon Baskin
Interviewed by Yosepha Tabib-Calif

Gershon Baskin was born in New York. He holds an MA and a PhD degree in International Relations from the University of Greenwich, London. He is also the co-founder and co-chief executive officer of *IPCRI* (the Israel Palestine Center for Research and Information). Baskin has written several books on the Israeli-Palestinian conflict, including *The Negotiator: Freeing Gilad Shalit from Hamas, In Pursuit of Peace in Israel and Palestine*, and *Reconciliation in the Middle East.*

We held the interview in Baskin's home in Kiryat Hayovel, Jerusalem. Baskin is an endless source of stories about the American Zionist Movement (AZM), immigration to Israel, living in an Arab village, holding talks with the *Palestinian Liberation Organization (PLO)* and *Hamas* members, and tales of how he has served as a consultant to several Israeli prime ministers. The many books Baskin has written regarding Israeli-Palestinian relations further indicate the extent of this man's familiarity with this issue. More personally, Baskin told me about his own daughter, who married an Israeli-born Jew and had her wedding in an Arab village, and who then left Israel for the south of France feeling that there was no hope for her in the Middle East. This provides yet another demonstration of how close Baskin is to his life's work.

It was interesting to watch Baskin constructing the narrative of his initiatives, mixing the conflict/peace narrative with his own life story. Through these stories, Baskin narrates himself as a key role participant who defines his own narrative.

Although written as a monologue, this interview was, in fact, a pleasant and open conversation, and near the end, Baskin's wife and one of his children joined us and offered some of their insights into their lives at his side. I have chosen to name this chapter *A Jewish Radical*, as this was the title of the American newspaper Baskin wrote for in the past and for how Baskin has chosen to define himself.

MY LIFE'S VALUES AND FOUNDATIONS: SHAPING A JEWISH AND IDEALISTIC IDENTITY

I was born in Brooklyn, New York, but when I was four, my parents moved us to Bellmore, in New York State. My life's values and foundations were formed in my childhood. I was raised in a secular home that was also very Jewish in terms of our self-awareness as Jews. My parents felt it was vital that we lived in a Jewish environment. Therefore, we lived in a neighborhood that was 90 percent Jewish, my parents' friends were all Jews, and we were all Jews at school, which was closed on Jewish holidays because no one attended. We all went to schul. Not to pray, really. It was more a social thing than a religious thing, and we were all members of the congregation. That's what we did. It was part of life in my neighborhood.

As a child, I also discovered the world. When I was eight or nine, we took a trip to the southern United States, where I first witnessed American racism. Traveling through Virginia, I saw a sign in a restaurant that read: "Whites only." That was several months before discrimination was outlawed in the USA. My mother, a teacher, brought me a library book that greatly influenced me, a life-changing book, *Black Like Me*. It was written by a white journalist who injected some material into his body that turned his skin black. It describes his travels as a black man in the American South in the late 1950s and early 1960s. It was a best-seller and had a substantial impact on me. When I was 10, I was already active in the struggle against the Vietnam War and knew our local congressman, who was a prominent figure in this regard. I even happened to meet Eugene McCarthy, a Vermont senator and a presidential candidate. So even though my home was not, I was very active politically from sixth grade. That was the late 1960s, at the height of the anti-war campaign.

In the 1970s, we relocated to a very un-Jewish neighborhood. There were some Jews on our street, but I went from a school with 90 percent Jews to a high school that was predominantly non-Jewish. In my first or second week there, a boy from my class – who had spent the previous summer in Israel and whose family had planned *Aliyah* – told me they were forming a branch of the Zionist youth movement Young Judaea in our neighborhood and said I should come. I did not know what it was. I knew that a group like this in my synagogue wasn't very serious and that I did not like it, but he invited me, and it was serious, and I liked it. I thought it would be a good place to meet Jewish girls. I think that was my primary motivation for joining.

Still, it was political too, exciting, and challenging. So in my tenth grade, I was elected as a member of the movement's regional secretariat. At eleventh grade I was placed in charge of the movement's educational activities, and in my twelfth grade I became the movement's regional secretary. When I was 13,

I dragged my entire family to Israel. This was before I was a Zionist activist. I don't know what hit me, but after my brother had his big bar-mitzvah party at the country club, I told my parents that I didn't want a party like that, but would like to visit Israel. I was raised on stories about my mom's cousin, a *Holocaust* survivor whose family had been murdered, but he managed to flee the Nazis. He arrived in Palestine on board an immigrant ship, but the British caught him. It was all just like in *Exodus* with Paul Newman and all those images. I was raised on such stories. The fact was that the cousin and the family had not been in touch until 1968, when my aunt went to Israel and found him. He came with his family to visit the USA a year later, and my bar-mitzvah was in the following year. So I said, let's go to Israel.

I remember our first Shabbat in Israel. We stayed with relatives in Givatayim, which is not a spiritual place. Still, I remember sitting on the balcony, looking at Givatayim and Tel Aviv, telling myself and my parents that this was my home. Between high school and university, I spent a year in Israel in the Young Judaea program. We spent six months in Kibbutz *Ein Harod Ihud* and another six studying in Jerusalem.

At the age of 16 I knew Israel would be my home. I was very young when I knew that. It had no rational explanation. Perhaps it was because I had grown up at a time of domestic alienation in American society due to the Vietnam War. Some of it must have been associated with that idealistic period that for us meant that Israel and Zionism were an attractive option. I grew up in a movement with friends who were my soul mates, and we were united. We formed groups to make Aliyah together. Indeed, that was an extraordinary generation in the movement. Many of my friends are in Israel now and are all very active in extremely important things. I believe that you will find many Young Judaea graduates in the environment-protection movement in Israel. For example, *Alon Tal*, *Jeremy Benstein*, and *Eilon Schwartz* are all some of my friends from the movement. We grew up together. Many members chose to study Jewish education or social work and then dedicate their lives to social issues. I am the only one who became a political activist.

CROSSING THE GREEN LINE: DISCOVERING THE CONFLICT

When I returned to the USA, I worked in the movement's Zionist summer camp for Jews. I did not want to be an instructor because I needed time to process the one-year experience I had had in Israel, so I worked in the kitchen. I was the camp cook's assistant. In my room, I hung up a map of the Land of Israel – the Greater Israeli map, including the *Sinai Peninsula* and the *West Bank*, and marked the places I'd visited with pins. One day, when I came back to my room, I discovered that someone had drawn the *Green Line* on my map.

My roommate Barak Berkowitz was the one who had drawn that Green Line. He was older than me and the founder of Choice (*Brera*), a movement established in 1975–1976 after the *Yom Kippur War*. This movement began asking questions such as: Do we really make certain decisions because we have no other choice? They concluded that there is always a choice. They were for establishing a dialogue with the Palestinians, acknowledging the PLO, and striving towards the two-state solution. These days, Berkowitz lives in San Francisco, a former Apple employee, still working in hi tech.

For me, the Green Line was a revelation. I looked at this map and saw Kibbutz Ein Harod and Highway 90, the Biqa Road, that I had taken so often. I realized then that though I'd spent a year of intensive study of the Zionist Movement, walked all over the Old City of Jerusalem, and was charmed by it, I had yet to have a single conversation with an Arab. Suddenly it hit me: There's a massive gap in my knowledge. In the following year, I started reading, covering some 100 books on the Israeli-Arab conflict, taking a few courses in university, and discussing it with other people.

A year later, in 1975, several friends and I contacted the PLO representative in the United Nations (UN). At the time, the PLO representative was an ambassador. The organization held observers' status at the UN. I worried that if we said we're from Young Judaea or the Zionist Movement he would not see us, so we invented a name for ourselves – The Socialist Zionist – and he agreed to meet us after working hours. We intended to tell him that the PLO should acknowledge the State of Israel and endorse the two-state platform. That was in 1976, and he rejected our ideas, of course. He said: "Listen, you Jews do not belong in our country. You robbed our land and expelled us from our homeland. Go back to where you came from and let us live." He even said, "Over my dead body," so I gathered there was no way to start an Israeli-Palestinian dialogue. That same year, I published my first article advocating the two-state solution in a beautiful paper published in Berkley, California, called *The Jewish Radical*. Since I could not find a starting point – mutual acknowledgment – for a dialogue with the Palestinians, I started studying Israeli Arabs. In March 1976, they marked their first *Land Day*, staging demonstrations in Sakhnin, Dir Hanna, the Negev, and the Triangle. Six young Arabs were killed that day.

A Reformist and social activist Rabbi named Bruce Cohen was in Israel during this time. He established an organization called Interns for Peace. The idea was to train people to become peace activists. He ran advertisements seeking Jewish-American university graduates who would volunteer to spend two years living in Israeli-Arab villages and engage in community work, creating ties between Jewish and Arab-Israeli citizens. At first, he tried to draft Israeli Jews but found it was impossible because people were either afraid or racist, and the psychological barriers were too high. He hoped that people without such baggage would do better.

That was my senior year at New York University, and I lived in a commune with guys from Young Judaea, which served as a platform for Aliyah. I was greatly troubled by my negative interactions with Israeli Jews before I made Aliyah. When I expressed my political views, Israelis would often say: Who are you to say that? You don't even know them, the Arabs. They kept telling me that, and it drove me crazy for two reasons. First: OK, I don't know them, but how could I? Second: I honestly believed that Israeli Jews did know Arabs – which was not true, of course, but it never stopped these Israelis from saying that they did, and I didn't.

Then I applied to do an MA at the American University of Beirut and they accepted me. They sent me plenty of material and letters that I needed to sign, waiving my rights and acknowledging there was war in Beirut and that the campus was shelled on occasion. So I said to myself: Man, you are mad, but not crazy. Just then, a friend of mine who was working for the Hebrew College in Boston saw a poster about Interns for Peace and said that this might be a good fit for me because she knew I wanted to do something in Israel. Interns for Peace had an office not far from New York University, and I went and signed up and was accepted – I was actually the first person accepted – and made Aliyah in 1978.

Together with the other interns, we spent six months in a training program on *Kibbutz Barkai*, and then I moved to the Arab village of *Kafr Qara*, where I spent two years doing community work. The local council rented an apartment for us. We were 14 members in that first group, spread over three Arab villages: Kafr Qara, Ar'ara, and *Tamra*. In Kafr Qara, we were four: myself, a married couple, and a woman. We did volunteer work there, including teaching English in schools. It was amusing at the beginning. The most radical movement at the time, according to the Israeli authorities, was the *Israeli Communist Party (Rakah)*, whose members were considered enemies of the people. They had a newspaper in Arabic called Al-Ittihad, and one of their reporters wrote that there was a group of CIA agents who came to live in Kafr Qara. When we heard this, we rushed to see Attorney Masarwi Mohammad, a lawyer and member of the Interns for Peace Executive Committee. He later became Israel's consul general in Atlanta and a judge in the Hadera District Court. He was one of the first Israeli-Arab graduates of the Hebrew University's Law Faculty. He decided to respond to that news story with a very satirical piece, claiming that the CIA is very interested in how the residents of Kafr Qara grow their cucumbers, so they sent four agents to spy on the farmers. That calmed everyone down.

During these years, I taught on a Jewish-Arab course for young instructors, following the example I learned in the Young Judaea youth movement. We even received a budget from the Ministry of Education, but it was a colossal flop, and I certainly did some damage. I am sure that the kids who attended the course learned to hate the other side because we did not know what we were doing. That experience taught me that goodwill is not enough. Dialogue between groups in conflict is a job for professionals and has to be studied. We should have a strategy, a methodology, and a pedagogy. Meetings must be structured and not just "let's get together and have some hummus, and all will be well." This could reinforce stereotypes just as powerfully as it could shatter them. It happens quite a lot.

The married couple left after three months. Life in the village did not work for them. The young woman quit after a year, and I was alone for several months. Then, the movement sent more people to be with me. I spent two more whole years in Kafr Qara. I still visit Kafr Qara, and I'm a celebrity there. They honor me. I did not know how much I would give, but I knew what I would receive. I wrote a journal and documented visits with local families. I visited more than 500 families during the two years I lived there. It happens less these days because everyone is driving, but at the time, I just walked the streets. When you passed by their houses, the villagers would always ask you politely: "*Tfadal!*" (Come in). They didn't always mean for you to step in, but I would go in when I was not too busy, so I got to know the entire village, all of 500 households and 7,500 residents. I remember nights when we would sit on the porch and the muezzin calls for prayer would echo from the surrounding mountains. It was like a choir.

BREAKING THROUGH: BRINGING PEOPLE TOGETHER IS THE STATE'S RESPONSIBILITY

In those years, we had a visit from a Los Angeles delegation that included a man who had worked for the Los Angeles County in bringing ethnic groups together. He told me that in the 1970s, more than 160 state employees were doing that in Los Angeles. This motivated me to examine how many people work for the State of Israel, the only democracy in the Middle East, bringing Jews and Arabs together. Naturally, I found none. I wrote a letter to then Prime Minister *Menachem Begin*, suggesting that I could assume such a role, and received an answer. I started a dialogue with the Ministry of Education and it took me another 14 months before I was able to make a breakthrough in creating such a position. At the time, the government put a freeze on hiring, so even though they had decided, in principle, that they wanted to hire me, there was no budget for this until an Arab Parliament member, Muhammad Wattad from the village of Jat, found a clause in the Absorption Ministry budget for this purpose. There's irony for you! They called it Project 200. The idea was to hire 200 immigrants from western countries. They were to work for other government ministries, and the ministry earmarked a budget for their salaries. That budget was supposed to finance their second year on the job. And here was this Arab Parliament member who told me: "I specialize in absorbing people who make Aliyah." He found the budget and got me a job with the Ministry of Education as a ranking supervisor. At the time, Zevulun Hammer was the minister of education and *National Religious Party* chairman, and Eliezer Shmueli was his director-general.

Shmueli issued a ministry memo. They introduced me to all of the sections and district managers in the ministry, and to Imanuel Kopolovich, who was head of the Arab Department, and who practically adopted me. He is a wonderful person, and I loved him a lot. He was not radical enough for me, but he was methodical and cautious. Knowing that his role was to promote the Israeli Arabs' education, he was familiar with the obstacles and worked very measuredly, wisely. He encouraged me and my views. We argued repeatedly, but that man is dear to my heart.

While on the job, I issued two director-general memos; one sought to encourage Jewish-Arab encounters, and the other acknowledged meetings between Jewish and Arab students at the School for Peace in *Neve Shalom* (*Wahat al-Salam*). Subsequently, Rabbi Yaacov Hadani, head of the Ministry of Education National-Religious Department, issued a statement contradicting that memo. He claimed that national-religious schools should be exempted from such meetings because he worried that encounters between Jewish and Arab students might lead to ethnic assimilation and perhaps even mixed marriages. I, who was only 25, 26 years old at the time, called for a meeting with the *Knesset* Education Committee, where I presented data which demonstrated that only 0.04 percent of all marriages were between Jews and Arabs. Ignoring the data, the minister, who was also the National Religious Party chairman, exempted the national-religious schools. Several other state schools contacted me, seeking programs and instructors for those meetings, but said they needed funds for them, and I had no budget. I went to see the director-general and told him I needed funds. He nearly chewed my head off. "You don't understand," he said. "What you're doing is cosmetic. We're doing this for the reputation of the State of Israel."

I had written two Foreign Ministry reports to the UN about Israeli initiatives for peace and coexistence. Yet, when the director-general of the Ministry of Education informed me that I was merely there to apply band-aids, I became furious. I looked for a way to attack this attitude without getting into too much trouble. I felt I should tell some reporter what the director-general had said to me. I knew the most unread newspaper in Israel was *Al-Hamishmar*, the National Kibbutz Movement's paper that I used to read on Kibbutz Barkai. I knew no one read it, but I thought it could make a splash. So I called the paper's education reporter, and the headline of the following Friday issue read: "The director-general of the Ministry of Education says working for coexistence is mere cosmetics." When I came to the office the next Sunday, my immediate boss Emanuel Kopolovich was waiting for me on the stairway. "You must report to the director-general's office now!" I went there with my heart pounding, and he yelled at me. His face turned all red, but I left his office with a reprimand and $15,000 to be allocated towards student transportation to Jewish-Arab meetings. I learned that you get nothing done in Israel unless you make some noise and bang on tables.

Later, they called me from the Prime Minister's Office, saying the German government had offered to finance a Jewish-Arab coexistence program. I sat down and wrote a program. I realized that as a state employee, I was rather restricted, so I suggested we establish an association with its own independent budget and with two representatives of the Prime Minister's Office and two from the Ministry of Education on the executive board. I also suggested that an institute for the education of Jewish-Arab coexistence be established, and this was accepted as well. A year later, I officially quit the Ministry of Education and started managing the institute, a position I would occupy for the next seven years.

I have always believed that I am a Jewish-Zionist Israeli, loyal to the State of Israel before anything else. Israel defines itself as the democratic state of the Jewish Nation, which assigns it some responsibility. Now, I do have plenty of reservations towards Menachem Begin (the prime minister at the time) and things he did, but he was a democrat and sincerely believed in democratic values. We met and I said that it was very nice that we have volunteers, organizations, and associations who work for coexistence, but where was the State of Israel in that story? I said the state was responsible for this, and he agreed. He did not argue with that.

This was when I joined the Army. I did not have to prepare for being drafted because, though I put it off as much as I could, I knew I would be drafted one day. I did not want to join a combat unit because that could have put me in a position where I might be forced to serve in the (Occupied) Territories or Lebanon. Instead, I decided to volunteer with the Israel Defense Forces' Commanders' College. There I served under the chief education officer and worked with his deputy, whose wife had worked with me on a coexistence project at the Hebrew University Secondary School in Jerusalem. She was active on our team and her husband joined us, and together we wrote an educational program on Jewish-Arab coexistence that the Army partly accepted. I also volunteered and spent two years running a course on Israeli society that was compulsory for officers ranking major. Of that three-week course, a week was devoted to Jewish-Arab coexistence, during which the officers spent a day in the Muslim town of *Umm al-Fahm*.

After I completed boot camp, which was outside *Jenin*, I was assigned to the Commanders' College on Mount Gilo, whose commander was Rabbi and Lieutenant-Colonel *Naftali Rothenberg*. He wanted me to become a course commander, but he had a problem because of my rank, I was a private, and the student soldiers he had were all majors. So he said: "You come in civilian clothes and sit with me at the commander's table in the dining room, and if anyone asks for your rank, say that you are a lieutenant-colonel." That's how I spent my military service. Later, running IPCRI, I was a reservist for the college, and for the next 15 years I gave lectures concerning the Jewish-Arab issue. The Army supplied me with plenty of opportunities to address not exactly friendly audiences.

TWO STATES FOR TWO NATIONS: IPCRI

The First *Intifada* (the Palestinian uprising) started in December 1987. I remember we had a teachers' training session in *Beersheba* one December evening, and these nice Jewish teachers began saying: "How could they do this to us? We were so good to them, building schools, universities, and hospitals for them." I heard the enlightened occupier speaking out of these teachers' throats. I, however, knew what went on in the territories. I asked my Arab co-instructor to forgive me and stepped out. I had to take some fresh air. Then, I realized I must see for myself what went on in the occupied Palestinian territories because something meaningful, different, and new was happening there. So, I started reading leaflets issued by the United Front of the intifada to this end.

In those days, there were no fax machines or WhatsApp messages. Instead, leaflets calling for rage days, strikes, or other activities were distributed twice a week, along with political messages that began to be formulated and distributed. Friends of mine would collect these leaflets translating their contents for me. One of the biggest mistakes of my life is that I had not studied Arabic systematically up to then. I started doing so only recently. After a while, I began realizing that the messages conveyed in the leaflets directly juxtaposed what the Palestinian UN ambassador had told me back in 1976. Now, they started speaking of establishing a Palestinian state in the territories occupied in *1967*. They did not talk of throwing Jews into the ocean or sending them back to where they came from. Theirs was an entirely different message.

In March 1988, I lived in the Jerusalem neighborhood of Talpiyot. On the first Sabbath of the month, I got on my Vespa and drove to the Deheisheh refugee camp. It was not the sanest thing to do then, but I wanted to hear some authentic, grassroots-level voices. I knew the leaders of the Israeli Arabs and had visited the Territories, but I didn't know a single Palestinian political leader or anyone else. There was a United Nations Relief and Works Agency

(*UNRWA*) school at the entrance to the camp. I parked outside, took off my helmet, and was immediately approached by several young men, who asked: "Who are you and what are you doing here?" I answered in my basic Arabic: "I am an Israeli who wants to know what this intifada is about. What are you fighting for?" This was during the fourth month of the Palestinian uprising. After we talked for some 20 minutes on the street, one of them said: "Come to my house." We entered the camp and sat for six hours in a very crowded room. I left there in the afternoon full of energy. I never once heard "Jews to the sea" or "go back," or "you have no right to exist," or "over my dead body." They said: "Get out of our lives and let us live ours. Give us independence and end the occupation," and they were talking about the 1967, not the 1948 occupation. I realized that the opening I was seeking in 1976 for some Israeli-Palestinian act was right here.

I resigned from the Jewish-Arab Coexistence Institute, wrote an advertisement, and went to East Jerusalem to have it published in three Palestinian newspapers: Al-Fajr, Al-Shab, and Al-Quds. Being culturally ignorant, I asked that the ad be posted on Friday. Why? Because Friday is the weekend edition and everyone reads papers. It is true for the Jews, but on the Palestinian street, Friday is the slowest press day. My ad read: "If you believe in the two-state solution, if you believe that Palestinians and Israelis can collaborate," and added, "If you have a college degree, please call me," and gave my home number. By Saturday night, some 45 people had called me and I arranged meetings with anyone who would sit with me. I spent five days in the yard of the American Colony Hotel and interviewed 23 people.

I'd written some text for them to read about what was behind the Israeli-Palestinian conflict. I argued that before the First Intifada, the Israeli-Palestinian conflict was about existence – us or them. The intifada changed that, and now the conflict was over seven issues: the Palestinian state and the nature of its sovereignty; the borderline between the two states; the road between the two Palestinian territories – the West Bank and the *Gaza Strip* – through the Israeli territory which resides in between; the future of Jerusalem; Palestinian refugees; economic relations; and water. I claimed that these seven issues must all be resolved if we want to end the Israeli-Palestinian conflict. It is a package deal. If we do everything but keep Jerusalem out, there would be no agreement; if we do everything but ignore the refugees, there would be no agreement. It is all or nothing. Today, I would add an eighth issue and name it the security problem or security arrangements, based on lessons learned from historical failures.

I asked these 23 people if they agreed with me, and all of them did. I told them that the next logical thing to do was sit down together and start working on the seven issues mentioned, trying to resolve them. I made two radical suggestions. Firstly, that we establish a common Israeli-Palestinian research institute and work within it as equals, sharing everything. We would have two managers and a shared executive committee. The second clause was even more radical. I said: "Let's not argue over the end result. We're talking about the two-state solution and we know where we are going. What's important now is that we decide how to get there." They all agreed. It took me a year to institutionalize this.

I started meeting Palestinian leaders and established contacts with the PLO, which was against the law at the time. Several months after I established IPCRI, I traveled abroad to raise funds with my daughter, who was four or five then. At the airport, after a security check, we reached passport control. I showed them our passports, and they told me: "You may not leave Israel. Sit there." I sat down, but every 10–15 minutes, I asked the police officers what was happening. After a while, a policewoman came and told me I would not be boarding my flight. I started crying. I didn't know what was happening, what I'd done to deserve this. Suddenly they came, took my daughter and me, put us in a car, and drove us to the plane. We went our way without any explanation, nothing. Apparently, I had been placed on a security list for four years and as a result I was detained every time I left or returned to Israel. In earlier times, I had shivers run down my spine whenever I saw the Israeli coast from the plane window. Shivers from overjoy as I was returning home! During this period, whenever I saw the coastline, I would break into a cold sweat, as I never knew if I would be permitted back into the country. I was outraged by this.

It all happened because I had ties with the PLO. I had an office in East Jerusalem, across from *Damascus Gate*. I was the only Israeli there during the First Intifada. Every time I phoned a PLO office abroad from my office – I would call Tunis via the Palestinian phone service in Cyprus or the PLO ambassador in Holland – as soon as I hung up, my phone would ring. When I picked up, there was no one on the other end. It was a message for me: "We're listening. We can hear you. Be careful and cross no red lines." Still, they never summoned or visited me nor gave me an explanation.

Each time I arrived at Ben-Gurion Airport, I asked why I was on that list. No one knew. They had a list of persons to detain, and I was on it. They would report back that I was there, and then they were probably instructed to let me go without questioning me at all. Sometimes, when I returned from some convention abroad, they would seize the papers, brochures, and books that I had brought with me. I guess they xeroxed them. Once I waited for three and a half hours before they let me go without an explanation. There were times when they just humiliated me by stripping me.

Before we started working, we formed three work groups: a Jerusalem group, an economic group, and a water group. *Yitzhak Shamir* was prime minister at the time, and I was summoned to the Foreign Ministry's Political

Research Department. Two people took me to some shed in the Foreign Ministry compound – that was the old compound, and those shacks once served the British Army – and told me: "This conversation never happened. If you tell anyone that you were called in and reported to the Foreign Ministry, we will deny it." That's how the conversation started. They wanted to know what was happening in my meetings with the Palestinians. Still, we agreed that no one reports that these meetings are taking place or who attends them and that we may use ideas raised in them, but without naming names. The idea was that we came up with thoughts on how to resolve the issues at hand.

Two years later, I happened to meet a man that I'd heard was from the General Security Service (GSS) or the *Mossad*. I had with me a pile of books and leaflets we had written, and he just sat there and told me: "We have that, and this one, and that, aha! We don't have that." This is how it went. They were very curious. The whole thing climaxed after the *Oslo Accords* were signed. I was still on the GSS list of people to detain at borders. Now, my family used to go to Sinai on our Hanukkah vacation together with another seven or eight families. At the Taba border crossing, they told me I could not leave, "but," they said, "we have no one to question you here either, so wait." The other families waited too. I told them to go, yet they stayed. Then two nice young GSS men in shorts and T-shirts showed up and took me to a trailer on the other side of the crossing. "They called us in from Eilat," they said. "Why are you going to Sinai? Who will you meet there?" I said: "I'm going to meet sand dunes, sunshine, music, and books. I'm on holiday." And they said: "Come on! Tell us who." "No one," I replied. "This is the vacation that I take each year with my friends." "So why are you on this list?" they asked. "Honestly," I said, "I've been asking the same question for the past four years. And now, let me ask you: How do I get myself off this list?" One of them said: "Why don't you write to the Israeli Police's legal advisor? Tell him your side of the story."

So I spent the entire vacation writing this letter in my head, and when I came home, I poured my heart out, relating my Jewish and Zionist history, how I love this state, and how I deeply believe that, out of this love, we must make peace with our neighbors. And I asked for a meeting with a GSS official to discuss my file. A month later, I received a phone call. "You wanted to meet a security official?" a man asked. "What? Yes!" I answered. And he said: "That's me." We arranged a meeting and talked for over two hours. I told him all about the things we did, things we were working on, and then I asked him: "Will you take me off that list?" he looked at me and said: "I cannot do that." So I said: "At least tell me why I am on it?" He then spoke about my Palestinian partner, whose name I did not mention. "You scare us." This is what he told me! "We don't care about your views at all, but unlike other left-wing people, you behave like an Arab. You know their culture and act like them. If you went abroad and Zakariyah Zbeidi asked you to take a package – and I'm not saying he is a bad person – you would not be able to say no." "I take packages from no one," I told him, "and if anyone ever gives me anything, I'd look for the first security officer I could find as soon as I reached the airport and say – listen, I got this package, and I don't know what's in it. Please, check it." And he said: "I'll recommend that you be taken off the list, with a heavy heart." I went abroad a couple of weeks after that meeting, and when I submitted my passport and heard them simply stamp it, it sounded like liberty bells.

FROM SECURITY THREAT TO PRIME MINISTER'S PEACE PROCESS ADVISOR

After Oslo and before the peace process with Jordan, we felt that business-people could play a significant role in promoting peace. We were busy with what we called peace building and peace making, where the former was about creating partnerships. Together with the Amsterdam Chamber of Commerce, we initiated an international business conference about the Israeli-Palestinian issue and named it 'Opportunities 94.' We thought we'd invite members of the Jordanian business community even though we did not have a peace accord with Jordan yet. I filed a request with the Interior Ministry to travel to Jordan via the Allenby Bridge and had a visa issued on my US passport by the Jordanian Embassy in London. The Interior Ministry failed to respond even after two–three weeks and told me it was under GSS inspection. I received the permit a week later; they gave me back my passport and asked me to deposit it at the Allenby Bridge crossing. So we went to Jordan and spent a wonderful week in that magical kingdom.

I remember sitting in the Jordan Rift Valley years before, looking over at Jordan and wondering what was happening there. We'd watch Jordanian television; saw the king going here or there, and here I was. On our last day there, we met with Marwan al-Kasim, the Royal Court chief and one of the men closest to King Hussein. I spent three hours with him. When I returned, I was interviewed by the *Haaretz* daily for its weekend edition. A week later, I was called in for security questioning at the Kirya, Israel's security headquarters. What about? I did not know. I arrived at the Sarona Gate, and my name was not on the list, nor did I have permission to enter. I came a bit early and was stressed and a bit anxious.

Then a soldier aged 40 or so, probably an intelligence officer in a service uniform and no insignia, led me to an old British Army barrack without windows, with just a table and two chairs. He pulled out a little notebook and a pen, ready to write, and asked: "Do you know why you are here?" "I've no idea," I said. "You went to Jordan," says he. "Yes, I had a GSS approval." He said: "Yes, but you did not notify your military unit." "What?!" I said, "Do you know what I do in the reserves? I speak about the Palestinian issue at the

Commanders' College." "OK," he said, "but you did not report that you were going to a hostile enemy state. You should have reported this." I said I was sorry. I did not know. At the time, you needed the Army's permission to go abroad, and I believe I had a three month pass stamped in my passport. I did not even think about it. Then he asked: "What did you do in Jordan?" I started telling him, and after 10 minutes or so, he closed his notebook and said: "Do you mind if we just talked?" I said: "I'd talk to anyone willing to talk to me." We talked for more than an hour. In the end, he asked: "Would you mind if I gave your name to some people who may want to speak with you?" and I said: "Sure. I'd talk to anyone willing to talk to me."

A week later, I received a call from a man who introduced himself as a member of the Prime Minister's Office's Research Department. *Yitzhak Rabin* was prime minister then, which was right after Oslo. The man told me he was working on the peace process and asked me to visit his department at the Shalom Tower, fifth floor. The first thing I did was research: What is the PMO's Research Department? I've never heard of it, and it turned out there was no such thing. Still, I went to the address he gave me and on the fifth floor saw a door with a sign: The Prime Minister's Office's Research Department. I opened it and saw small interview rooms inside. They told me the prime minister formed a team of five people from various branches of the intelligence community whose role was to advise the prime minister on the peace process. It was a secret team because Rabin feared he might be accused of using the intelligence services for political purposes. He did not trust the political echelons and did not like or have confidence in his cabinet members. He trusted the Army, but the chief of staff, Amnon Lipkin-Shahak, had told him that the Army did not know how to make peace. The Army only knew how to make war, therefore, he should look for other people. Now, that's an honest man. So Rabin established that team, and they found me, and later, secretly, I served as an advisor for them up to *Benjamin Netanyahu*'s rise to power, or rather up until a few months after he was elected. Thus, I went from being 'a threat to the State of Israel's security' to the prime minister's advisor on peace affairs.

I spent more than 200 hours with that team. It really was like a James Bond movie: We'd agree on a time for our meeting, then I'd get a call that same morning, telling me at which hotel room I needed to be, and I had to enter that room without being noticed by anyone. When room service brought up soft drinks, I had to hide in the bathroom. It was crazy. When the team was eventually dispersed, they gave me a present and said I should know that my fingerprints were all over the agreement with the Palestinians, that I had a real impact. When we first met, they offered to give me cash, but I said I wanted no payment. They told me to take the money, buy some books or subscribe to a magazine, but I said I did not want to, that I was doing my job, which was influencing the peace process.

This is how I always work. Once I take their money, they own me, and I don't want that. I am independent. I last met my contact after the demonstration in which Rabin was murdered. I had seen him before, at the demonstration. I knew the entire team, and when I suddenly saw him passing, I said: "What are you doing here? You are a GSS man. You cannot be here." He said: "I am only watching," and went on.

Later, when Netanyahu was already prime minister, the team wished to upgrade my security clearance. I was instructed by a GSS man ahead of my lie detector test, which was part of a six hour security debriefing. He told me that the most important thing was for me to tell the truth, so I had to admit that I had smoked pot when I was younger and so on. He told me that they would ask questions, and they would know if I was lying. A day or two later, my contact called and said Netanyahu had dissolved the team. I have not seen this GSS contact since. I have been looking for him and the other four members of the team, but they vanished into thin air. I have spoken to three former Mossad heads since, and *Yuval Rabin*, *Dalia Rabin*, and *Eitan Haber* as well, and it seems that the people of that team no longer exist, it is as if they never did. When I started working with them, I signed a paper pledging not to write about them for 30 years.

Dan (Danny) Yatom told me that the name my contact gave me could have been fictitious, which is why he could not be found. Haber said that though Rabin had weekly meetings with a small team, Haber never attended them nor asked the prime minister about the team's purpose. "I don't know. I did not ask too many questions about who or what they were. There was this understanding that there are things you don't ask." Several years later, I wrote to Prime Minister *Ariel Sharon* and asked him to reconvene the team. He wrote to me that he had other means of collecting the information he needs.

I was also involved in the attempt to bring *Gilad Shalit* home. A year before Shalit was abducted, Sasson Nuriel, my wife's cousin, was kidnapped and murdered by Hamas in September 2005. He was a businessman who owned a factory on Mishor Adumim, and there was a complicated story involving the GSS in this regard. Never mind. A few days after he disappeared, the family asked me to use my contacts to find him. I tried but failed. A few days later, Hamas aired a videotape showing Sasson in handcuffs, and it was clear he'd been tortured. It was shocking. His body was found a week later. Attending his funeral in Jerusalem, I swore that if ever anyone asked me for help of that kind, I'd do anything and would not rest. When Shalit was kidnapped, and for the duration of his five years and four months in captivity, I remember myself standing over Sasson's grave. I don't remember precisely, but my wife says that the body was decomposing, and it smelled terrible. I don't remember the smell, only the feeling of standing over the grave.

While Shalit was in captivity, I tried to reach my Palestinian contacts. I was acquainted with a Hamas member that I'd met in Cairo and tried to create an Israeli-Hamas dialogue. Six days after Shalit was abducted, the man I met in Cairo called me and said we had to do something. He reached out to me! On that day, I had my first conversation with *Ismail Haniyeh* and his political advisor, and that's how it all began. The Hamas member suggested holding a conversation with the soldier's father. It took me a few hours to trace the Shalit family's home number. When I did, I left a message on their answering machine and they called me back. I talked to both Noam and Aviva Shalit. Noam talked to the Hamas man that very day, and both parents came to see me in Jerusalem the next day, a week after the abduction.

JERUSALEM

So this is the story. I established IPCRI and managed it for 25 years. I have mediated over 2,000 Israeli-Palestinian meetings and have overseen work-groups with experts in security, agriculture, tourism, antiquities, economy, water, and science. I have no doubts concerning how to achieve this peace. It is all known, written, thought of. Anyone who wants to, can. I don't doubt this. What we lack today is political will.

I was IPCRI's directorate chairman until a few months ago when I quit. Two young people run IPCRI today. Regrettably, they don't have the resources to be there fully. Our annual budget reached $1.5 million at our peak, but today IPCRI cannot even pay for a full-time staff or an office. They raise funds for projects, obtaining a few thousand only, not much more. It is very hard.

I quit because I wanted the Palestinian residents of East Jerusalem to run in the Jerusalem municipal elections, but the IPCRI team feared this. I stated that we'd try to form an Israeli-Palestinian list to run for mayor and City Council with a Palestinian heading it and me as no. 2. That was not the first time I tried to get into politics and make a difference from there. At the time, there was the Green Movement, established by Young Judaea members. I tried to fit in, and we were very optimistic that we would be able to create the right dynamics with environmental issues and get into the Jerusalem City Council, but we failed. I am an inactive member of Meretz's Party because I am not cut out for party work. I wanted to run for the Jerusalem City Council and believed that our joint party could win many votes. Some 30 percent of Jerusalem residents don't vote in the local elections, and I knew we could get the votes of previously indifferent people, including many Palestinians. There are 175,000 potential voters there, but only 1 percent voted in the last municipal elections. I knew they would be very excited about this idea. Still, I realized that after 50 years of Palestinian boycott of the municipal government, the leap to a joint Palestinian-Jewish list was too big.

This is why we are forming a Palestinian list to run in the elections, and I established a new association to help 'get out the votes.' It is named *Hakukna* (Arabic: our rights), and these days we are forming a Palestinian list of candidates, including one for mayor, who will probably not be an Israeli citizen, only a resident. Such a person cannot be mayor by law, so we intend to appeal to the High Court of Justice, knowing we will lose. The idea is to place the local story of the Jerusalem City Council on the *New York Times'* front page. That's the story here. We want to see if we can succeed in encouraging the Palestinians to stand up for their rights and challenge the assertion whereby the united City of Jerusalem is the eternal capital of only the Jewish Nation. This is a lie, of course. Still, the young people who presently run IPCRI were in disagreement over the Jerusalem issue, and I realized that I needed to step down because Jerusalem is more important to me than the organization.

NOW WHAT?

In the short run, I am not optimistic. I feel we are in the worst place I can remember. I have a friend, Bradley Burston, who writes for *Haaretz*'s English edition. He is a wise man and his wife is very active politically. A few days ago, in a Facebook post, she wrote it was the thirty-second anniversary of her Aliyah and wondered, if she could immigrate to the State of Israel today, should she? The answer was, no, probably not. I wrote a response: "Varda, I'm so much in that same place today. On the 28th of September, 2018, I marked 40 years of living in Israel, and I'm telling you that the situation today is the worst I can remember in four decades." This scares me, and the fact that there is nowhere in the world I'd rather be.

My daughter ran away from here last summer. She and her husband and my first granddaughter moved to the south of France. They bought a house in Provence, because of the political situation and the economy. They tried to buy an apartment here and found nothing below 1.5 million shekels. In Provence, they found an amazing house with a garden for €200,000. They can always come back, but it makes me very sad. This is very hard for me. I have two sons who study at the Hebrew University of Jerusalem. One came back to live with us, and the other does not want to leave the house. They both studied mathematics, nothing political. My wife comes from the scientific field. It's not that she works in this field, but it's that she is more realistic than I am.

I also teach a course at Hebrew University, a month-long summer class on Israeli-Palestinian relations. Instead of focusing on the conflict, I speak of negotiations, agreements, failures, reasons for them, and what can be done next. I often invite guest speakers, Israelis and Palestinians, and no one has ever refused me, even though they are not paid. All I know is that I call people, and they accept. One of the reasons is that I very rarely refuse when I am asked to help. I believe we are under an existential threat today, and if we want to be the democratic state of the Jewish Nation, which is what we'd chosen for ourselves, we have to do something. I believe that today, we are back at an existential conflict – not between the Palestinians and us, but within ourselves. We may want a democratic state for the Jewish Nation, but after 70 years of existence and 50 years of occupation, we are neither democratic nor Jewish. Thus, for the State of Israel, this is an existential question.

I believe that the most important thing today is to create a situation in which we have partners. This is not theoretical. This is highly practical. It is very, very hard for both sides to form such partnerships. It is harder on the Palestinian side because they are caught in a populist struggle against normalization, and people pay the price for things like that. We need to learn how to do this and protect the people who do it. Nevertheless, I am certain that a majority of up to 70 percent on both sides wants and is willing to make the necessary compromises, provided that it believes there is someone to do this with on the other side.

After Camp David negotiations, *Ehud Barak* created the myth that "there is no partner for peace," which is very strong and is fed daily to citizens by leaders on both sides. It is tough to break this myth. Both sides give us enough reasons each day to believe there is no partner, but as a partner in marriage myself, I argue that partnership starts with a decision to form one, and then it has to be cultivated daily. What we have here, however, is a decision on both sides that there is no partner. They prefer it like that, which gives us an excuse to do whatever we feel like doing.

We need to know how to reconstruct the belief in the possibility of forming a partnership. When the Second Intifada started, *Ron Pundak* and I established the Forum of Palestinian-Israeli Peace non-governmental organizations. It started as a support group because we were under real attacks. People were killed on both sides, but we believed we must keep up the dialogue and maintain ties. We established a forum of Israeli peace organizations and demanded that our Palestinian partners establish a similar forum for Palestinian peace groups. Then, we founded the Forum. It is only a support group, but we knew that we could not do it alone, that we needed partners from our side and the other. This is what we need to work on today.

ONCE I START, I CANNOT STOP UNTIL I SUCCEED

Today I travel freely all over the West Bank, visiting villages and refugee camps. I'm also trying to bring back two Israeli soldiers' bodies and two Israeli civilians held in Gaza. Last Friday, ITV carried a report by Ayala Hasson, showing her visiting the Al-Am'ari refugee camp in *Ramallah*. She made it look like some covert military operation. For me, this is normal. I drive there in my car and go wherever I please even on foot in the center of *Hebron* or anywhere else. Israelis sometimes call to ask me if it is OK to go to Ramallah. I always tell them: "First of all, it is against the law so if you do, know that you are violating the law. And if you still do it, don't go alone. Make sure you go with a local, someone who'd meet you at the checkpoint because you don't know where you want to go." Then they ask me if they should take a gun with them, to which I say: "What for? Do you want to be a target? I go there with peaceful intentions and meet the same on the other side."

When I cross checkpoints, I am accompanied by a young man, a graduate of Al-Quds University who has an MA in environmental studies and works with me in the business of energy. He lives in Se'ir, a village outside Hebron. I drove him home after a visit to the south Hebron region. It was dark, and we arrived at a checkpoint they sometimes erect outside his village. They stopped us and asked for our identification. A young soldier of Russian origin looked at my ID card and said: "What? You are Jewish?" I said I was, and he asked: "What are you doing here? It is dangerous?" I said: "What's dangerous? I visit here all the time." "You cannot do that!" he said. "It is risky. They will kill you!" I said: "Listen, how old are you?" He said he was 20 years old. I said: "I've been visiting villages here for the past 40 years – that's twice your age – and you want to tell me it is dangerous?" He just could not stomach this. He called his commander, who came and started asking me questions, but this was not in *Area A*, but in Area B, where Israelis may travel, and it is not a felony.

So I sometimes get across checkpoints, and sometimes I am detained, but I show them my journalist card and they let me through. A month ago, I examined the *Bethlehem* checkpoint, and they detained me there for an hour and gave me some warning form to sign. I even have a permit to visit the Knesset and go anywhere there, including the Parliament's dining hall. Last year, I needed to renew the permit so they gave me this security questionnaire to fill out, some 20 pages that I had filed several times before. They asked me to write down all the foreign countries I'd visited. Now, I've been to 52 countries, and I was not going to list them all. Then they asked if I had been to enemy states and yes, I have. "Did you visit Jordan or Egypt?" "Sure, I go to Egypt four times a year; I've been there more than 50 times now. I am not going to list all of them." The last time I went to the Knesset, they told me that my permit had expired and that I should go to the Security Department. I went there, and they extended my permit by a month, which happened every month until I received no summons, and then they renewed it until 2021. For the past five years, I've been trying to promote solar energy projects in the Palestinian Authority and Egypt because I decided I wanted to build something, not just talk. Yesterday, I spent all day in Ramallah. I have a permit to construct solar fields and I am trying. I hope we'll close the finances for our first field in Egypt in the next two weeks, and then we'll sign contracts with the Palestinian

Authority for two projects in southern West Bank. Today, the Palestinians do not control the electricity. It is all in Israeli hands. In theory, they have control, but it is minimal. It is all in the Army's hands. This Druze officer in the Civil Administration is in charge of electricity and is practically the Palestinians' electricity king. He is a good man, but this is a military system, and he is a state official, and they're on strike now. I called him yesterday and he said: "We're on strike. I cannot talk to you." I want to bring in dozens of millions of dollars to invest in solar energy. It is a considerable challenge and had I known how long it would take, I would not have started it, but once I started, I could not stop until I succeeded, and I will succeed.

In recent years, I've been writing a book that tells the tale of the Israeli-Palestinian conflict through my life story, the experiences I have had, and the lessons I've learned by doing what I have done. It is a very optimistic story.

5. Small initiatives with great impact

Ghadeer Hani
Interviewed by Haneen Sameer Magadlah

For many years, I had heard about Ghadeer but never met her. People asked: "How come you have not met her? There is no way you are not familiar with her yet." I recall researching her name on the internet, trying to understand who this person was and why I needed to know her.

In 2019, I read a newspaper article informing that Ghadeer had received the *Sami Michael Prize* for Equality and Social Justice. It said: "We did not imagine there was another nominee who deserved the prize more than her!" I told myself: "We need to meet!"

I met Ghadeer in the office of *AJEEC-NISPED* where she worked. On our way to the office, I noticed that everyone we encountered welcomed her with much love. We sat in a room with a round table. Before starting the interview, she looked at me and said: "Haneen, I love people so much. Before we start, could you please tell me more about yourself, who are you, and what do you do?"

She gave me a big cup of Arabic coffee, which I love, expressed genuine interest, and looked deeply into my eyes. I thought to myself: "How come I have not met her earlier?" There was a moment of silence and then she asked: "Are you aware that what you are doing is very important? Writing these stories and listening to these voices are very crucial, especially these days, while the hope is lost. We are living in a stage of hopelessness."

Our conversation lasted three hours. I learned about her tremendous initiatives and projects and hope and lack of it. She claimed: "We don't survive without hope, we must keep the hope alive, always do remember this." I left feeling recharged with a tremendous amount of hope and positive energy. Since that day, I have followed her work and achievements passionately. Her latest accomplishment was winning the *Israeli President Hope Prize* for 2020.

CONNECTING WITH MY IDENTITY AT A VERY YOUNG AGE

I am 43 years old, from Akko/*Acre*, in the north of Israel. I've been living in the Naqab/Negev area, in the south of Israel, for almost 20 years. I work in economic development and tourism, and I am socially and politically active in the fights for peace and coexistence in Palestine/Israel, for women's rights, and against gender-based violence and polygyny.

I felt like a child until the age of 12. Even though I was the eldest, I felt as if I was forever a child. At the age of 13, I started becoming more aware of my various identities, particularly, my Palestinian national identity, and wanted to know more about who I was. I recall one time I drew the Palestinian flag. A colleague of my father saw it and asked him what this meant. Our household was never a political one, but my father, a bit confused, answered that it was a drawing of his daughter, without having an issue with it. But then again, at the time, peace was not on the horizon.

I used to be a very active member of our community center. I participated in some sort of competition and won a bunch of books about Palestine, one of them was by *Muhammad Ali Taha*. From that point forward, I started feeling more connected to my Palestinian identity, doing so by reading books about various Palestinian matters and the issue of the depopulated villages.

I used to read so much, to the extent that my teachers would introduce me to older students to show them how knowledgeable I was. I used to pick up the political books to read, written by *Mahmoud Darwish* and *Samih al-Qasim*. I have this memory of when Samih al-Qasim was supposed to come to visit my school in Akko/Acre to read one of Mahmud Darwish's poems at a ceremony. He ended up not attending the event, so I was asked to read in his place. I felt great pride that night.

I covered my head with a *hijab* when I was in seventh grade. It was during the month of *Ramadan*. For me, it was another thing that was associated with my identity. Everyone asked me why I did it, stressing I was 'too young' to cover my head, but I didn't listen, it was what I wanted, and no one forced me to do it.

The question of identity did not end in my youth and remained important in later stages of my life. Each time I was learning about local geography or history, I searched for information about Arab villages that existed previously in certain areas, about towns that were depopulated, and wondered about the people that lived in these now-empty spaces. My grandmother is from the depopulated village of *Al-Zeeb*. She used to tell me stories about how Jewish soldiers came to their village to kill everyone, and how my grandfather pretended to be dead so they wouldn't shoot him. I remember these stories every time we visit *Al-Kabri*.

When I was in eleventh grade we had to have self-discipline as we were studying individually to prepare for our Bagrut exams (matriculation certificate). Because time was in my hands, I started working and volunteering in several places. My first paycheck was from the community center, where I worked with little children. It was a very satisfying experience that made me learn that I wanted to do community work. Thus, I became enrolled in social and political activism, and I joined al-Jabha, the Hadash political party, the Democratic Front for Peace and Equality.

A CANDIDATE FOR THE ELECTIONS AT 21

My parents were always non-partisan, they used to vote, but I never really asked them who they were voting for and why. My girlfriends and their parents were strong supporters of Al-Jabha, and I felt as if this particular party represented me and my beliefs.

When I first started getting involved with activism and community work, the community center I worked for organized a summer camp that some children could not afford to join because it was a bit pricey. Therefore, my colleagues and I organized an alternative summer camp. We raised donations from various people and raised all the food and transportation fees as support from our communities. We also received some financial aid from the municipal council that helped us pay for country clubs and other activities. We set up a summer camp where each kid paid a minimal symbolic fee of 60–70 NIS, and everyone came and had a blast. This particular experience was a game changer for me, and I became really involved with the youth movement. It was exciting.

At the youth movement meetings, we used to have a book club where we discussed various articles and literature, and I genuinely loved these discussions. Later, in the 1998/1999 elections, I was not even 21 when I was a city council electoral candidate, the fourth or fifth on the list. They ended up canceling my candidacy due to my young age as it made me ineligible. During that time, the *Islamic Movement* (political party) in Akko/Acre saw me as a threat to their candidacy because I, as a girl wearing hijab, could steal votes from them. It was the first time that I made a public statement addressing a social issue; I did it because I was confident in who I was and what I believed. In the statement, I declared that I had decided to put on a hijab all by myself, that I had decided to run for the elections all by myself, and that I was an independent, strong individual who would not let anyone step over me or question the integrity of my intentions.

A DELEGATE OF CHANGE

I found a new job opportunity in the Naqab/Negev area in the southern part of Israel. I started working in a community center there, and it was such a difficult time for me. I was more independent than ever before and was living alone. I had a rough time understanding the Bedouin dialect even though I made a significant effort to learn the different words and pronunciations to the point that I wrote everything down. Still, it was challenging to understand most of the conversations. The dialect was simply so different from where I came from. I used to cry every day.

I started working in a very politically unstable period. A few months later the Second *Intifada* broke, and I was asking myself "What am I doing? Can I be an activist? Am I an activist?" I used to hear people scream, "Watch out! She has explosives in her bag!" wherever I went, and it was extremely uncomfortable and scary for me. Being an Arab was a threat to people, I was treated as if I wasn't even human, which shocked me. I understood that there were not many Arabs living in the area but did people really think every Arab person was a terrorist? It just did not make any sense to me.

It was there and then that I began to realize that Arabs and Jews not only did not live together, but they rarely communicated. I felt a responsibility to form bridges between Arabs and Jews and use my privilege as someone who spoke Hebrew to connect people. I also thought about how I could take part in helping Arab women who could not speak Hebrew so they could go and work, study, or even start an academic journey. I truly believed that through education, we could bridge the gap between Arabs and Jews so that they could see us as equals.

Then I met *Amal Saleh*, who came to me with a suggestion. She asked me: "What do you think about organizing meetings that bring together Muslim and Jewish women? In such meetings, we could discuss religion and religious connections between the two." And so we did. I found the meetings to be very successful, and we discussed a different topic each time. In that framework, I used my Hebrew-speaking ability to create connections because many Muslim women there couldn't speak the language. The meetings stopped at one point, but they encouraged me to go and learn group facilitation because I genuinely believed in the effectiveness of group meetings.

In Acre though, things were a bit different. Arabs and Jews communicated and connected more than they did in the Naqab/Negev. In high school in Givat Haviva, Jews and Arabs would always have sleepovers. Therefore, for me, this kind of bridge between the two people was not strange and I knew how it felt from a very young age.

LONELINESS

When I was 30, I felt as if I was utterly alone. My cousin came to work for a year in Beer el-Sabea'/*Beer Sheva* and then went back to the north. And I lived here for six months, and then I moved to *Hura*. I started feeling lonesome, even though I had roommates. I started thinking about how much I wanted to have a family and kids, but it was far from being an option at the time. I guess I just gave up on the idea of having a family and looked for other things to do instead. Two years later, I was working with AJEEC full time. I was always busy with activities and programs to the extent that I used to get home only at 23:00 each day. I was fully aware that I kept myself busy all the time just because I did not want to feel lonely. Until this very day, these feelings of loneliness are present in me, especially before I fall asleep. Before I moved from Hura to Beer el-Sabea'/Beer Sheva in July, I used to get annoyed by the screams and voices of the neighborhood children during the summer holidays, and I would not be able to sleep. But now that I am here, I really miss those kids' presence.

Sometimes the feelings of loneliness intensify. For instance, I had many neighbors that I used to chat with, even though we had nothing to talk about really. What would I talk to them about? My job? They wouldn't be interested in hearing what I do. Still, they would tell me how lucky I was because I was a free woman with no restraints, no family, and no kids, and I would say to them how lucky they were because they had warmth from their husbands and their children. I would insist that families bring joy and security, and they would end up agreeing with me and tell me that I made them realize how important having a family was to them. In such moments these feelings of loneliness intensify because even though they say that I am lucky, I am simply not.

THE COMMON GROUND IS THAT EVERYBODY WANTS TO LIVE

I started working with AJEEC in 2009 during *Operation Cast Lead*. The office of the organization was in a hotel building, and Arabs and Jews used to meet every day, see each other in the elevator, eat at the same table but never speak to one another. I found it insane that we didn't even greet each other "Good morning"; I was annoyed and bothered to say the least.

I assume it was because of fear. I remember a rocket falling next to Tal al-Sabea'/Tel Sheva, and a girl told me that she wished it would fall on Beer al-Sabea'/Beer Sheva so we'd all die and get this over with. Here in the Naqab/Negev, many people have family and relatives in Gaza, and so it was tough for them to deal with this reality. At the time, I organized, together with Amal, the second chief executive officer of AJEEC, a series of workshops to address these hardships, discuss them, and to frame our feelings and emotions regarding our reality. I believe that these workshops were necessary for all of us. They created connections, which are the main element that leads to problem solving. Of course, during that time, my sense of identity intensified, and it was imperative for me always to say that I was a Palestinian Arab woman.

When I finished school, I joined the local youth movement and we traveled to France and Germany. There was a big discussion in our group regarding identity, our Palestinian identity in particular. My teammates argued that I shouldn't say that I was Palestinian in the airport (they were afraid), and I insisted that they were wrong. It was simply who I was, why should I hide who I was and where I came from?

At AJEEC, when we reevaluated our organizational vision, we insisted on emphasizing our Palestinian identity. We were fully aware of the consequences and funding challenges we might face because of such a decision, but AJEEC's mission and work areas had expanded beyond al-Naqab/Negev. We started reaching out to other Arab villages, such as Lod, Qalansuwa, and Shefa-'Amr. Even when we held a meeting in *Jaffa*, it was essential for us to state that we were Palestinians, because it was simply empowering. I do not believe that it clashes with peacemaking and coexistence work.

During the assault on Gaza, before *Operation Protective Edge*, I participated as a translator in group meetings between Israeli and Palestinian women. Even though there was an Arab facilitator, they still needed me for when they split into smaller groups. I enjoyed being part of that group, even as a translator and observer. I saw how significant joint work is and how meaningful being attentive can be, just listening.

A year later, the same group of women met in Jerusalem. The topic of the discussions once again was the war. *Women Wage Peace* set up a tent next to the Israeli President's Residence that they named 'Stead Fasting,' fasting against the war crimes that were being committed, fasting in resistance for 72 hours. We joined them in their opposition and when the Palestinian women came in, I helped with translation there as well, and I recognized my significant role as a Palestinian Arab woman who is a citizen in this country.

The solution will not come from the *Oslo Accords*, nor from the Geneva Accords; we – Israeli Arabs and Palestinians – have a role to play. Because our Palestinian brothers in the occupied territories did not care about us as partners in their struggle and the Jews never allowed us to be part of anything, they never gave us a chance. I felt as if we, Palestinian citizens of Israel, had a vital role to play, our opinions mattered, our relationships mattered, and I did not need to have family in Gaza to care because they were still my people dying there.

Therefore, when I say that Hebrew is a 'bridge,' what I mean is that we as Palestinians who live in Israel can use this language to build connections and bridges of peace and serenity. Some would tell me not to use the term 'bridge' as a way to describe it because people step over bridges, and I would always reply: "people can step over it all they want when peace is achieved." There's so much suffering on both sides. For how long will this go on?

I cry very often, but I mostly try to hide my tears because people might think I'm pretending. I'm so emotional when it comes to this conflict. I can't look at the suffering of the kids in Gaza without crying. One might think that the Jewish kids here also suffer. Here they are scared of balloons, and there they are … Never mind. There's no need to compare. Why compare? But when will people have the chance to talk and communicate for God's sake? I mean, I had the privilege to meet and speak with Jewish people, and it shaped how I see education and bilingualism. I mean, I'm part of the board of *Hajar School* even though I don't have kids, it's just that these things are significant to me.

LANGUAGE IS IDENTITY

Through Women Wage Peace, I came to acknowledge the role of women in social and political activism. Jewish women would often say: "I'm scared of the day I hear a knock on my door, the day I open the door to the dead body of my son." For me, any child in the world is a child of mine. There is nothing I would wish for my little nephew that I would not want for any child. So for me, it was essential to get that message across through Women Wage Peace's Facebook page in Arabic. I was willing to make it my responsibility to translate everything to Arabic because language is identity. My language is part of who I am, and I want my message to reach my people, my Palestinian Arab-speaking people, in Arabic. Do not get me wrong, we had a lot of negative feedback, but much positive feedback as well, as many want peace too.

Translating is surely draining for me but it is something that is really, really, really important for me. At times I even care more about the Arabic version to be completed before the Hebrew one. For example, when the Nation-State Law was passed, I felt as if I had been robbed. When they decided that Arabic was not an official language in Israel anymore, I felt like I didn't have much to lose anymore. If my language is not recognized, then nothing that I am is. Nor my identity, my existence, or my history.

Women Wage Peace are now considering making some changes in order for them to translate their entire publications into Arabic. I genuinely can't keep doing it because it's a lot of work. Therefore there is a need for an external company that translates the content to Arabic to maintain that section of the publication. I am happy that my efforts brought about this acknowledgment.

Another initiative I was part of is *Project Wadi Attir* where we planted trees in Hura. It was also a project about peace, and I was very active there because that makes people get closer and connect. But there were many challenges. I never imagined that I would be in the same movement with right-wing women or settlers. I never imagined I would sit with a woman settler in the same room out of my own free will. Never.

For me, if you're a settler, living on the stolen land of my people, you don't even have the right to approach me. Yet my experience in Women Wage Peace changed me a little, for better or worse. I feel that I am part of something bigger now, and I have a message to pass. I feel it most when I speak with my friend Liora who is from the *Alei Zahav* settlement. When we talk, we disagree about 90 percent of the things, but there is the other 10 percent where we agree, and I try to hold on to those 10 percent. I started seeing that there is more than one truth. My truth is different from hers, regardless of whether I consider her truth as legitimate or not.

So, for example, I'm Ghadeer, a Palestinian Arab woman who lives here, but also I can understand why Ariela doesn't want to leave the land she's holding, and this is where we can start our conversation. She once saw a picture of my father with my nephews before taking off for *Umrah*, so she asked who it was in the picture, and I answered. Then she proceeded to ask me about Mecca, Medina, the *Prophet Mosque*, *Al-Masjid an-Nabawī*, Al-Aqsa Mosque, Dome of the Rock, and their importance to me. I answered, and she was shocked because the things she knew about all of these places were different from what I had told her, which prompted her to do research about it all. It's crazy how our beliefs are shaped by the misinformation that we have and the partial knowledge we are exposed to. That's why I believe that through conversation so much can change because when a right-wing woman hears me out and listens to what I have to say and tries to understand where I come from, it might instigate something in her and maybe make her think differently or question a thing or two.

ALL THAT WE DO IS FOR NOTHING

When they were trying to pass the Nation-State Law, I stayed up until dawn to watch the news, the debates, and the modifications they were making to the law. At some point, I closed my eyes to rest them for a little. It was only a matter of seconds, and when I opened them, I saw that they had already voted for the law. I was shocked. I felt as if all that we do is for nothing. I was leaving for work around 07:00, and my aunt called me crying. I started worrying, and I asked her what was wrong. She said she was sad because of me, so I became super stressed and said: "Oh my god auntie, what happened?" She answered:

"All your work and efforts and those of your girlfriends were in vain, it was all for nothing … God damn them."

All the left-wing parties disappointed me because they did not take this new law seriously, and they could have done more, but then I thought about it. The votes were 55-62 in favor of the racist law, which means the difference was only seven – that comforted me, but it also stressed me out.

I spoke with my girlfriends, and told them to forget about me, that Ghadeer who belonged to the past, along with Women Wage Peace, *Other Voice*, *Standing Together*, and all these other organizations. Coexistence and joint work were over for me. Peace was not an option anymore, and regarding my Jewish colleagues, I'd do what I had to do, but nothing beyond, I was over it all. Many tried to speak with me. Others left me alone because they did not want to stress me out, but I was utterly devastated. On that same day, Women Wage Peace had a tent put up for the last day of the mothers' training program that ran that summer. The aim was to finish it with a demonstration near the presidential residence, and everyone asked me to join them to lead the group in Arabic. I ended up agreeing. I asked them to send me all the materials that needed translation, and I finished everything in time.

There were not many Arabs there, and we were only four Arab women at the demonstration. It was important for me to hug all of them before the rally. When we reached the president's residence, I experienced something similar to an anxiety attack, but I insisted on continuing. I told myself: "Ghadeer, you have to keep going. This is something you believe in despite everything else." Yes, I have to keep empowering myself, but I sometimes ask my girlfriends to empower me because I have difficulty talking about my feelings. It was very empowering for us to volunteer and work together in creating new spaces for us to express our thoughts, opinions, and share experiences, not from a victim's perspective, but from a stand of empowerment and demand for justice. I even changed my name on Facebook and wrote it in Arabic, and I stated that whoever wants to find me has to learn Arabic.

Many people added me on Facebook afterward and asked me to help them change their names to Arabic. It was a movement of some sort to protest the new law. Overnight, I had over 2,000 people asking me to help them change their names, most of them from abroad.

During the demonstration against the Nation-State Law and afterward, I suggested that we translate all of our posts online to Arabic to have more Palestinians joining us. I volunteered to recruit activists and participants for these activities. I also suggested taking care of booking buses to pick people up from Jerusalem because many Jewish folks wanted to come but did not have transportation. Many people cared about the Arabic language and came to protest the passing of the new racist law, and it was my duty to help everyone get there. Four full buses transported activists from all around the country, as not many people had a way to commute to Tel Aviv, and others worried about finding a parking spot. By arranging transportation, we showed everyone that we were all together and looked out for one another. The whole experience affirmed that I was in the right direction.

Some people said that the demonstration was 50/50, half Arabs and half Jews. Others said it was 60/40 in favor of Arabs, I somewhat saw it was 40/60 in favor of Jews. But anyway, that demonstration in Tel Aviv restored the hope within me. It showed me that we must go on. We must spread awareness and talk about these things at any given opportunity. I started researching how I could make a good impact and change, and whether I could change the law and what I needed to do.

My friend Leila spoke to me one day while I was dragging my luggage on the platform in the train station, getting ready to leave. She said she was thinking of forming a political party that was fully based on joint work between Arabs and Jews, and that I was the first person she thought of to join this party. I immediately said yes.

YOU WILL FIND ME WHEREVER PEACEMAKING IS

I won the Sami Michael Prize. I was emotional to see that such awards existed, but I also felt weird about it because if God created us as social beings, why should we receive prizes for being normal, decent human beings? I realized that the world we live in has more things that separate us than things that bring us together; there are more divisions than bridges. At some point, I wanted to tell them that I don't want to receive this prize because these acts should be normalized; they should be the status quo. But I felt that overall it was a token of appreciation, and it would be embarrassing to decline. Surely, though, this prize made me feel a greater sense of responsibility.

Luckily enough, during the time I was part of Women Wage Peace, I represented the organization in a conference in Italy. There I met with a left-wing Israeli woman who was part of Standing Together –an Arab-Jewish movement for equality, social justice, and peace. Of course, they were against settlements and strive to end the occupation. She asked me to join their movement, and I did, and honestly? Standing Together is the reason why I was still in Women Wage Peace, because in Standing Together I could do radical activism because they are leftist, and I didn't have to compromise on my ideology. But also I bring a lot of feminist perspectives and women-related issues that are discussed in Women Wage Peace to Standing Together.

For example, in Women Wage Peace, there was a program called 'Initial Talk,' a framework where two women discuss a specific topic or event. There I learned how to communicate better and how to ask questions. For instance, instead of asking "why?" and "what should you do?" it is better to propose suggestions and ask about opinions. I support these methods because they have proved themselves as successful and efficient.

Recently, I joined Other Voice, which was founded ten years ago after the blockade on Gaza. They have been protesting every week at Yad Mordechai Junction, in the southern part of Israel, to stop and dismantle the siege on Gaza. At these demonstrations, people curse them, yell at them, throw coffee in their faces, and sometimes splash them with urine. I am so scared for their lives. I always fear they might get shot by some violent fanatic. Most of them live around the Gaza separation wall or in Sderot. We organized group meetings of people from different organizations to discuss how to reconstruct Gaza and repair the life there once the blockade was over. We started proposing ideas and alternatives, with the cooperation and collaboration of people from Gaza. That was such a fantastic experience, something that gave me hope. That people who were suffering themselves – though not as much as the Gazans – wanted to do something about the blockade, was an authentic act of solidarity because they knew that this reality was not good for anyone involved. They appreciated this collaboration.

There was another initiative by a young man from Kibbutz *Be'eri* that was titled the Lighthouse Project for Gaza. It did not involve politics but instead focused on philanthropic financial contributions sent by some of the settlers to Gazan workers that had previously worked for them. This also instigated so much hope within me, and it is worth sharing and talking about. People need to hear and know that Gazans are sick of this reality and don't want war. They just want to live in peace. Once Israelis allow them to speak and give themselves the chance to hear them out, they come to new a realization.

Wherever I go now, people tell me that I am famous. Some people are surprised that I am still active with all of this determined energy. Every day I wake up, I do it to make peace possible, break dogmas and stereotypes about us Palestinians, about us as Arabs, because this is how peace can become an option. This is why we vote during the elections. Because we believe that some people can represent us and make a change, and we keep on trying. I also started being active in religious activities. For example, recently I celebrated Hanukkah, the Jewish holiday, in a synagogue in a program called 'Three Women,' which hosted a Christian lady and me. And later on, I participated in the same project in a church in Beer al-Sabe'/Beer Sheva. People relate throughout these initiatives because they suddenly see that people from different religions are still similar because they care about the same values and pillars.

I rarely say no to requests to participate in such programs and initiatives, not that I have time, but I usually sleep three–four hours and sometimes even less. I sleep only because my body demands rest at some point and because I need to dream to go on and continue with what I do. Dreams fuel my efforts to make peace possible because if peace happens here, peace can happen everywhere.

I started many different and small initiatives as well. No matter how small they might be, they have so much significance. I once organized a group for Iftar during Ramadan where many Christians, Muslims, and Jews joined in eating on one table. Some people were concerned about *kosher* food, so I asked each person to bring something they could eat, and we set up different tables for different types of food. We spoke of the importance of fasting for the three Abrahamic religions, and everyone left after learning something new. I once also organized a talk about the significance and status of women in Islam, Christianity, and Judaism to provide a cultural context about these religions.

A year ago, as I was on my way back from London, a soldier from Tel Aviv was shot in Arad in the southern part of Israel. I saw the news about the trial, and the father of the soldier spoke on national television and said that he still believed in coexistence despite everything. I don't use the term coexistence. I prefer 'joint life.' When I saw the news, I wondered, how can I reach the mother of the dead soldier and send her my condolences? I knew that the court hadn't yet decided who had killed him, and they were still investigating the reasons and motives that had led to his death, so nothing was clear but still, as a peace activist, I wanted to meet her. A few minutes after I saw the father on television, a Jewish friend from Jerusalem called me and asked about my trip. I told her that the trip was good but that I had suffered during the airport check-in because I was racially profiled and discriminated against. I asked how she was doing, and she said that the political climate there was worrying because of the death of a soldier. I told her that I had just watched the news about him and my desire to reach out to his mother. It turned out the soldier was her son's classmate in elementary school and she knew the soldier's family. She was excited about connecting me with the mother, and was a bit emotional. We decided to make it happen.

When I spoke with the soldier's mother on the phone, she asked me about Women Wage Peace. She wanted to know about our activities and said she might join some of them. I suggested that as part of *Arbor Day* activities, during which we plant trees, we would plant trees in honor of her son. I spoke with Women Wage Peace to make it happen. She talked to the municipal council there and proposed the idea. They got back to her saying that it would be difficult to organize such an activity on the proposed date because on the same day there would be police forces and representatives from *Kekren Keyemet LeIsrael*. I asked for her permission to approach the municipal council myself. I spoke with the secretary, and we had a woman-to-woman talk. Five minutes later, she called me and said that the mayor was available that afternoon if we could make it. I said yes. At 17:00 we went on the bus and met with the mayor, we met with the gardeners, and, of course, the mother of the dead soldier, and we arranged everything.

By the time the event started, the family was involved with the trial and was planning to raise money to encourage Bedouins to serve in the army. I was afraid that the event would not give voice to my beliefs and could reflect poorly on me as an Arab/Palestinian activist. I thought to myself: "OMG Ghadeer, what did you do? Are you recruiting Bedouins for the army right now?" I just didn't know what to do anymore. The entire situation was confusing. I consulted with Women Wage Peace, and we decided not to mention Women Wage Peace so that the whole event could be about the dead soldier. Eventually, many Arab council members came to the event to show support, so Jews and Arabs were there together. The mother gave a beautiful speech, and the father spoke about coexistence. It was a meaningful experience despite all my misgivings, and I felt it was meant to happen.

I love people, love connections with others. I am a person of connections. In order to build connections with people, one must build respect, respect their place and who they are. For example, when we first started working on Project Wadi Attir which was an environmental sustainability project and a tourism-oriented project and one that needed a lot of resources from funders and mainly community donations, I told the people in the project that I didn't want other feminist organizations in the area to feel threatened by us in terms of taking away their resources that come from crowdfunding. I told them that individuals in the Naqab/Negev were living in challenging socio-economic realities and that many people had a hard time in providing food for their families. Many mothers feared for the future of their children because they never knew what to expect. People were generally living in despair and hopelessness. Resources are a challenging thing to take care of, especially in our community.

I NEED TO TRUST YOU TO MAKE PEACE

I feel like I have less influence on Palestinians than the impact I have on Jews, and it saddens me because I am fully aware of the socio-economic reality that stops us from having any hope. Sometimes I feel that I am standing on a delicate thread between hope and despair.

Sometimes I wish that the number of Palestinians in Israel who are active would be at least relatively similar to our population's percentage in the country. Sometimes I feel like crying, and I immediately look for something to keep me hopeful, to prevent me from feeling down and helpless. One of the things that keep me going is that my parents are proud of me, really proud.

Despite all the bad news and the things that put me down like the Nation-State Law, nothing makes me happier than volunteering and being active. I do not feel proud to talk about my work. I feel proud of working. The Sami Michael

Prize was 7,000 NIS, and I gave all of that money back to the organizations and movements that I work with through workshops and initiatives. Because this is where it is supposed to go, in return for all the experience and knowledge these organizations have provided me. I owe them everything, and as long as I do this work I will always feel like I want to give more.

Peace is created through building trust, and trust is achieved through knowledge and familiarity. I need to know who you are to trust you, and I need to trust you to make peace with you. So for me, things are simple. My activity fuels me, and as much as I do, I want to keep doing. When I speak about peace, I do not just mean between Palestine and Israel, but peace between us as human beings, as individuals who share a space and live together, peace for the region. Peace in the way in which we think about our joint collective future and how to make it better, how to make each other better, and that peace is built on trust.

6. The freedom to choose

Hadassah Froman
Interviewed by Nechumi Yaffe and Lital Myers

We interviewed Hadassah Froman to shed light on the activism of religious and settler women who seek a path to peace through conducting dialogues and meaningful work that bring together people of both sides. It was not easy to get hold of her or make an appointment, but we insisted. At first, we wanted to talk to her in her home in the settlement of *Tekoa*, believing it would be appropriate and interesting to see her in her natural environment. Several days before the scheduled date, however, we were informed by the university that we were not permitted to travel to her home, which was in the heart of the settlement area, due to the current security guidelines. Thus we asked her to meet us in Jerusalem. We feared that changing the venue might cause Hadassah to cancel the interview or that if we held it, it might be pre-charged with tensions unrelated to the three of us. Fortunately, the change of venue seems to have had no impact on the conversation or the interaction between us.

We met Hadassah at the National Library on the Edmond J. Safra Campus in Givat Ram, which was filled with loud students and construction work. We felt like we were meeting a woman who lived in a different sphere, outside our noisy and anxious world. All through the five hour interview, Hadassah gave an air of calm and ease, a feeling of old and open familiarity. We felt like Hadassah was pulling us into her world, to a different place where people lived with uplifting values and ideals. The meeting elated us, taking us out of everyday banal reality. We realized that the strong personal ideals embedded in Hadassah's soul allowed her to live heroically and gave her the power to deal with the numerous complexities and challenges that characterized her life. This chapter tells the story of Hadassah Froman's life from childhood; a story of a woman with moving and empowering insights about the complexity of life; a story that left us with thoughts about activism for the benefit of others and the common good, even while paying the dearest personal prices.

THE KIBBUTZ: EXTERNAL CALM, INTERNAL NOISE

I was born on *Kibbutz Lavi* in the Lower Galilee in 1949, two years after the *1948 War of Independence*. The country grew, and I grew up with it on a northern kibbutz, surrounded by Arab villages. The only other Jewish town near us was *Tiberias*. I was raised on the idea of the great *Aliyah* resumption. All of our parents were refugees who came from different countries and were not really Israelis. When I was small, people on my kibbutz spoke English and were not connected with the Israeli reality, but slowly and in their own way, they connected. Living on a kibbutz, I was a girl who loved nature and vistas. Our family hiked a lot. At the same time, I realized very early on that I would not be like most kibbutz members. I could not stand the social intensity and living right on top of each other. It was not for me. We lived in a *children's house* and visited our parents for two hours each day, which did not suit me at all. As a little girl, I remember still being in kindergarten, waking up at night and going alone and barefoot in the mud – we did not have real paths yet – to my parents' home. Dad must have smacked my behind – it was still OK then – scolded me or something and took me back to the children's house. Mom says that when they served lunch in kindergarten, I used to take my plate to my room, sit on my bed, and eat there because I could not stand the noise. Society, as a whole, was noisy for me.

The first kibbutz rabbi was Moshe Levinger. He was the first to open my eyes. He introduced us to the Land of Israel teachings of *Rabbi Kook*, which I found amazing. I was 11 or 12 then, and suddenly I heard someone speak to my inner world, addressing the experiences of something that happens around us but has no words. It was fascinating. That was his fight. The entire kibbutz was against him, but he left an enduring impression on me that affected how my life evolved.

On the one hand, I have memories of growing up where new things were happening, even nationally – a nation discovering itself and its land. These were extraordinary experiences that people who live today don't have. On the other hand, the kibbutz and eventually the family framework – and I had terrific though strict parents – painted the world in a certain way. Later, I chose a very different path.

MY JOURNEY

After I graduated from grammar school, I moved to the *Jezreel Valley* communal high school, where I got a room and my independent life started. My early freedom was very significant to me. One of the reasons kibbutz life, and later some religious issues, did not suit me has to do with freedom. Ever since

I was a little girl, freedom, being in motion and liberated, was a meaningful core of my being. I knew then that freedom would be the condition for my entire existence. In high school, I took liberties as a student. I was very central in class but also disobedient. I did not study much. After I graduated from high school, I joined the army. There was no other choice then. The army was OK, but where was my freedom?! Kibbutz members often become commanders in the military, so I became a commander in the *Nahal Brigade*. I served on new Jewish settlements, which were called strongholds then. We were involved in establishing settlements in the Jordan Rift Valley, and we were shelled every night.

I graduated from a squad commanders' course, and my Nahal commander called me for a personal meeting and said they want to give me some responsibilities because I excelled socially – though not in my studies. She said they wanted to establish a new form of Nahal core group, a mixed group of religious and secular soldiers, who would serve as a core group that would form a new settlement. I was chosen because I was a religious girl from a religious kibbutz. But I felt ambivalent because I knew that I was not a friendly person, and religion is all about socializing, so inside, I rebelled against it. I don't know what the Nahal commander was thinking, but she said: "I want you to have this gift. Accept this challenge." That was the first time they designed such a group, and for me that was the first time I accepted such a challenge, which was the root of all that has happened in my life since. At the same time, I started studying, mainly Jewish philosophy. I had this yearning to find a root, connect to one. That was a deep search that I followed from my disagreement with the type of religiousness I was raised in.

As most kibbutzniks do, I served another year after the army, and then I went to university. I walked around the Hebrew University thinking about studying Jewish philosophy. At the same time, I toured Jerusalem and started joining all kinds of study groups. Then I left the university and attended the Michlala College for Women in Jerusalem. I truly wanted to study Jewish philosophy texts, and the university is a bit heavy, making you go through hell before you get to a text, and I had no patience for that. The college was ultra-orthodox by nature. After the army, I went there with another girl, and *Rabbi Cooperman* accepted me at once, after a personal interview. He told me: "I am accepting you based only on our conversation, but I will not find you a husband." Later, we conflicted. During the *Yom Kippur War*, David Ben-Gurion died, and a memorial siren was sounded. He said we would not stand still in honor of his memory because this was a gentile's custom. "OK," I said, "so let's read a chapter of Psalms together." He said: "No. We'll not do that either." So I took the Book of Psalms and left the classroom. That started a scandal in the college. I spent two years there, during which time I met Menachem (*Rabbi Menachem Froman*, later my husband), and my life changed forever.

MENACHEM – THE LIGHT OF MY LIFE

We met when I visited a man with whom he used to study. He showed up at some stage, went to the kitchen to make coffee, made it with a spoon of salt instead of sugar, and started laughing. The minute I heard his voice, his laughter, I knew that this was the man of my life. I knew that even before I talked to him. I knew that this man would save me from life's banality. He blew my mind. I felt his presence and proposed to him right away. He used to attend the *Merkaz Harav Yeshiva*. I called him and said: "Listen, I felt there was something in your presence, that we have a common path, and that's a divine decree." Not that I fell in love with him, but I just felt there was something greater. And indeed, my life changed in an instant.

I don't look like it now, but I was a timid girl then, blushing and stammering. I felt strongly that if I didn't make a move, without Menachem I'd have nothing to live for. I knew that very strongly. He said: "Sorry, but I'm seeing someone, and I will probably marry her." I said: "Well, we'll see!" Then he went looking for me and found me in one of the Jerusalem study groups I attended, and our relationship started. We had a bond out of this world, and I mean that in two aspects: a very, very strong one and very, very difficult one. For example, I was the eldest granddaughter of my grandma. Before my wedding, she bought me a fully furnished flat in Rehavia, but I did not live there for even one day. Menachem said: "We don't need it. It is not appropriate for us," and I had no problem with that. I was totally dedicated to our story. Until that moment, I had never listened to or followed anyone. I only did what I felt like doing. With him, things changed drastically, and it was hard, but I realized this was something else and was bound to happen.

I did what he wanted about the wedding, too. There were weddings on the kibbutz, but Menachem said it was not necessary, not right. So we got married at the Wailing Wall, without caterers, a band, or photographers. Nothing. That's how we got married. He was the light of my life. He was so different, so extraordinary that there was no other way to get along with him. He had his own ideas of how things should be, and I knew we'd succeed as a couple only if we did things his way, which was not a simple way to live.

As a student, I used to wear a skirt to college, but put on trousers as soon as I got home because I was from the kibbutz. Once, Menachem came in and saw me dressed like that and said: "What is this? Go change." And I, like … well, quickly changed. I kept telling myself: "What's this? Are you paying attention to what you're doing?" I mean, never before had anyone told me what to do. It was on my mind for a long time, and it was not simple.

Additionally, Menachem led a wholly committed and very engaged way of life and was terribly dedicated to his own ideas. There are all kinds of norms in life, such as celebrating Bar Mitzvah or Bat Mitzvah, which you have to follow, but he often did not care. I shifted between those things and felt that my role was to mediate him to the world, a full-time job. Then, I became his secretary and I could not manage paperwork and such. It was not simple for me; the roles I undertook were not simple – managing our finance and things like that. It was not for me. Even managing a home was not for me, and I had ten children! He did not mind hiring help, and at some point, I got help in various things, but I may not have let myself have enough.

In the army, I was associated with the core group of *Rabbi Levinger*, who established [the Jewish settlement in] *Hebron* – the real hardcore of the *Gush Emunim* settlement movement. I used to visit Rabbi Levinger where they settled, in the Military Government House in Hebron – I was a sergeant in a miniskirt then – and study *Orot Kodesh* (Lights of Holiness, a book by Rabbi Kook) all night. Menachem came from a very different background. He was a vital member of the *Labor Movement* and wrote for the [left-wing] dailies of *Davar*, *Al-Hamishmar*, and *Haaretz*. He was raised in a home that you may call secular because it was secular socially, but he was soaked in Hassidism from his parents. They had this unique combination with *Kfar Hasidim* – a village built by *Hasidim* who became Mapainiks, as in members of *Mapay*, and then a group from *Benei Akiva* joined them. Menachem was a unique product of that mixture of cultures. He was associated with the Labor Movement, and because of me, he naturally joined Gush Emunim. That was a meeting of worlds. In the beginning, we used to fight about this and almost broke up, but after we got married, it became clear that it could work. At first, that seed of Menachem's special activities was formed when we, too, joined a settlement. However, the concepts of the left, and peace, and that they could work together were also part of our lives as a couple.

We were a total couple. We were characterized as a couple that was in total symbiotic alignment, both spiritually and philosophically, and were physically together all the time. We started studying together right from the start: Lots of *Gemara* at first, *Maimonides* a bit later, and after we got married we studied *Melachim u Milhamot* (Kings and Wars), the *Sota Tractate*, which ends with "A Priest Anointed for War" (Book of Deuteronomy, 20: 2), after which he went to fight in the Yom Kippur (October 1973) War. Men were drafted for five months. It was traumatic, and everywhere his battalion went I followed, spending five months with him on all fronts and studying together.

WE BELONG TO THE LAND RATHER THAN 'THE LAND BELONGS TO US'

When we returned from the war, we lived for several years in a house above the Wailing Wall. Bar-Ilan University had a building where we conducted cultural activities and started forming relationships with the Palestinians, which was in Menachem's blood. We lived inside the *Muslim Quarter*.

We spent three beautiful years in the Old City of Jerusalem, where two of our children were born. Still, I did not want to live in the Old City because there was no sunshine or space there, and I keep asking myself: Why did we stay there as long as we did? Menachem used to say: "Ever since Eve drove Adam out of the Garden of Eden, no one did that except you." He followed me gladly when we moved to Mevaseret, a suburb of Jerusalem, a place with sunshine and space. Then, Menachem met Shilo Gal, then *Gush Etzion Regional Council* head, who told him: "Come, build a kibbutz in Gush Etzion," and Menachem loved the idea. He was a Labor Movement man, a member of the first peace movements, and an idealist who loved the land. He was very excited, but I said: "A kibbutz? You want to start a kibbutz?" It took me years to leave my own kibbutz, and now I was following him into another. He was very enthusiastic, and I said to myself that life brings you whatever you need, so I don't need a house or any other assets. I decided to believe that whatever I needed would be available, and I should not worry about it. That became my rule in life. So I said: "OK, let's go to the kibbutz, and if we don't like it, we'll leave." And so we established Kibbutz Migdal Oz with a group of young people in the Gush Etzion Regional Council. Menachem went wild with all kinds of kibbutz ideas because he was a little closer to that way of thinking, living on kibbutzes during and after his military service.

We had enough of the kibbutz after three years. Menachem realized it was becoming too stable and no longer suited us. If you ask me what I did, I would say: I gave myself fully and totally both to the idea and the establishment of settlement after settlement. We were into starting settlements. They offered Menachem the rabbi's position in several places, though he still was a very young rabbi. Then, Menachem told me: "Look, the relations between the religious and the secular will be the main issue of Israeli society." I remember it surprised me because, at the time, the gap between the two populations was not yet that crazy. He saw something that I could not. Therefore, we decided to establish a mixed settlement. People came from Tekoa with two pick-up trucks, collected our belongings, and placed us in Tekoa. At the time, it was a very remote place of secular immigrants from Russia. We did not just live there, Menachem was the rabbi, and I was a teacher. Connecting religious and secular Israelis was our mission, but the interest in the association with the Palestinian identity started to emerge. Menachem started forming all kinds of connections, believing at first that was his Zionist mission.

I tell this story whenever I speak, about a formative moment that stayed with me. Before we moved in, we were invited to see the house assigned to us in Migdal Oz. On the door, there was this sticker: "The Land of Israel belongs to the Nation of Israel." As I was about to enter the house, all rejoicing and happy, Menachem told me: "Remove this. I will not enter a house that has this sticker." And I said: "What's wrong with that? We are settling the Land of Israel, are we not?" He said: "No! It should be the other way around: The Nation of Israel belongs to the Land of Israel." I remember this well because it was a mental turning point for me. I was under the influence of Rabbi Levinger, genuinely believing that the land was ours and that we were settling it because we had every right to do so, and it meant that the Arabs' right was not as real as ours. Menachem believed that we belonged (to the land of Israel), but there may be others who belonged too. Also, belonging to the land is nothing like owning the land, as if one is masculine and the other feminine. That's where he started believing that Zionism is a feminine movement. Originally, Zionism was a (feminine) movement of surrendering and dedication, not a (masculine) movement of penetration. Not a movement of occupation, but one of submission. You give in and try hard to make it yours, but you don't reject others for that purpose. Menachem started taking that path and, slowly but surely, trouble started, and then the *intifada* broke out.

SETTLEMENTS ARE A FINGER EXTENDED FOR PEACE

We built Tekoa with our own ten fingers, but the society we established there was not really ours. People did not understand us. That became clear when the *Jewish Underground* story broke. At the time, Menachem was a member of the Gush Emunim Secretariat. He was a leader already – a bit eccentric, but a leader. After the Jewish Underground was uncovered, it turned out they had tried to recruit him twice because they felt he had an underground personality, a nonconformist with original views. When the Jewish Underground became known to the public, Menachem strongly criticized it. He tried to convince Tekoa people to sign a petition against the Underground, and that started a rift between him and them. He decided to quit the Gush Emunim Secretariat, and they accepted his resignation and told him that he really was not the right person for the post. Now, we built the place, and it was very dear to us. Being thrown out of there felt like we were ripped away, but the society that formed there was not truly with us. People did not really understand us.

All along the way, I followed his ideas. He was my teacher for life. What can I say about my great teacher? I learned from him and worried that he might be cast out of the religious sector. It was a very delicate game. On the one hand, Menachem stood up against almost everything that the settlers' sector produced; on the other, he was very connected to it, and if he left it, his work would lose its meaning because he wanted to bring change from within. That started many, many years of hardship. Everything became harder and harder, and he encountered a lot of resistance in the settlement and the whole world.

Hardly anyone agreed with him, both in the left and the right wings. He was viewed as 'the crazy rabbi' or a traitor, or something. It was hard on the family, and our children grew up against a backdrop of 20 years of opposition to their father. They had to cope, but some of them did not and still carry the scars. It was not simple for them to watch him being humiliated at the synagogue, having stones thrown at their home, or reading abusive graffiti. When the children grew up and started hitching rides, they were asked: "Where are you from?" And they said: "Tekoa." "Aha, so this rabbi of yours is so and so." Before they got out of the car, they would say: "I'll have you know – he is my father!"

Things were hard for many years, but Menachem did not care about anyone. He kept writing his articles and creating real scandals in Israeli society, making sure things were published. For example, it turned out that he used to visit Sheikh *Ahmed Yassin* in prison. That created a massive scandal in Israel. He was ostracized by the settlers, the society where we lived, but the Israeli left wing attacked him too. He used to say that the settlements were a finger extended for peace. He did not believe in separation, claiming that a war would start once the separation was introduced. After all, no such separation is possible in the Galilee or Jerusalem, and an artificial separation would lead to a war, so we need to learn to live together. He even dared to say that the association between Jews and Palestinians would come about through the deep cultural connection and mutual religious interests. They asked him: "What are you talking about?" But he was very persistent. He knew Muslim society very well. Some of his activities scared me quite a bit. I mean, his meetings with Sheikh Ahmed Yassin were unusual in every respect. I feared he crossed a line there, but I was his student, and a student follows her teacher. We were a solid couple and had a powerful love, but I was his student, too. So, I said, I will not decide now. Everything new he did in this field became part of my world, my spiritual world, until he became ill.

THE DISEASE

Menachem became ill and felt his end was near. This strongly motivated him to see his path through. In every respect, it was crazy to do everything he did when his body was weakening and withering away. It was very, very hard, and he did it big time! Shivi, my son, who joined us, also has Menachem's 'wow,' a strong internal power, and he just took Menachem under his care and pushed him on. They did a lot of things in that period, and he helped him through it. He embarked upon a voyage from this world to the world beyond. He taught it and shared his feelings with others. For me, too, learning about these tools was like preparing for our next stage. It was a separation process.

We tried to understand the passage between the worlds of the living and the dead. For the prior 20 years, Menachem had taught the *Zohar*, teaching that deals with that all the time. It is all about the transition between worlds, speaking a lot about death and passages. We were deeply into it. Menachem made me swear that I would not run away even when he died. He did not want me to skip the place of death. It is a junction, a significant spot in the transition between the worlds. In any event, at the moment of death, I was behind him, not beside him. Shuvia, our ultra-Orthodox daughter, was beside him, but I saw his spirit the moment he died. I never doubted that he was the most incredible human being I had ever met. I knew him thoroughly, and his spirit went through me and told me: "Come, come, we are going on." I realized I was joining him on a journey with different tools, that I had no idea how I'd do that, but that something would happen there. It was as if I had gained another perspective of what I was doing, what was happening there, and a language of 'between the worlds' started forming in a very interesting way.

AS LAND SURRENDERS TO THE SKY: PEACE INITIATIVES AFTER MENACHEM'S DEATH

After Menachem passed away, I had no idea what to do next. We had this gathering – my children and his most devoted students – and each one said: I'll take this, I'll take that, and I did not know what I'd take. I had no idea. I was staring at a void and had no words. Slowly, things crystallized. Menachem was very busy with peace and coexistence. He met and talked with Palestinians. It was evident to me that I could not take his place because he was an extrovert who spoke to people, and I was not. I don't enjoy talking to audiences. I have a different type of way in the world, and I did not know how to promote peace and coexistence in my own way.

Then, Palestinians approached me. A woman whose son was in (an Israeli) prison came to see me with her other son. They did not know if we'd agree to cooperate. They tried to approach various peace organizations, saying: "We want to make peace with you the settlers, and you are the main issue, you are the subject matter." Many in the Palestinian society knew Menachem. Every time he visited *Yasser Arafat* – and he went there a lot – they had a camera and showed him on television, and so he became known in the Palestinian world. They said then: "He was our teacher. Let's do something together."

We formed a shared plot in the Gush Etzion Regional Council – *Roots-Shorashim-Judur*. It started with a small group of settlers and Palestinians, who would meet and talk, and then more people followed. Anyone who wanted peace in the region, including settlers and national-religious people, arrived, and many more came for an extended period. Slowly, more and more circles were formed in which we tried to make connections and create an interest (in the topic of connecting and coexistence). The link was seen and felt. I found the connection by acting from my position as a settler and as a religious person. As Jews, we understand the sadness and share histor-ical and cultural stories. We meet and study together, cook with others, or do pottery. Today, we mainly focus on Jewish and Palestinian youth groups that meet and do things together. Slowly, these gatherings are increasing, turning into many activities and circles, and thousands of people who come, groups from Israel and abroad. We are busy all the time, and I am completely into it.

I was more involved at first, and now I have more and more circles, and I am busy touching other sides of society as well. I feel it is imperative to make an impact on the Israeli secular society. Today, I am very involved in discussion groups with the Israeli secular society. This is one thing we do, and it takes up much of my time. Also, Menachem was a teacher of the Zohar, and we started Zohar Chai schools – we now have ten such schools all over Israel, named after him, as he used to call himself Chai Shalom (living for peace). That truly is a way to study the Torah by bringing in every segment of Israeli society with plenty of creativity. We have a preparatory school and a theater – he loved theater – with several plays. This is growing in various directions. We have a lot of work, a lot of work.

When nationality obtains an aspect of power or ideology, it turns into nationalism, and we have to be very sensitive and cautious about that. We are here with this beautiful thing: We returned to our land and built this wonderful thing here. Once it assumed some aspect of force and pride, we would lose everything. Menachem used to say that there was a stage of physically building this state, which lasted until around *1967* and the occupation of the Western Wall. Then, our mission changed. Now, our mission is to build a spiritual edifice of meaning for the Nation of Israel right here, in the center of the world, and to develop our responsibility for the entire world. Our task is to introduce the entire world to the most basic humanistic values of peace, compassion, love, and accepting foreigners. Of course, our primary national tasks are not done. They still exist, but they need to serve that mission.

In our society, however, it is the opposite: Some people are attached to the land, so they worry about themselves and reject others, or even want to drive them away; others worry about humanitarian rights, so they reject the land and are not connected to it. Menachem turned this around: He who feels attached to the land must serve the fundamental values, and this is the role of the Jewish Nation as a leader in this world. Since the two things are often perceived as mutually exclusive, it is not simple to present these ideas to the public. However, I believe in this simple idea: Those who are connected to the land, those who feel a deep religious connection with the land and the sky, are saying that the Lord placed them here. And just as land devotes itself to the skies, they devote themselves to God Almighty, and through their faith, they must take responsibility and create partnerships.

I live in a world of action, and among other things, I have to meet with military men and politicians. When I meet with them, I speak practically to drive the message home. God gave me a clear vision, and practical talk, the ability to remain focused and speak of nothing else, and I do that.

GOING TO PLACES THAT GIVE ME LIFE

I have no plans. I go to places where I feel there is life, to what gives me life. Learning is powerful in my life. I cannot even stand a day in which I do not study. This is a solid habit I got from Menachem. I guess I, too, am built this way. I am a creating artist. I feel I am evolving in all the learning frameworks. These tracks also pull me into Israeli society. I tell myself each morning: "So if you faithfully obey … Be careful, or you will be enticed" (The book of Deuteronomy, 11: 13–16). I become very fearful and tell myself that there are challenges, and I need to open up to them. I am alive. Menachem strongly felt the Nation of Israel, and I strongly feel that I continuously meet challenges that arise. After all, these are all exciting things. Recently, I have been approached by several army veterans who completed their military service. They are now hiking across Israel, seeking certain people and places. Instead of traveling to India or starting a career, they travel and seek for meaning together. This is interesting. I feel reality keeps bringing these opportunities, such that I could devote myself to.

I am almost 70 – I mean, take me seriously! 70 is quite an age that allows you to observe life. I have a lot to say about my life with my partner and my motherhood. Sometimes I think back to my university days, wondering if today I would do things differently and study more seriously. Before I made my decisions, I thought about studying art, but I did not. I criticize myself a lot for my decisions in life. I have a studio where I do some pottery. In pottery, the natural process is that you try to work with the material, and it scatters; it is hard to control it and mold it into the form you want. Life scatters like in pottery, so do relationships and motherhood, and one needs to shape and reshape them constantly. Now it is pottery, but it could have been something else, and perhaps I'll develop it in other directions.

7. No one can occupy my heart, my mind, and my identity

Huda Abu Arqoub
Interviewed by Haneen Sameer Magadlah

Huda has been the regional director of the Alliance for Middle East Peace (*ALLMEP*) since 2014. Previously, Huda worked as a teacher, trainer, and consultant for the Palestinian Ministry of Education. Huda has years of experience in conflict resolution, non-governmental organization leadership, social change education, and activism. Additionally, Huda has expressed a life-long commitment to building healthy person-to-person, Israeli-Palestinian relationships. She is a well-known speaker whose areas of expertise include Middle East politics and the Israeli-Palestinian conflict. She is a co-founder of the Center for Transformative Education and has taught and trained hundreds of students in Israel and the United States.

I heard about Huda from various people – Palestinians, Jews, and persons worldwide. Many months went by before I, as an interviewer, was able to arrange a meeting with her. She is a very busy woman who gives you the feeling that she carries the world on her shoulders.

Eventually, we were able to meet each other halfway at Tentor monastery, located between *Bethlehem* and Jerusalem. That day there was a general lockdown on Palestinian cities, the roads were not safe to travel on, and I did not believe that she would take the risk of meeting me, nor did I imagine she would make it to the monastery. On the one hand, I did not want her to take the risk. On the other hand, I looked forward to meeting her. I waited patiently until she arrived. She was exhausted from the journey and the checkpoints, yet she was noble and full of positive energy.

The conversation with Huda flowed yet was also very intense and overwhelming. Often, I stopped recording as we needed to relax and take a deep breath. Huda's eyes were filled with tears almost throughout the interview. However, her voice was strong and clear, and it resonated with me days after I met her.

I LEARNED FROM MY GRANDMOTHERS

I was born in 1970 in Jerusalem and grew up in *Hebron*. I learned a lot from my grandmothers. My grandmother had to single-handedly run the house and raise the children because the British military took my grandfather to fight in Germany during World War I for seven years. Everyone treated her as a widow because her husband was absent for so long. Someone even wanted to take custody of her and her children, but she refused. She also fought not to lose her inheritance rights, for women commonly did, in her traditional society. Although my grandmother had no formal education, she insisted that her daughters go to school. I believe that this was her central vision and strategy. Along with other women, she creatively preserved her Palestinian identity, including her identity as a woman and mother. Many women in the 1930s, 1940s, and 1950s were deprived of any education due to the *British Mandate* and the predominant Palestinian culture. These women insisted on educating their daughters, and through this, they placed the cornerstone for Palestinian identity: survival and education.

I was raised in a family that had a rich library in the house and which also had beautiful music playing in the background. In the 1980s, when Israeli tanks stood next to our home, our parents would light a candle instead of using electric lights to read. We would also play mind games and enjoy poetry. My parents kept telling us that tomorrow would be better and that we must invest in a good education to create a better future. My dad would teach and explain Islam in a way that made me proud to be a Muslim. Unfortunately, some people interpret Islam in a different way today.

I really appreciate my parents' and grandparents' abilities. My grandfather on my mother's side graduated from Oxford in the 1930s, even though we were only a middle-class family. My mother used to teach English in the 1970s and expressed socialist ideas and thoughts. My father was also open-minded and had a liberal interpretation of Islam. In my childhood home, we would hear stories of success, hope, and resilience. We were taught about the importance of representing one's self even during the hardest of times. I carried these precious values with me into my adolescence and beyond. We thus perceived education as our 'salvation.'

DISCOVERING MY PALESTINIAN IDENTITY: I KNEW WHO I WAS

Our education was based on a Jordanian curriculum, so our school did not provide us with opportunities to know ourselves as Palestinians. One of my uncles was imprisoned by the Jordanians just because he rejected how the

Jordanian curriculum portrayed *Mahmoud Darwish* as a Jordanian poet. The Israeli occupation authorities also detained him for similar reasons: Mahmoud Darwish poems. This was another expression of resistance – to protect our Palestinian identity.

The period in which the *Sabra and Shatila Massacre* took place, 1982, was one of the most challenging times for us. We did not see much about it on the news, but the Jordanian television channel showed a documentary about what happened in Lebanon. My parents did not allow us to see the documentary, yet we watched it behind their backs. On that day, the Israeli authorities turned off the electricity in the whole city, but some young people gathered together to watch the documentary about the massacre nonetheless. At the time, our house was the only one with a television, so the guys brought an electricity generator and turned on the electricity. Almost everyone from my neighborhood came to our house to watch the documentary while my siblings were sleeping in the other room.

The Israeli television channel would always show films about the *Holocaust*. But as a child, I thought that the photos of the Jewish Holocaust were actually those of the Sabra and Shatila Massacre. Of course, Israelis would feel offended if I said this in front of them. They would say: "How dare you make a comparison between the Holocaust and the Sabra and Shatila Massacre?!" As a 12 year old, I could not distinguish between these two events since I did not know how to compare them, and I did not ask questions like "Who did that?" and "How is this related to Israel, Lebanese Christians, and *Ariel Sharon*?" Ergo, I saw a remarkable similarity between these two events, such as the countless dead people laid on the ground or the similar walls which surrounded these camps. After looking at the pictures, I lost my appetite and couldn't eat or drink anything for three days.

With the First *Intifada* outbreak, we were exposed to severe violence by the occupation forces, although my parents did their best to protect us. One day, my father, a school principal, came back home, carrying a Palestinian flag. The school students raised the Palestinian flag, and this was considered a crime at the time. My father would go to school early in the morning to take down the flags so that the Israeli forces would not close down the school. Of course, he considered education to be the ultimate redemption for youth because it provides them with great opportunities. One day, he brought home a Palestinian flag, and I saw him hiding it because it was forbidden to have the flag back then. At night, I took the flag from the drawer where he hid it. This was the first time I had seen a Palestinian flag, and its colors and design fascinated me. That evening, I hugged the flag and started weeping. I was only 14 or 15 years old at the time. I was crying because I knew who I was. Despite the unjust occupation, its attacks on my neighborhood, the killing of my colleague, and the imprisonment of my uncle, at that moment I understood what it meant to be

Palestinian and what the colors of the Palestinian flag symbolized. Afterward, I discussed with my parents why they hid the flag and why they did not tell us who we were. We are not Jordanian. We are Palestinian! Thus, we had to struggle to familiarize people with their identity. We had to fight to teach people about the Palestinian narrative.

This period was not easy. During this time, the Israeli Army would break into your house with dogs to search it. I am very fond of dogs but became cynophobic (fearful of dogs) due to these violent experiences. To these days, dogs scare me. They remind me of the dark and humid nights in which Israeli soldiers, all dressed in green uniforms, would break into our house with lethal weapons, and my dad would try to calm us down. I was the oldest amongst 12 siblings. My parents created a very peaceful environment for us and tried to shelter us from the harsh reality outside. They transformed the house into a cultural and social paradise where our grandmother would tell us amazing stories. However, the Israeli forces would break into our home and arrest my father, forcing him to take down the Palestinian flags. My father was a great and respectable man in our society, so it was humiliating for him to be forced to take down the Palestinian flags. At times, we wondered whether our father would ever come back, and we were also scared that our younger siblings would be attacked or killed by the occupation forces because many kids were being targeted at the time.

MULTIPLE MARGINALITIES: THE RISE OF THE RADICAL ISLAMIC MOVEMENT – SUDDENLY, EVERYTHING CHANGED

When the First Intifada erupted, schools closed down, and the situation became scary for girls both in terms of the struggle against the occupation and the radical Islamic movement. Things started changing rapidly, and the radical Islamic way of living took over. Suddenly, women were no longer allowed to go out of the house, and female activists were being threatened and attacked with eggs and nitric acid by radical Islamic activists. The radical people brought about a new Islamic identity: women were asked to stay at home, wear the *hijab*, and were prohibited from participating in games and sports. All of this started in 1988–1989. Up to 1987, my teachers did not wear the hijab and our weddings were celebrated by women and men together, even though we were all Muslims from the village of *Dura*. However, everything started to take a different shape.

The teacher in my religion class no longer allowed me to join the class because I was not wearing a hijab. He would complain about this to my father, and my father would answer that a girl should not be coerced, but make this decision for herself. Eventually, my dad forced me to wear a hijab because of the pressure he had to deal with. It was too much for him to take. In my class, Muslim girls started bullying my classmates, socially pressuring them into covering their hair with a hijab. I see this wave of Islamic conservatism as one of the worst things that affected our Palestinian struggle: 51 percent of the people (Palestinian women) were suddenly marginalized and ordered to stay home. Unfortunately, many women accepted these new rules, and I realized how women could sometimes be the worst enemies of other women. Some women not only strictly adhered to the new Islamic regime, they also started forcing all the other women to stay at home, encouraging them to marry young.

Suddenly, my environment turned upside down. People abandoned the old ideals of knowledge like reading, education, building the national character, freedom, etc. The Palestinian struggle became a monopoly for men. Women were not allowed to leave their houses and were told to cover up their bodies because "we have an enemy around us, and we should not expose our women to the enemy." During these times, I witnessed people being killed and imprisoned by the Israelis and watched as the terrible inner change in our social practices took hold. The concept of 'struggle' became more related to money than to resilience and steadfastness. The political parties would pay the youth to demonstrate on *Fatah*'s founding day, while others would push us to celebrate Hamas day. Given the importance of education, schools were trapped in this inner political struggle and affected by the factions within Palestinian society. In my opinion, this was another factor that negatively affected our understanding of the Palestinian identity and struggles for freedom.

It is worth noting that the occupation challenges us to preserve our collective identity and culture. However, the inner political division and the extremist religious views affected us negatively. They interrupted the educational paths, for all schools and universities were locked down, and we found ourselves in a trap. Suddenly we changed, our society took a different structure. Men and women could not talk, women could not be freely active, and the education system was not functioning. Eventually, all this led to the *Madrid Conference* and the *Oslo Accords*, and an internal division between Palestinians. Such stress leads to disappointment and pressure and steers towards mistakes in actions and decision making. The Palestinians are still paying a heavy price for this trajectory, as it harmed the collective Palestinian identity and our resilience. It is also unfortunate to see that the internal divisions within Palestinian society are ever deepening.

SEEING THE WORLD: FROM POWERLESS TO POWERFUL

In 1992, I moved to Jordan to study for one semester. My sister was studying at *Yarmouk University* during this time and received a scholarship to pursue her studies there. And because I did not get a scholarship, I had to return to Palestine and pursue my studies at *Dar Al-Mu'allimat* institute in *Ramallah*. I also worked as a teacher at the same time. Following the Madrid Conference and the Oslo Accords, there were international efforts to bring together Palestinians and Israelis from similar professions or disciplines. In 1997, I had my first encounter with Israelis. This was the first time I ever saw an Israeli who was not in a military uniform. I was 27 years old at the time, which is not a young age. The meeting was held in Austria, and the Palestinian Ministry of Education approved the arrangements. We were part of a delegation of Palestinian teachers, comprised of both men and women, and the facilitators were both Palestinian and Israeli. The seminar included some Austrian teachers. We aimed to defend the Palestinian cause and confront the occupation. All of us wore a *keffiyeh* following the example of the late President *Yasser Arafat*, and I was surprised to see that the Israeli teachers who were in the room did not have a problem with that. On the contrary, the Israeli teachers supported the Palestinian cause and were against the occupation – the left wing in Israel was strong at the time.

When we started sharing the problems that we were facing with students and education, both in the Palestinian and Israeli contexts, I was surprised to see that we were struggling with very similar problems. After looking at the great working conditions and high quality of life enjoyed by teachers in Austria, we realized how teachers' conditions are also related to social justice. The Austrian teachers were treated fairly; they were well compensated and enjoyed significant budgets for professional development. Yet, both Palestinian and Israeli teachers were underpaid and were hardly offered any opportunities for professional development. Before going to the meeting in Austria, I read an important book written by *Paulo Freire*, and I was impressed by the idea of being strong even under occupation. He claims that it is your responsibility to liberate yourself and liberate others. This led me to perceive the concept of power differently, and I started seeing myself as the powerful one. Instead of seeing things in black and white, I shifted away from the 'either us or them' mentality. I also started seeing things from a more humanitarian perspective. Moreover, I recognized the importance of changing ourselves to be free. Since 1997, I have been trying to perceive myself as a free woman, although it is not easy to define what 'freedom' really means for women.

Indeed, I live under occupation, but I see myself as a free human being. No one can change my mind and occupy my heart, convictions, or identity. The physical, forceful occupation is still here, but through my steadfastness, education, culture, and social awareness, I can prevent the occupation from penetrating the pillars of my resilience. Therefore, I am free and determined to take part in liberating this land. This change in my thinking encouraged me to develop conflict-resolution skills, so I applied for a scholarship to specialize in the field of peace and conflict resolution.

Between 1999 and 2006, I traveled a lot to the United States and Austria to participate in various initiatives. I received a *Fulbright scholarship* from 2004 until 2006 and studied at the Eastern Mennonite University in Virginia. The program there was one of the best globally, and I learned with other students who came from oppressed societies in various conflict zones worldwide. Imagine being in a room with 25 people from 25 different conflict zones. You would then realize that the conflict, as you experience it, is actually easier than others. All the conflicts created by the British Empire were represented in the classroom, and my presentations were highly respected and appreciated. Unfortunately, this respect and appreciation were missing in my community, and people did not know your value as a teacher. When you are in an environment where people respect and value what you say, your self-confidence is enhanced, strengthening your pursuit of freedom.

I lived in the United States for seven years, worked in the educational field, and spoke about the Palestinian cause. I was also the executive director of a non-governmental organization there. Yet, I felt like a stranger abroad. I was disconnected from my country. Hence, I chose to come back and look for a job in the educational field.

PALESTINE: MY MAIN CAUSE AND PLACE OF RESIDENCE

I returned to Palestine because I had great hopes and a sense of belonging to this country. I am currently the regional director of ALLMEP, a network of more than 110 organizations that works in Israel, Palestine, and Jordan. The network's main objective is to strengthen the relations between people, regardless of their identity, be it "Israeli-Palestinian," "Palestinian-Palestinian," or "Israeli-Israeli." Each organization has its own approach for bringing about change, but the ultimate goal is to establish a coexistence model that preserves all people's culture and identity. We also recognize that the Palestinian people have a historical connection and a historic right to this land. We must admit that all of us are injured. We all suffer from trauma, whether it is trauma which emanates from the British Mandate, the Israeli occupation, or the Holocaust. I am always interested to hear the stories of marginalized people, either in Israel, in Palestine, or in other places in the world.

In my current job, I provide consultancy services and assist in building programs that secure and provide financial and other resources to marginalized people through our offices in Paris and Washington, DC. My work is quite diverse, and it involves a great deal of communication with people from different backgrounds. I started a dialogue group between women and I set up joint projects for Arab and Jewish women. I am also in touch with women who have been subjected to rape and persecution in places like Bosnia and Herzegovina and Africa. These women paid a heavy price, and I sometimes visit them and learn from their valuable experiences.

In Palestine, we advocate in favor of open dialogue and the protection of human dignity. As such, we create discussion groups that tackle various issues, encouraging dialogue between peoples. Further, our organization does a lot of volunteer work. Some of our volunteer groups confront biases against women in various religious circles, while others fight against the so-called *honor killings*. Additionally, our volunteers also demonstrate how Quranic verses do, in fact, support women's rights. The Quran actually supports women and grants them various rights. For example, the Islamic religious narrative portrays our prophet Muhammad as working for Khadijah, who later proposes to him. She was much older than he was, very affluent, and the first to believe in his message. Therefore, one wonders why the presence of women in current Islamic religious discourse is so lacking. The Quran itself mentions women and gives them rights, but other human beings have taken these rights away from us.

I mainly meet ordinary citizens through my work, but I sometimes meet diplomats and Palestinian Authority representatives. I do not meet with Israeli officials because we are not ready to deal with them. The Palestinian Authority represents us and communicates with the Israeli side when needed, but it is all formal. We need to have an informal level of communication, as well. We need ordinary people and a place for everyone. We must secure this channel. We need to enhance the representation of people in different areas and not only on an official level. From what I have witnessed so far, I genuinely believe that women have a tremendous capacity to bring about change.

I have managed to change myself, and this change is what allows me to affect others and direct them toward making a change. I cannot ask people to change without first changing myself. Therefore, I see that my transformation process has enabled me to talk to others about change. For example, I cannot approach people with a 'victim's mentality' and tell them that they need to change society. Instead, I first inform them that we must stop seeing ourselves as victims and perceive ourselves as survivors. We should see ourselves as strong people, and we must never give up. We should also always appreciate life and being alive. I have personally passed through a process of inner change and abandoned the victim mentality, and I have chosen to confront the other side instead of running away. This gives me a sense of legitimacy and credibility, even though I understand the many challenges that we, the Palestinians, face. I also believe in 'leadership by example' and try to apply this within my society. We should never live a defeated life. We have a great responsibility towards the younger generation.

I receive generous support from my family, neighbors, and community, as well as the Palestinian Authority. I have no fear because I do not have a hidden agenda. I do not want to become a prime minister or part of the upper-class elite. I am just an ordinary person who likes to sit with her mother at the end of the day and watch television. I would like to run for office after Palestine becomes an independent state and we are liberated from the occupation. I would like to do so someday, when all of us become one, regardless of our location, and when the Palestinian refugees in Lebanon can study, work, and travel freely. This will probably happen only many years from now – maybe by the time I am 100 years old. But for now, elections and politics are a game of deception and involve many concessions of our identity. Hence, I do not want to join them. My current mission pertains to the groundwork, and my strength is in education and raising awareness.

I am very proud to be resilient and steadfast and have chosen Palestine as my main cause and residence. Being Palestinian is not necessarily linked to a place, but it is connected to culture. I never pretend to represent all Palestinians; I only represent myself and my name. However, I believe that my religion is one reason for my political activism, and it is the source of my actions. I am also proud that I managed to finance my education without having my parents bear the expenses. I worked hard to get a scholarship. Moreover, I am proud of my grandmothers because they represent the true identity of Palestine.

OUTSIDE OF CLOSED ROOMS

Women Wage Peace is a great initiative that represents me. It encourages women to participate in political activism and combats the exclusion of the other. This includes what is called feminist inclusive political activism. Of course, this also involves men who participate in these activities. I feel represented by the 100+ organizations with which I cooperate. For example, Holy Land Trust is a great organization that works for change and calls for non-violence. Another great initiative is Creativity for Peace. These initiatives aim to help people achieve self-liberation and positivity. I also work with other initiatives, such as *Combatants for Peace*, Bereaved Families for Peace, and religious dialogue initiatives.

The first time I met women from Women Wage Peace, I asked them: "Are you a leftist organization?" They said: "Yes, kind of." I said: "I am sorry, but the left has failed both in terms of reaching out to Israeli society, and in terms of mitigating the conflict. We need people who can reach out to Orthodox and right-wing Jews who fear us and want the Palestinians to disappear. Also, we do not need you as our representatives because we Palestinians can represent ourselves well." Later on, I discovered this organization's remarkable capacity and the Israeli left's aptitude as a whole. In October 2017, I stood in the middle of a protest and spoke in front of 45,000 people about peace activism. Within our circles as peace activists, I see that we sometimes isolate ourselves from reality and live in 'our little bubble.' We speak and travel abroad and share knowledge in our circles, without being strongly connected to the people outside our circles. Therefore, I always insist on being 'on the ground' and staying connected to reality and society.

Our biggest failure would be if we stopped resisting injustice. If we accept injustice as a reality and try to escape it by playing video games or watching soap operas in closed rooms, we are our total defeat. Of course, I am not arguing against having time to rest, but I see that the most significant failure is a people's idleness and acceptance of injustice. I thereby carry additional responsibility. I am here to help people and support future peace activists who are suffering from desperation. I am here to support those who, due to depression, prefer to go back to their closed rooms without doing anything real in the field by encouraging them to get back out there.

If we keep having dialogues between people who are already convinced inside closed rooms, we will not have a real impact on real life. Therefore, we must reach out to people outside of our closed room, to the people who are not convinced that we need peace-related dialogues.

To remain in this land, our land, we must continuously seek peace between Palestinians and Israelis. The current approach will not lead to peace. Only once Israelis realize that their existence, peace, and security are positively related to mine, we will be able to live together in equality and create a system that gives equal rights to all. The Jewish-Israeli white man must recognize that he is part of a broader culture and should not impose his white culture on us. Israelis should consider themselves part of the greater Middle East and adapt to Middle Eastern culture. The new generation in Israel has the opportunity to become a part of the Middle East. Throughout history, Palestinians, Jews, Christians, and Muslims have coexisted together and have had access to the same places, including worship houses. The Wailing Wall had Jewish women and men praying together by it, and it was never segregated based on gender before *1948*. No religion should have a monopoly on this land because the land belongs to everyone. The problem can be solved when the Western Jews consider third- or fourth-generation Jews born in Palestine as Palestinian Jews. That way, we would all become one people instead of enemies who try to wipe each other off the map. The work for change is very exhausting, and it requires a strong feeling of identity.

I do not fear the enemy. On the contrary, my mission is to liberate the enemy. This is an amazing power when one feels it. I also feel encouraged when I see other women and men joining forces, so I do not feel alone. This is the legacy that I chose to build to bring about change. Of course, many things can make you feel bad on a day-to-day basis: feeling frustrated or that your heart is tearing. My sense of responsibility is what helps me keep on going. I have 28 nephews and nieces who are a great source of inspiration for me, and they give me the energy to wake up early and pass the checkpoint from Hebron to Jerusalem every day. This is not easy. I did not get married or have children of my own. That was my choice – maybe this is the price of my activism.

I do not see myself as a leader and do not seek to become one; I am just a person who knows how to communicate with people even in times of anger and frustration. The women who work as peace activists must realize that we will never make a real impact if we remain afraid of establishing dialogues outside closed rooms. I emphasize this when I work with different organizations. Many outside our closed rooms are not familiar with our significant projects, such as projects that call for mutual acceptance and recognition. We must be close to the people at all times and use a language of sincerity and dedication. This must be done at all costs, even if some people blame us for normalizing relations with the Israeli side by accusing us of participating in projects involving Palestinians and Israelis, whether or not these explicitly aim to expose and resist the occupation. I would respect this point of view, but I would tell them that they are wrong. This is my way of thinking.

RESILIENCE REQUIRES THAT WE RUN AN INTERNAL DIALOGUE

I am a proponent of creating dialogues with Israeli society, especially with its women. These dialogues add significant value, although it takes years to accomplish them. There are approximately 12 million Palestinians around the world. We must strengthen the internal dialogue amongst ourselves, too. The Palestinians in the *West Bank* must be in touch with the people from the *Gaza Strip*, for instance, and the Gazans should have better dialogue and communication with the people of Baqa Al-Gharbiyye, Kafr Qasim, and other Arab towns and villages within the *Green Line*. We should communicate with our Palestinian brothers and sisters in refugee camps in Lebanon and Jordan and the Palestinian diaspora scattered around the world.

Nowadays, Palestinian society discriminates between Christians and Muslims. Before the *Nakba*, the percentage of Christians within Palestine was 33.5 percent. Now, it is less than 1 percent, so the Christian identity is disappearing in Palestine. There are many reasons for this: the occupation, the feeling of being a minority, and more. This affects our struggle negatively. We Palestinians believe that Jesus was Palestinian. We see him as part of the Palestinian identity. During Christmas, I put a Christmas tree up at home, buy gifts for children, and wear a Santa Claus hat to celebrate the holiday with Christians. Because Christianity is part of our Palestinian collective identity, there should never be any form of discrimination in Palestine.

I also believe that the Palestinians inside the Green Line are the last defense line for the Palestinian identity. It has been proven throughout the years. In my opinion, they are the only ones who have a real sense of the Palestinian collective identity and have impressively preserved it and our language. Their population consists of around 2 million today. These people struggle more than all of us, being in a complicated situation. Despite this, some Palestinians here disregard them saying that "they have an Israeli ID, so they live the good life since they have freedom of movement." No one knows how much they suffer to keep their identity alive, and very few people understand their political struggle and their successful journey towards joining the *Knesset*, regardless of whether the Arab parties are influential or not. Their presence poses a challenge to the notion of a Jewish state, politically and legally.

All of us belong to the same land, and this land needs us. The land does not only need our blood, which is being spilt in vain. It primarily needs our strong presence. For this reason, I aim to establish a robust internal Palestinian dialogue that can raise us from the bottom and make us proud of our identity, diversity, and steadfastness again. However, I see that this is the beginning of the end for Palestine, not in terms of the land but in terms of the people's belonging to the land, declining cultural practices, and loss of self-consciousness.

Unfortunately, our society does not appreciate any form of struggle. We have reached a state of indifference. Most people care only for their house, car, spouse, and kids. People throw garbage in the streets without hesitation. People party while the people of Gaza are being killed in cold blood. Things were not like this in the past. I am not against people celebrating, yet it seems that we have reached a state of total apathy towards each other. After about 12 years of the siege on Gaza, none of us think to call and speak to Gazans and ask them how they are doing. Resilience through care is the solution, and it requires that we start talking among ourselves.

FEMINIST POLITICAL ACTIVISM

It is the preservation of our Palestinian identity and culture that has made us visible. I genuinely believe in our youth, both men and women, and feel that we have an excellent opportunity for making change happen. I also see that men are victims, especially since they are continually subjected to physical violence by the occupation. However, men tend to have a one-direction mindset, while women are more inclusive because they are used to embracing children of different personalities. Imagine a woman with five children who are all very different: the first child is bad-tempered, the second is calm, the third is ill, and so on. The mother embraces them all and listens to them without being biased against any of them. Men do not think inclusively as women do, like this. Men have more of a linear way of thinking and a 'black or white' kind of division. I have better hopes of working with women, for I feel that they are more motivated to liberate themselves and communicate with their inner selves. On the other hand, men tend to be concerned about the harsh and hostile circumstances around us and about what they can do to change it – which is almost impossible.

Feminism offers another form of inclusive leadership. It requires being open to others even if you disagree with them politically, culturally, or socially. To illustrate, Palestinian workers who cross the checkpoint every day undergo different forms of oppression. Yet, they manage to maintain their self-control in order to be permitted to enter Israel, to work, to make a living, and to be able to send their daughters to school. These men sometimes mistreat and abuse their wives at home. Still, I see their self-control at the checkpoint, as they make their journey to earn a living to send their daughters to school, another practice of liberation. Therefore, we should not exclude them or judge them negatively just because they 'serve the enemy' and make money out of it. If we were in their places for one day, we would know how hard it is to stand in line through these horrendous checkpoints, struggling for survival.

When the 1948 Nakba took place, men and women who traveled to obtain an education and live in different locations worldwide talked about the Palestinian identity and the Palestinian narrative. They shared their stories so that everyone would know that there are people called Palestinians. In my opinion, the most tremendous Palestinian success in our struggle for freedom is our persistence and resilience, and the older Palestinian women are the most resilient of us all. Of course, Palestinian men are also resilient, but, similar to other men around the world, they try to find a way out when life gets hard and, as a result of desperation, end up dead or in prison. Accordingly, women are those who take care of their households. They are the most substantial base.

Following the Oslo Accords, the establishment of the Palestinian Authority led to a great decline in the political role of women. Palestinian Authority officials respect Palestinian women. We have a ministry dedicated to women's affairs. We also have some female representatives. Yet, this representation does not encompass all elements of Palestinian society. This is one of the greatest tragedies that our nation is confronting, standing as an obstacle in the way of freedom. This is also a huge threat to our Palestinian identity and our collective narrative. My main goal is to promote female political activists for change. I believe that Israeli society also needs this type of change.

We Palestinians must reclaim our collective identity, which respects us all, women, men, Muslims, Christians, I mean all of us, and respect our heritage, our shared space. We must all acknowledge that we have a shared history for all religions. The moment we go back to these roots, we will be able to change our future.

8. To solve the puzzle

Khaled Abu Awwad
Interviewed by Shakked Lubotzky and
Amalya Oliver-Lumerman

We met Khaled Abu Awwad on a summer morning at the *Roots-Shorashim-Judur* Center – an old house on the Abu Awwad plot of land. The center conducts extensive activities that aim at promoting dialogues and familiarity between the Jewish and Palestinian residents of Gush Etzion. No activities took place there that morning. We sat on the porch, watched the dogs, cats, and chickens in the yard below, and heard cows and horses in the distance. It all seemed very pastoral so that anyone who randomly walked by could not imagine just how complicated and bloody reality is in that region.

Khaled is a busy man whose hands are always full. He oversees the family plot and, together with Palestinian and Jewish partners, gives lectures and leads joint learning and discussion groups that slowly and cautiously spread the Roots-Shorashim-Judur message. Khaled believes in nonviolent resistance, modeled on Mahatma Gandhi, Martin Luther King, and Nelson Mandela. At the interview, he outlined the chronology of how his worldview was formed. The interview with him was painful and not simple at all, often making us shift uneasily in our chairs. Still, his life story leaves no one indifferent. He can sure tell a story and his rhetoric was impressive. Time passed by quickly.

In our minds, we followed Khaled to his birthplace and his life in a family of refugees. He is a working man, a bereaved brother, and an angry man who learned how to channel his anger into beneficial action. The first part of the interview that mainly dealt with his life story lasted two and a half hours. We met again later to learn about the establishment and activities of the Roots Center.

Our meeting was both moving and painful. Khaled spoke like a man who is deeply immersed in his inner world, with eyes half-closed, sitting or reclining, and smoked an entire pack of cigarettes during the interview. We rarely interrupted his speech with questions because he was very focused and had a complete worldview and lore.

Before we left, he suggested that we sample some figs from the tree in the yard, and their sweetness helped somewhat to alleviate the pain and hardship that accompanied the interview.

YOU ARE BORN WITH NOTHING

I am 52. You are born with nothing. You are nothing. The village, the land, everything you inherited from your father and grandfather is gone, and then you are born and must start your life from scratch. Before I even came into this world, my village, family lands and home, and everything that serves as one's familial foundation – including one's grandmother and grandfather – were all gone. I was born into the death of my village, home, and lands. I was born a refugee, a man in a new world, the first generation of myself, with nothing. I was born in a room deep inside the woods in Gush Etzion. The room was not in our family home, but in a house my father was given because he was a forester.

REFUGEES, PALESTINIAN LIBERATION ORGANIZATION, AND INTIFADA

I was born in the late 1960s and did not know much of what went on around me in my early childhood. I knew there was a war. I know from family stories that Gush Etzion came under heavy [Israeli] Air Force attack and that the Jordanian Army was there too. I know we were hit one night, and then we – my parents, my siblings, and I – went to Jordan for only seven or 10 days, and then returned. I don't remember that. It was before the age of memories.

My real childhood started after we returned. It was a difficult childhood in a family of refugees, living in a village full of local farmers who all had land and houses, and only we were refugees. In 1977–78, we managed to buy some land and built a house in *Beit Ummar*. That was our house after the forest cabin we had at Gush Etzion. We bought it from a Christian family that, as far as I know, had left for the United States and sold their land. We purchased that plot from them, and then my father, my brother, and I started working the land, which had not been cultivated before. We bought tractors and made it right. I was maybe seven or eight and my brother was older, perhaps 12. We used to come here with Dad, clear the rocks, build levees. The tractor cleared the large stones, while we moved away the smaller ones. Thus we became farmers again, which we were originally.

I had a difficult childhood. First of all, we are a familial culture. When you live in a village, you fight with other kids, but every time I was in a fight, my parents – mainly Dad – told me: Don't fight with anyone because we are the

minority here. We have no one. We are outsiders. Everyone here has a family
– clans of 500 or 600 or even 1,000 people – but we do not.

Of course, there was no government or authority here. There was nothing
except for a military government, which was indifferent to what happened
among the Palestinians, and only cared about the political or military aspects.
The civilian aspects of Palestinian life matter to them only as a means of con-
trolling us. I mean, if you need a document such as an identification card, you
must go there because they need to log in your data so that if you commit some
security offense, they can detain you. Violent disputes between Palestinian
families are none of their business. So we grew up learning to keep our mouths
shut and not react. That is true for all Palestinians – we learned to shut up, not
respond, and always be the party that gives up. Life is hard when you feel you
live where you don't belong to the place and with the others who live there.
Those who live there consider you an unwelcome guest who came to take
some of their land, work, and village.

We were eight siblings. I am the second son and have only one older brother.
In 1983, he got fed up and expressed his anger and pain by going to Lebanon,
where he joined the *Palestinian Liberation Organization (PLO)*. They sent him
to Yugoslavia to train as a fighter pilot. He had good ties with *Yasser Arafat*.
He studied there, graduated, and received an 'excellent pilot' certificate, but
could not come back here or find a job other than serving with the PLO. He
went wherever they did: to Lebanon, Tunis, and even Yemen, where he spent
time with Arafat. All the while, our life here continued as before.

SHATTERING DREAMS

When I was in high school, the *Islamic Jihad Movement* had branches everywhere, preparing to establish something. I, too, was drafted when I was 11 or
12. I was invited to join classes and study the Quran and its interpretations. If
I attended prayer, I'd receive a good grade from my teacher of Islam religion
studies. When school ended each day, we followed him to the mosque, running
there so that he could see us praying and give us a good grade. They then
started saying to me: "Come for prayer," or later in the evening: "Come to
study the holy book of the Quran." At the time, I must have felt they were my
extended family. I began feeling empowered because they had my back. With
time, I felt I belonged to a large and influential family. I started believing in
religion and the clergy and all of the Quran studies. I remember I trusted them
not 100 but 1 million percent. To me, everything they said was God's word,
and I believed it all without having to think.

My own family was not wealthy. We barely supported ourselves. If my
pants were torn, we sowed a piece of fabric to them. Once, they gave me
money for a new pair of trousers. One of the group's religious leaders, who

was also a teacher, had a clothing store. I decided I would buy my pants from him because he would give me the best pair. I went there, gave him my money, and said: "Give me the best you have." He took the money and chose a pair of trousers for me. I went home and put them on, and everyone laughed at me. "What did you buy? This is nylon cloth. It is garbage, not the best, but the cheapest." That was the first time I was shocked. My family's reaction was terrible and hurt me, but I was twice as hurt because the man I trusted betrayed me. How could it be? I remember thinking: "You are a religious man. I asked you to choose the best for me, and you gave me this piece of crap?!"

Since childhood, I have been thinking about that incident, and how it influenced my life, how he treated me, and what I did wrong. The trousers story made me doubt every group that I felt was my extended family. I started wondering: How could members of the clergy – people who believed in God, leaders who represented God for me – act like that? And why did God choose such people to represent him?!

I proceeded on my spiritual path alone. I continued praying and started reading, trying to understand what the Quran said and what religion was, but my way. I ceased attending their meetings and said I would like to reconsider things such as: Is this the right direction? Are these the right people? Then I had a period without religion during which I engaged in studies and thought of myself, my private life, and then I graduated high school.

I went to study at what today is known as the Al-Quds University but was named then the College of Science and Technology. I studied mathematics and computer science and became a teacher, but then the *intifada* started. When it broke out, a new stage started in my life, during which I was always full of rage and pain: "Why did it happen to me? Why did they take away everything I had before I was even born? Why was my family scattered? Why do I live with just a small part of my family when the rest are in Jordan, Nabulus, *Ramallah*, Kalandia, and all places? Who caused that?" These thoughts were all aimed at a single foe called Israel, believing it caused that suffering and was my no. 1 enemy.

When the intifada first started, all of us went out to demonstrate. We said: No to the occupation; We are fed up! That's how it was everywhere. At the time, the entire village – women, men, small and big children – took to the streets, hurled rocks, and clashed with the army. It was chaos, and we did not care about our lives. They might or might not kill us, but we would not retract our demands for rights, life, and liberty. Several months after the riots broke out, I was arrested for the first time and charged with partaking in demonstrations and being a member of illegal organizations. They put me in jail though they had no witnesses against me, and they did not accuse me of felonies that led to extended jail time. I spent 18 months in jail, but intermittently – two months here, three there.

After my first detention, I reverted to working as a teacher. The school was far away. I had to walk 5 km every morning because no cars went there. It was the kind of place where a car drove by every two to four hours. So I walked there and often walked back, too. On my first day back in school, I said hello to everyone and taught my classes. At the end of the day, the principal summoned me to his office. "How are you?" he asked. "Fine," I said. He took out a letter and said: "I received this from the Israeli Civil Administration. It says that they are firing you. According to this letter, I should not have let you teach here today, but out of respect for you, I ignored what they said, and I let you. If they hear about this, I could lose my job for letting you spend a day in school. I do not care. Let them do whatever they want, but this letter says you are done." The principal was in tears, and I was facing him, thinking: Here again, they are ruining it for you. You studied and found a job, and now you have nothing again. You are out. And once more, it was done by the same party and people – the State of Israel.

That was one of the most challenging days of my life. I went back home in a state of shock, not knowing what to do next. There were no private schools at the time, only Civil Administration schools, so if they fired you as a teacher, you had nowhere to work. Only Jerusalem had a few Jordanian-owned schools. The intifada and all that was happening convinced me that we needed to resist, to fight. We could not let them keep dominating our lives like that. They were wrong, and they were condescending: You have no rights; you are not even human; you must do what they tell you, and you will be punished for the tiniest deviation. That was my punishment. I started studying a new profession and began trading in grapes, which I bought from the farmers. I also purchased a small Fiat 128.

COMMERCE, TEACHING, RESIGNING

That Fiat was an old and cheap car. Someone sold it to me, but it was in poor condition. It broke down every time I drove it, and when it did, it was as if I was selling the produce just for gas money. Only after I filled the gas tank could I think of other things. Even that did not always work. I would take a few crates of grapes to sell, but then the car got stuck, so I had to sell the goods, give the farmers their money, and was left with a little money for gas and a little for me. I used to take the produce to Jerusalem, where supermarkets paid us well, seeking our merchandise. Jerusalem was a good market for us. It was before they erected all those roadblocks, we could go anywhere. I had my regular clients, and I learned the business. Next, I started collecting used boxes and sold them to the farmers.

It was through that job that I learned about private schools and teachers, who told me: "They are looking for a math teacher. You should apply. It is a good opportunity for you because it is rare and wanted by all schools." I applied, and they interviewed me. I went to that interview, but I did not believe they would hire me, and I no longer cared. Then they said: "You can start tomorrow." I thought about it and agreed. I believed I'd be able to go on with my work and work for them. I earned 90 Jordanian dinars a month, 180 shekels, when a Palestinian laborer who worked in Israel earned some 1,000–1,200 shekels. I said, fine. I used to leave home at 4 am, pick up produce from farmers, drive to Jerusalem, and sell it to supermarkets, and I'd arrive in school some 30–60 minutes before it opened, have a coffee, and start the second part of my day. After the school day was over, I made my rounds again, collected the money for the grapes, drove back, and paid the farmers. It went on like that for three years.

I remember how one day the army broke into the school while the children were in a recess between classes. The army arrived and just made a mess. The teachers ran to their room to hide, leaving the children alone in the yard. They were running around, some crying and some in tears because the soldiers fired tear gas. I went out to calm them, and then I went up to the gate and started cursing the soldiers and arguing with them: "What do you want? These are children! Go away!" That calmed the troops a little, and they said: "OK, but make sure no one throws stones or anything." I said: "I promise. Just leave!" They asked me again, and I promised again. And they said: "Fine. We're leaving, but if anything happened here, we'd break in and arrest children!" I said: "Nothing will happen. Go!"

After that incident, the children looked up to me as the hero who defended them. After recess, they formed lines and entered the classroom. There, I told them: "This is a place of study, not of war. We must keep it that way. If you throw a rock from inside the school, you don't hit the Israelis. It is as if you throw it at us, harming the school and your own studies. It is more vital that you study than fight. It is too early for you to be warriors. Study, get to know the world, and then you can decide what you want to do." They said: "Fine. We're with you, Teacher Khaled." After that, I was their go-to man.

One day, a boy entered the class, crying. When I inquired about it, he told me the principal had hit him. I went right to the principal's office, grabbed him by the tie, and said: "Who are you to hit children?" He thought I had gone mad. I said: "If you ever raise your hand to a child again, I'll cut your arm off!" He filed a complaint with the general manager of the private education system that owned the school, and they sent me a cautionary letter. I took the letter, went to the school management in Jerusalem, and asked for the general manager. They told me it was Hosni al-Ashraf, and that he was a powerful man and I should calm down before I saw him. He was in a meeting, but I shoved everyone away, knocked on his door, and placed the letter on his desk, asking: "What is this?" "Who are you?" he asked. "I am one of your teachers." "OK," he said,

"What do you want? Why are you acting like this?" I said: "Give me a piece of paper. I quit." I signed it, tossed it on his desk, and bid him farewell.

WHEN RABIN WAS MURDERED

In the 1989 Intifada, we did not yet have political parties. We did not have the *Unified National Leadership of the Uprising*, *Fatah* (PLO), *Hamas*, or the Islamic Jihad Movement. Only in 1989, some two years after the intifada had started, parties began forming. Everyone wanted their share in our leadership, and we had to choose. Our choice was clear. We chose the PLO, which was Fatah. That was our party, so that when the *Oslo Accords* were signed in 1993, my family accepted that as our win; we fought, and we won. We celebrated and felt particularly joyous. We truly believed everything would change. We felt a duty to defend the accords.

Hamas, which did not sign the accords, became our no. 1 enemy. We hate it more than we hate the Israelis. Hamas is unacceptable for us and its leaders are viewed as evil men who want to kill our joy, our accords, and our victory. They did not do any of the work, they only started to get involved in 1989. Thus we resisted Hamas and attempted to protect the accords. We sent our people and stopped Hamas and Islamic Jihad people from hurling rocks and perpetrating terror attacks. We felt like every attack Hamas perpetrated was stabbing us in the back. I remember thinking that both the Jews in Kiryat Arba (*Hebron*) and Hamas do not want peace, so they must be collaborating. I even believed that Hamas took money from the extremist Jews of *Gush Emunim* and that they coordinated attacks because when Hamas harmed Jews, it was actually hurting us, the Palestinians. Indeed, the terror attacks that Hamas and Jihad carried out did break our backs, just as they broke the backs of our Israeli partners, *Yitzhak Rabin* and *Shimon Peres*. Every such attack hurt us, the Israeli left leaders, and other peace activists, and was a gift to every extremist. Hamas made it look like we were all terrorists, violent, nonhuman. They did things that shamed our nation, destroyed our international image, and ruined our future and the accords we had attained.

That was when things started to deteriorate. It was a time of despair. How can you make peace when Hamas and Jihad do that? Can nothing convince them, or set them straight? How can they be educated otherwise? How can we stop them from being like this? Inside me, I blamed mainly them and was full of anger at them.

And then came the night they shot Rabin. I was home that night, watching television, and I remember that one minute after midnight, they announced his death. I cried in tears for that leader who had lent his hand to a historic agreement. I felt anger and pain and realized that you Jews also have your own Hamas, your own extremists. I had heard them before, but there still is a gap between words and acts. The Rabin murder marked a much more advanced and serious stage: They had turned their threats and words into action and they actually succeeded.

That only exacerbated my despair. I thought there would never be peace, that it would take a miracle from God. I tried to dissociate myself and my life from all that, to live here without actually being here, to live among people without being a part of them. I tried to create my own world and stopped thinking about what was going on or even to be interested in it. I did not want to know even when I came home and the television news was on. If anyone in our village was killed, I left the village to avoid the funeral and even the subsequent need to pay my respects to the bereaved family. I made myself a bubble to live in. Still, I kept thinking to myself: When is this going to end? How long will we live like this? Hamas only wants to fight, and the Israelis do not want peace. The latter are cheaters and only trying to buy time, but Hamas are cheaters too, and do not want peace, and do not care about the Palestinian Nation. So Hamas and Israel – you are both the same. You are both our enemies. So I don't care anymore. Keep fighting each other, kill each other. I have had enough. And then Youssef was killed.

WHEN MY BROTHER YOUSSEF WAS KILLED

When my brother Youssef was killed, I suffered yet another shock. An Israeli soldier shot him in our village. It is a sad story. In the 1990s, they started erecting roadblocks, and we were not allowed to enter Israel without permits. I worked in Israel and had a hard time obtaining permits and overcoming those roadblocks. I could not enter Israel in my car, so I employed Youssef as my driver. He used to drop me off in the village of Beit Omar, where I crossed the border on foot, and an Israeli driver waited for me there and took me to work and back. I usually finished work at 6 or 7 pm, but that night I finished earlier, at 5. On my way back, I phoned Youssef to come to get me, but there was no answer. Then his friend Shibli answered the phone. "Where is Youssef? Why does he not answer?" I asked. "I am on my way and soon will be at the border. You cannot linger there because you cross on foot and must get away fast. Where are you?" he asked. "I am coming to get you." "Why?" I asked. "Where is Youssef?" And he said: "Something happened. Youssef, he … is wounded." "Wounded?" I said. "No, no. He is fine. Mildly wounded. He's in the hospital now. I'll come to get you, and we'll go there to see him." He came, and we went to Hebron, and I did not know that the back seat of that car was soaked with Youssef's blood. When we arrived at the hospital, I saw the entire family, my brother, my sisters, and my friends, crying. "What happened?" I asked. "Youssef is dead," they said. I leaned against the wall and then went down on my knees. I did not cry or anything, but after a few minutes in that posture,

I said: "I want to see him." "You cannot. You'd better not," they said. "They shot him in the head." They said I should wait until they prepped him, and then I could see him, not now. We went home, which was full of people, and some members of the Palestinian leadership approached me and asked: "What are you going to do?" I said I didn't know.

Earlier that day, Youssef was at home, waiting for my call. He went to see a friend, had a cup of coffee with him, and left. Then he met a widow who wanted to see her parents, so he picked her up. When they arrived at her parents' house, children were demonstrating, and the army was there. The children hurled rocks, and the soldiers erected a roadblock. Youssef was the first to be stopped there. They ordered him to park. The woman left and walked to her parents while he stayed behind. The soldiers fired tear gas, and the children threw stones, some of which hit his car. Youssef got out of his car and yelled at the children to stop throwing rocks at the soldiers, not because he wanted to protect them, but because he worried about his car. He meant that he did not mind if they kept throwing things after they released him. The children stopped. Then one of the soldiers started hurling rocks at Youssef's car because he saw it annoyed him enough to order the kids to stop. I don't know what that soldier was thinking. Perhaps his pride was hurt when he saw he could not stop the children with his gun, yet Youssef only talked to them, and they stopped. I am just trying to understand what was going through his mind. When the soldier started throwing rocks at Youssef's car, Youssef lost it. He got out of his car and yelled: "What do you want from me? You told me to pull over and stop the engine, and I did that. Why are you throwing rocks at me?" The soldier started cursing him, ran toward Youssef, and aimed his gun at Youssef's head, point-blank! Youssef said: "What do you want?" But the soldier pulled the trigger, and Youssef died on the spot. People told me that. It all took place right under the balcony of this house and the villagers who live there related their exchange, word for word. They said that the soldier's officer got really mad afterward. He ran to the soldier, shoved him, screamed, "What did you do to me?!" and hit him. The other soldiers pushed the crowd away by force and then left the village, heading for the main road. Then the villagers approached Youssef, but he was no longer alive. They put him in my car and took him to the Hebron hospital.

After we returned from the hospital, people and some Palestinian Authority (PA) leaders came over and said: "This was murder. We should take Youssef to *Abu Dis* for an autopsy. Once they issue a forensic report, we could file a complaint." The family was against it, but I said: "Yes, I will send him." That was in late 2000, and there were many roadblocks everywhere because the Al-Aqsa Intifada was in full force, and everything was a mess. We took him and did everything we could. We had a news conference, and leaders were invited too, through the PA and the university there, because the center is inside the university, so they invited all kinds of human rights organizations. Then, we had to return him, and there were demonstrations and barriers everywhere. We were in the ambulance, trying to find a way through. We took the body over all kinds of dirt roads, going around the village so that the army would not seize the body. We tried to avoid roadblocks because we knew that they would take the body and send it to the Forensic Institute in Abu Kabir outside Tel Aviv, and we did not want that because we knew they would keep it there, which is a kind of abuse. We managed to reach my village and my house, where we took out the body. We brought it out again for the noon prayer at the mosque, and from there, we went to the cemetery. The entire village was there, some 10,000 to 15,000 people. The army placed tanks and cars everywhere on the main road. When we reached the cemetery, the soldiers started firing tear-gas canisters and the people threw rocks at the road and the soldiers. In the end, some 10 people remained until we buried him. Everyone else fled the gas.

A SYMBOL OF PALESTINIAN NATIONALITY

I did not work for nearly a year. I was in such despair that I felt life was not worth living. It was impossible to live in such a bad situation, constantly wondering what to do next. My mother became very ill, and her health deteriorated further out of anger and pain for Youssef. My father deteriorated too, but not as much. My siblings and I became very close, always sitting together, talking, thinking. We gained in status – in the village and the PA as a whole – turning into a symbol of Palestinian nationality. So much so that anyone who wanted to show they identified with a strong national Palestinian identity sought the family's proximity.

As a family, we became leaders of the intifada, representing Fatah. Youssef was viewed as the fallen son of a family that had fought for and grown with a peace flag, supported Oslo, and had now lost a member. My family went through every station in the history of the Palestinians. Other families lost their dear ones too, but they were local. Refugee families lost loves ones too, but did not fight as we did nor hold leadership roles; and some lost no one. We were part of the leadership. All the PA leaders you hear about today were our friends or were with us in the struggle.

My mother was a brave woman. She took part in our activities and made contacts, even reaching Yasser Arafat. My brother Jamil was like her. We used to hold conversations with Arafat even during the intifada. Once, we went to see him in *Bethlehem*. His office had a floor for receptions and another concealed floor, where there was a darkened room, with no lights or windows, a cordless phone on the desk, and a hidden staircase. We had to look around, make sure no one was there, and only then did we go upstairs. Even if the whole world came, they would not know there was someone upstairs. In that room, there was a phone to talk to Arafat, but he was not there. That was before Oslo. We used to go to Gaza, Ramallah, Nablus, and *Jenin*, meet with leaders, and discuss our next steps. None of them held a formal role in the intifada. People were more or less active, but we as a family – particularly my mother – were at the most involved end. Also, there were disputes and arguments, anger, and even dissociations, particularly among women. They used to fight each other a lot, and sometimes they would hug. There were many things, but all in all, that was the leadership – a strong and leading body of women. And those women could lead!

For the population as a whole and our village specifically, it was as if: Look, you fought, you were for peace, and now you see what happened! You have that agenda, and you have the entire Palestinian history in one family, so of course, people supported you. But what will you do now? Will you keep believing in that peace you upheld and your party promoted? Do you still believe you are headed in the right direction? Here, this is the price. Now, let's see how you deal with that, and how you respond, and what you think of Israel and the Israelis now after you signed and supported the Accords. They told us: We follow you and believe in you. The right direction is what your family decides. As for other parties or the extremists who don't believe in peace – that's the wrong direction.

PICKING THE PIECES AND HEADING OUT

After Youssef was killed, my initial reaction was: "I will never forget." I had met Jews from work. One of them called my home, and when they answered, he said he would like to talk to Khaled, to comfort him. They came to me and said: A friend from work called for you. I said, tell him I am not here and that I don't want to talk to Jews. They hung up. I spoke to no one for a while and busied myself asking people: "What is that soldier's name? What does he look like, that soldier who shot Youssef? What is he – an Arab, a Sephardi Jew, Bedouin, Jewish, Druze, black, white, tall, short?" I asked all kinds of questions as if I wanted revenge, as if inside me I tried to eat him alive, chop him to pieces. Nothing mattered but that soldier. As for all other Israelis, I cut them off. I did not want them in my life anymore. I wanted nothing to do with them, not even work. I would find work here.

Then my story with *Yitzhak Frankenthal* started. People told me he would like to pay me a condolence visit. I did not know who he was and said: "Give me a break. Why are you bringing garbage in? What do you want? Leave me alone!" Still, Frankenthal came every few days, explaining that he was a strong person who believed that the Palestinian Nation had rights. I said: "Leave me alone. That's a lie." For my brothers and sisters, I was the family leader, so if Khaled was against, they all were – except for our greatly respected mother. So they told my mother: "That Jew wants to come to your house with a bus full of Israeli families that want to comfort you, support you, and stand by your side." Mom said: "Fine. Let them come." That started a debate, but she said: "What have we got to lose? Youssef is already dead." She did not mind a busload of Israelis or Palestinians inside her house. It was all the same to her. Youssef's death destroyed her from the inside, really broke her spirit. For her, all things were just the same.

Next, we started coordinating that visit. The intifada was still raging, and the situation in the territories was terrible. Jews' arrival in the region was unacceptable. It was even risky, particularly after the *Ramallah lynching of 2000* and all that. So the coordinators asked me if it was OK for them to come to the village if it was not dangerous. Why should it be dangerous? I asked. They are coming to visit us. Who in our village would dare attack guests of ours? Our status is strong. They came, a full bus. The village was closed because the army had erected piles of dirt on our main roads, so we took them over back dirt roads to our house. They came in, and some of our friends and neighbors came to see them, too. They started a conversation, a normal conversation. Just people sitting and – as I am sitting here, telling you how Youssef was killed – the visiting families started relating their tales. These were Israeli families – Jews, Arabs, and Druze – and each had its story. I sat with them, listening, and could not believe my ears. So this is not only happening here! It is there too! What is going on here?! So I listened to the families and wondered: Why? Why did it happen to them? Why did it happen to us? Why is this happening at all? Before the meeting, there was that person. He was guilty and, as far as you are concerned, he should be punished and placed behind bars. And now, here, the party you have been blaming is a victim, too.

The first thing that came to my mind was the political map of this region. In my political map, the distinction between Israelis and Palestinians had been clear – criminals and victims – but that meeting erased the borderlines. What is going on here? These are not criminals, and we are not victims because there are victims on the side I believed was criminal. So I started asking: Who is the victim? Who is guilty? Who wants peace, and who does not? It was as if I had a puzzle solved one way, but that meeting reshuffled everything, and I had to solve the puzzle all over again – differently, I realized, but how? That is the question: Which piece goes where? What is the new distinction between us? I thought to myself that this was not only the story of Youssef and that soldier whose name I don't know. Youssef and the soldier represent the two nations. It was not personal. Youssef did not know the soldier, and the soldier did not know Youssef. They had no personal history between them or anything that would make one hate the other enough to kill him, so what caused it? Why was the soldier so full of hate or rage? And the family that came to see me, why did they kill their daughter? There was a mom and dad from Tel Mond, whose daughter went out with her friends to Dizengoff Center, and a terror attack took place, and the girl did not return home. This was the *terrorist attack at Dizengoff Center*. I told myself that their story is worse and what happened to that mother was more challenging, yet she came here. She was neither looking for revenge nor filled with hatred. Thus I had to ask myself, who wants peace, and who does not? That was the first datum when rearranging the new puzzle. Who accepts the borders, and who does not? I had to think of all the parties involved – the clergy, settlers, Israelis, Palestinians, the world. I thought of everyone and tried to see the full picture of what was happening. It was like watching a match and managing to stop yourself from seeing just your side, looking at the bigger picture, and trying to understand the situation anew.

That started a new quest in my own and my family's life. I knew we had to stop this together. The operative word that echoed in my head was – together, together, together! I believed it during that meeting, and I still do – together! That is the way to overcome the boundaries of nation, nationality, and religion. We could turn the good people into a single family where we support one another, ease each other's pain, and help each other. With time, this belief and approach grew stronger in me. Every time I met new people, heard what they had to say and what they had been through, listened to their view of the conflict, and their genuine desire, my approach gained strength. The same holds for the opposition. Their very resistance proved to me that we were on the right path.

FINDING AND FOUNDING *AL-TARIQ* – THE WAY

That is why, in 2006 – which was very hard politically for me, my family, and our friends because we had lost the elections that year and grieved! We really grieved! – I decided to establish the *Al-Tariq* Movement, The Way, the Palestinian Institution for Development and Democracy. I chose that name because after six years of experience going in the direction I had been following since that meeting at our house, I had become confident that there was no other way, and that was the only way, so I simply named it The Way. I kept thinking, this is the way. We should not deviate from it left or right and must stay on its course. We did quite a lot before we established Roots.

Al-Tariq is an intra-Palestinian social movement based on nonviolence, reconciliation, and civic participation. If it had maintained the size it reached at some point, it could have changed the fate of this entire region. We appeared on Palestinian television, in the media, in the press. We ran a robust campaign, but our leadership worried that a powerful body was growing there, so we met plenty of resistance. I was summoned for a thousand interrogations, but I endured. That is a shame because many good things are destroyed like that. Still, I kept holding on and holding on. I received a *UNESCO* award and put the entire sum into the movement. I sold the car I had to pay for an office, the staff, and trips all over the *West Bank*. I hung on like that for nearly five years, until 2011. Regrettably, funds have always been our problem, and I could not keep supporting it properly. I had my friends and supporters, but none of us was a millionaire. We were simple people, and the situation would not let us do as much as we had done before. We reached economic instability. The international community supported and funded us, but only as it saw fit. So we were unable to continue.

At some point, I took part in the negotiations between the Shalit family and Hamas. Gilad's father, *Noam Shalit*, came to my place, as did Hamas representatives. I sat with them for a while, and then I left, closed the door behind me, and let them try to solve the problem. It was amazing! To save someone's life, I kept my office open for everyone all the time and barely had time to sleep. I was in Ramallah and went home once a fortnight to see my children.

ROOTS-SHORASHIM-JUDUR

Speaking of the Israeli-Palestinian problem – which resulted in the conflict and violence in this land where both Israelis and Palestinians live – I believe that the solution will not come from politics. The solution requires that we do some fundamental work to change the way each side perceives the other. The history of both nations over the past thousand years created a very negative way of how they see each other. Both sides formed an image of the other side that is very dark, full of hate and mistrust.

The signing of the peace accords started a new era that required changes in perceptions. The agreements addressed the lands, geography, demography, and resources. They spoke less of emotions and the attitude of the Palestinian nation or the Arab world as a whole toward the Jews and the other way around. It has been 26 years since the accords were signed, and we are still stuck. Each side blames the other: the Palestinian leader blames the Israeli leader and vice versa. The army, the security officers, the politicians – each works on their side, trying to find solutions and deal with the current situation, but we see no change. Things move in waves, going up and down, but I cannot say that anything some leaders did brought about change. Things remain as before. I believe that we need to change worldviews if we want to change the situation, and for that to happen, we need to get the two people to meet without preconditions. We need meetings where we ask and learn more about each other, creating trust. In the families' forum, Al-Tariq, and other activities I was involved with, I did that between people of all areas, Palestinians and Israelis.

One door did not open – the one leading to talks with the [Israeli] extreme right, and the settlers are extreme right. There, we hit red lines and values that banned talks between Palestinians and settlers. The Palestinians would not talk to them because the settlers are our primary enemy and the main problem that hinders the application of the peace accords. To this, I say: If they are the reason that hinders peace, it is all the more reason we talk to them; and if they are not, we should examine that – but how can we examine it without talking? How can we study and learn who they are and what they want, or why living in Gush Etzion, Nabulus, or Hebron is so important to them? Is it really meant to prevent peace, or do they have other reasons?

In the Roots-Shorashim-Judur Center, we initiated conversations between us as Palestinians and the settlers, our geographic neighbors. They live right next to our homes and are the closest to our everyday life on the roads, at home, in fields, plantations, and farming lands. We meet them everywhere, but not as friends. We do not meet them and talk. We do not see them as humans, and they don't see us as humans either. When we meet, we keep physical distance between us, for various reasons: We don't believe each other; we fear one another; we see the other as creatures from another planet. So we started addressing this up close.

We started meeting some of them, and they began meeting us, and we saw that our needs and opinions were not very different and that there was an option to make a change that could help us accept and respect each other. I began to realize that as humans, we all have natural needs: to eat and drink, to play and cry, and we have spiritual needs and our particular group ideologies. Being a Muslim, I have an affiliation with Mecca, Medina, and Jerusalem. I also feel connected to Abraham, Isaac, Jacob, King David, and King Solomon. Inside me, there is this spiritual connection and constant pull. I would like to visit Mecca and Medina; I'd like to see where Muhammad the Prophet lived and walked, follow his journey from Mecca to Medina. Inside me, I am attached to everything associated with his history, and I need to get close to this, know more, touch it.

Similarly, I considered Jews who live here and asked myself, what are they doing here? What are they talking about? They, too, try to touch, know, and be close to satisfying the needs that I have as a religious person: They want to be close to their roots – Abraham, Isaac, and Jacob; their pilgrimage to Jerusalem, the Temple, and the Ark of the Covenant; things that were, historical tales and where they took place; and things that happened here, there, and over there.

You see, externally, it seems like people here are turning themselves into obstacles on the road to peace – which to the world is the Oslo Accords. Then I began wondering whether these accords answered their needs. Did the Oslo Accords truly meet the needs of the entire Palestinian Nation? The whole Jewish or the Israeli Nation? Initially, we said that Roots and Oslo could not work together. It is not that I disqualify Oslo. The accords started a new era, and some of its text is fine and positive. The positive thing is that we began to understand that the solution would be reached only through negotiations, not through violence and war. The positive thing is that the Oslo Accords put an end not only to Palestinian declarations that this entire land is ours and they have no rights; but also to the Israeli assertion that this land is entirely theirs and that there is no Palestinian Nation. The Oslo Accords created a kind of partnership in struggling against all types of violence while offering the Palestinians a small opening of hope, a chance that there is a solution. Nevertheless, the accords failed to resolve the conflict because other issues – such as a Palestinian state within the *1967* boundaries, and an Israeli state within the *1948* borders, and territorial distribution – were not resolved. Thus, we in Roots-Shorashim-Judur said that we have to respect the parts that Oslo addressed – that the State of Israel, the Palestinian state, and the PA exist – and other things still need changing.

THE RECONCILIATION JOURNEY

Roots is one station on my reconciliation journey, which started in 2001 with the families' forum, Al-Tariq, and other activities towards creating peace and reconciliation. Roots is a station on that road. Me, my brother Ali, my family, and several other people who spent some time on the Israeli side felt a need to really meet Israelis such as *Hadassah Froman*, who is a leader on the Jewish side.

Back in 2003 or 2004, I met the late *Rabbi Menachem Froman*. We happened to attend the same conferences and activities, and then we suddenly met and introduced ourselves. He invited me to his place, and I came to partake in discussions on the Israeli-Palestinian or the Israeli-Arab conflict. I happen to have a friend who is an American priest who used to talk with us and, at the same time, maintained close relationships with people in the Gush Etzion. He knows us, so he is aware that we, as a family or group of activists (my brother Ali, me, other people here), are open to meetings and conversations and that some of our members are ripe for it. Thus, he made the initial connection. That first encounter laid the foundation for several other subsequent meetings and, before long, we were a group that undertook to promote local changes in our region. Each side, us and the Israelis, invited their friends and acquaintances from their villages and families. Thus, slowly but surely, we realized that we were not alone and that many in our region felt that meetings and familiarization with the other side was important, and that they did not want to harm people on the other side, nor would they have others do it.

I believe that today, the Roots-Shorashim-Judur extended circle – by that I mean people associated with Roots, Palestinians and Israelis – comprises some 600–700 people in our region. Some of us maintain contact and are very active, while others appear every two or three months, but we are all associated with Roots, and I believe that anyone associated with Roots is an opportunity wherever they are because Roots is there too.

We represent Roots on the Palestinian side and see that what we do is much respected, not because people are convinced it is the right way to go, but because they see no other way. In any case, neither of us knows for sure which is wrong and which is correct. All I know for sure is that what we have here is a connection between people who respect each other, and that helps people around them look and see that perhaps this is an option. I believe this is the secret of the solution. We have an active group of young, teenage members in Roots. They are very active, holding intense and amazing meetings, and greatly impact our surroundings. Our success here attracted attention elsewhere. Jews who live in the Jordan Valley came here for a year of talks. They asked for our help in promoting Roots on their side, and so we did help some 18 months ago. That is how the circle expands and amazingly grows, encompassing Israeli and Palestinian settlements around Jericho. There is also a great demand for Roots in the northern region. Many who had visited here are now corresponding with us, asking us to find the time to come to them and help them move forward. They want the same feeling we have here.

Roots answers some of the residents' needs, and to me, the fact that others want this on their side means success. The truth is that we attend every conference, and even if it is not ours and we did not initiate it, you will always see a group from Roots attending meetings between Palestinians and Israelis who live in the region. It always comes up – in elections, in the council, in the *Efrat* municipality. We have contacts with the Efrat mayor. He does not share our views, but he is not against them. We can be found at every key event, in every neighborhood of the Israeli locality, and almost every village or neighborhood of the Palestinian locality. I feel that Roots is an example that proves that partnership between us over this land and state is possible and positive.

The majority of the Palestinian Nation and the majority of the Israeli Nation want to live in peace. I do not doubt that. Nevertheless, I am also confident that in order to live in peace, we must first understand what living in peace means, how it is done, and what is required of us.

If we fail to introduce education for peace and peace values, it will not be worth it. If I want to succeed, I do not have to change you. All I ask of you is that you try to change whatever hinders coexistence – which may be one state, two states, or even 10 states. I make the same demand of myself.

9. To make a change, we must be willing to change

Shiri Levinas
Interviewed by Roni Mikel Arieli

In July 2018, I was busy writing the concluding chapter of my doctorate thesis on *Holocaust* memory in South Africa from the early years of apartheid through to that nation's transition to democracy (1948–1994). The chapter starts with a review of moves that characterized the last decade of the twentieth century in South Africa – from the formation of the national unity government under Nelson Mandela in 1994 to the establishment of the Truth and Reconciliation Commission, based on the Promotion of National Unity and Reconciliation Act, No. 34, enacted in 1995. The commission was the national cornerstone of the new South African democracy, which mediated individuals' personal traumas while promoting a uniform narrative, framed in terms of the shared collective memory of the new nation. As a cultural historian of South Africa, and mainly as an Israeli researcher and citizen, I kept asking myself: Is it possible to develop transitional justice apparatuses to suit the Israeli context of a lasting conflict? Can such an initiative emerge from Israel's civil society?

These questions were on my mind on the Sunday morning of July 29, 2018, when I met Shiri Levinas in her home to hear about Women Wage Peace (WWP), a movement she formed with other women in 2014. WWP was established during the charged period that followed *Operation Protective Edge* and intended to promote a diplomatic agreement as a strategic solution to the Israeli-Palestinian conflict, while placing women in decision-making positions. United Nations (UN) Resolution 1325, made in October 2000, accentuated the importance of women's participation in decision-making centers for the promotion of solutions for violent conflicts. While the UN resolution focused on the need to attain women's involvement in peace and security processes, Levinas, a self-proclaimed feminist since childhood, argued that women were being marginalized on these very issues all over the world, and even more so in militaristic Israel. Levinas further argued that peace would come only if it was "wrapped in the Israeli flag", while focusing her efforts on creating a feminine discourse in Israeli society that would guarantee that the entire social discourse became more inclusive. In our meeting, Levinas mainly spoke of her social activities, which is why she skipped the story of her childhood and spoke only of her adult life. This interview offers a peek into the life of Levinas, an inspiring woman whose tale shifts between despair and hope, and includes numerous insights about women and femininity, gender, and conflict resolution.

I DID NOT INITIATE OR ESTABLISH WOMEN WAGE PEACE; WE DID

I want this to be very, very clear: I did not establish WWP; I merely took part in its establishment.

The initiators of WWP were attorneys *Michal Barak* and Irit Tamir. They each had an idea and they met by chance – in *Geneva Initiative*, I believe – and said: Come on, let's do something. That was the end of August 2014, following the incident of the *kidnapped boys*. Israel was on fire after three Jewish teenagers were abducted and murdered by Palestinians, and the Israel Defense Forces launched Operation Protective Edge in Gaza in which both sides sustained casualties. At the time, there were plenty of women's initiatives. Michal and Irit sent emails to friends. I had known neither before. They happened to watch, on *Israel Social TV*, a clip I made from a lecture on gender and conflicts that I'd delivered at the Tel Aviv Cinematheque, addressing the *Bereaved Families Forum*, the Palestinian and Israeli families for peace. As fate would have it, Irit became ill three weeks later and left to care for herself, leaving Michal alone. We were quite close by then and Michal, humble as always, told me: "I am not ready to lead. You do that." I said: "I don't wish to lead. This is not my agenda and I think it is not right." Then we started hearing other women: "I want to!" "I can do it." "I am ready." We both became a bit concerned and she asked: "Shiri, what do we do?" I said: "Michal, I have a brilliant idea: we're forming a flat movement." This is how all that Wow! around WWP and the flat movement started [laughing]. So this came out of our distress and the need to find a creative solution for a real problem in a way that would not deflate the move we were trying to make, while avoiding ego clashes and having people become poster girls. So Michal and I announced it would be a flat movement and this is how it has worked until now. This is how the structure and the DNA of the movement was formed. Then we wrote our set of principles, and we passed it along to broader circles. This is why I said right from the start that it was not I who initiated or established WWP. It was us. A team of wonderful and worthy women working together.

DEVELOPING MY FEMINIST AWARENESS

The seeds of my involvement in the establishment of WWP were sown years ago, having to do with the development of my feminist awareness. My feminist activism started when I was a child on Kibbutz Eyal (in central Israel). I was a reverse feminist, believing I was stronger and better than all of the boys. I refused all girly trappings and would not wear dresses or play with dolls. When I was six, visiting relatives from the city brought me a golden necklace. I was so insulted that right there and then, before their amazed eyes, I tossed it in the sewer [laughing]. I got into fights, joined bike races, played football, and generally let no one be more a 'boy' than me, so no one could say I was any less. I intuitively understood how the power balance worked at a very young age and decided that if this was the game to play, I would be on the winning side.

Still, my feminist mindset was further shaped when I lived in New York. I arrived there after working in Israel as director of international conferences for a major tourism company. My brother Ram was killed in what became known as the *Naval Commando (Shayetet) Disaster* and I felt I could not breathe in Israel; I could not grieve and had to play act all the time. I did not have a moment to myself. I was fully dedicated to looking after my siblings, doing this, fixing that, and I felt I would soon just disappear. I wanted to move to New York even before Ram was killed, but I knew I could not make that move soon after it happened. Only two years later, when I was 29, I summoned the courage and moved. While in Israel, I produced a conference for Nurit Berman, chief executive officer of the Emda Company that was part of an international head-hunters' network. When I decided to move to New York, I had no visa, job, or anything, only my father who lived in New Jersey. Nurit urged me to meet her American partner Fred Siegel, chief executive officer of Conex Intersearch. I knew he worked with conference producers, and when I met him, I said: "I want you to help me work in conferences in the USA." First he said that we should have lunch and talk about it. Then he asked me to meet his other partner, and after dragging me around for a week, said: "How about working for us?" and I was like: "What do you want from me? What do I know? I know nothing about your business or about HR. I've never worked in marketing, and have no idea about business collaborations." He said: "I have a feeling you should work here." I said: "You know what? Write me an offer and we'll talk." As soon as I arrived at my dad's place, a FedEx package arrived with an offer I could not refuse, given my age and social status [laughing].

That was a school for life. Fred, an amazing native New Yorker Jew, served as aid to the New York City mayor for several years and as dean of the New

York University Business School. An interesting man. I learned a lot from him and Nurit, and made plenty of money, being in charge of collaborations with Israel. So there I was, a 29-year-old girl, sitting with venture capitalists and startupists from Israel, with embassy people and such. The first thing Fred did was send me to buy some clothes [laughing]. "Take $1000," he said, "and please: get dressed."

So I lived in New York, made good money, and volunteered in the Bronx Zoo. I have always wavered between working with people or animals. While forming business ventures, I was also a holistic healer. I learned reiki, energy reading, guided imagery, and so on. Next, I joined a group of peace circles – an organization of Christians, Jews, and Muslims. I got to know people from the Palestinian and Syrian communities in New York. I learned plenty from those meetings and my volunteering activities. I remember I went to a party on some roof. There was a very cute DJ there. We started talking and I asked him where he was from. "Syria," he said, "and you?" I said: "I come from the country you hate the most." "Don't know what you're talking about," he said. "Israel," I said, and he replied: "You are so arrogant. Syria has far greater troubles than Israel. For example, the wars between the Kurds and the Alawites." He gave me a review of the situation in Syria, things I'd never heard before, and we became good friends.

While in New York, I met very strong, independent, and opinionated women with agendas that really surprised me. For example, women who chose not to give birth. I am ashamed to say it, but I – the great feminist and scholar of gender studies today – met once with a beautiful, rich, and talented woman who had chosen not to bring children into this world. I could not understand this, so I asked: "Why? Do you have a problem?" When I hear someone pose a question like this today, I roll my eyes and click my tongue, but I did ask it myself. I can't deny it. She answered: "No. I just don't want to raise children. I love my life. It is very convenient, and I don't believe it would be better with children, nor do I believe I'd be the best mother." I still remember how amazing I felt. Her response made me see things differently and start thinking.

Next, I met a Swedish woman, Fanny Söderbäck, who came to New York to write her doctorate on gender and literature. We became very close friends and she became my teacher of feminist theories. She brought up questions I'd never asked myself. It was like someone had pulled a veil off my eyes. I began to understand the power balance and the gaps in attributed values in our society. For example, how come our parents are cared for by lowly foreigners who we pay minimum wages, while a person who sits on Wall Street, selling and buying shares on his computer and making millions, has supreme status in our society? My daily New York experiences helped me develop feminist awareness and views on global power balances, categories, and social psychology that I later studied. It all started there.

Then New York became too cold for me and I decided to leave. One friend of my brother Ram was a skipper who needed a crewperson to take a yacht to the Caribbean islands. He asked if I would join and I thought it sounded great. In just three days, I locked my apartment, quit my job, and sent emails to my clients. They were sure I had got married or something [laughing], and vanished. The sea voyage lasted three months – an experience I would not recommend and certainly will not repeat. I toured the islands for a while by myself. One day, my other brother came there to see me and said: "I am bored. Let's do something even cooler." I said: "Fine, but I am not moving away from the Caribbean Sea." We went to a tourist agency and asked: "What else is there?" They said: "Mexico, Cancun, Playa del Carmen, Caribbean Mexico." I said let's go, bought a ticket, and went to Mexico. As soon as I arrived, I knew that I was staying, and I had enough money not to work for a while from my New York earnings.

MEXICO – THE COCOON FROM WHICH MY BUTTERFLY SPRANG

I believe Mexico was an excellent cocoon for my butterfly to spring from. The two years I spent there and things I did in Mexico actually for the first time combined gender with conflict. Being away from everything I had known or belonged to, being absolutely detached, created the potential for things I realized later, when I returned to Israel. I believe that without that period, I would not have been able to act at all.

One day, after I left an internet café, an American woman walked up to me: "May I join you?" "Sure." "What do you do?" "Nothing," I said. And she said: "No. When you do things, what do you do?" I told her I was a holistic healer, and she said: "I knew it! I need you!" "What do you need me for?" I wondered. "We're establishing a project named Angel Notion Clinic, organizing delegations of American doctors who come here to treat the children." At the time, I lived in Playa del Carmen, a resort town where the Mayans' descendants used to live. These are natives who still preserve parts of their traditional lifestyle, having suffered years of conflict with the government over rights to their land in Chiapas. They are transparent, have no rights to their land, no rights to their homes. The natives are oppressed by their own government. This is very sad to see. So she told me: "We're forming a community center for them that will bring in delegations of physicians and teach alternative medicine to the locals. I need partners and I want you to be one." I said: "Fine. I'll be a partner."

So me, a Mexican psychologist, and a Mexican psychiatrist, who later became my closest friend, established that center together and it is still working today. The center has saved the lives of quite a few children. If they had heart problems, we sent them to the USA. Delegations of plastic surgeons, oral and maxillofacial surgeons, and orthopedists would come to Playa and treat them, while we covered the patients' medical follow-ups and support procedures. One of the finest lessons I learned there was the way we managed to get the entire town involved in the project. When we brought in medical delegations, hotels gave them free rooms, restaurants fed them for nothing, and the bus company drove them around free of charge. It was because the town comprised many foreigners that we managed to create a state of mind of caring and responsibility for the place, and establish a self-supporting project that did not need donations or handouts. All local employees were paid in full for their work at the center. No local was asked to volunteer, and we had no big donors. It was all about local initiatives by individuals and tourists who visited the town and realized they were responsible and needed to give back, and not just use what was easily exploitable in Mexico.

When I lived in New York, it became clear to me that I wished to focus on working with women and gender. Then, when I arrived in Mexico, I joined the Angel Notion Clinic and started working with groups of women who were victims of the Chiapas conflict. Our goal was – I don't like the word 'empowerment'; 'autonomy' is better – to help them find their autonomy and defend their rights as well as their presence as meaningful women in their families, communities, and society.

Work there rattled me. We are familiar with our conflict here. Where is the greatest pain of the Israeli society from our conflict? Bereaved mothers and families – a world I knew all too well, regrettably. In Mexico, I met women whose pain was very much alive: women whose faces were sliced, whose fingers were broken, who had been raped. Women whose children were taken away and killed. Horrors you'd never think you could stand to be around, and suddenly they were out there, in the sunlight, with nowhere to escape because we had to deal with just that. It was shocking to see the imbalance, the abnormal and insane price of inequality and, at the same time, understand the privilege I had and the gaps between us. It was there that my life-long commitment to work with women and gender issues was formed.

I became interested in privilege and started investigating what it meant to be privileged, the meaning of power relations between women, and how one created common spaces when social gaps were so vast. The tough questions I had, which started there, became even harder when I returned to Israel. After all, it is rather easy and convenient, and it feels good, to help in places where you are a foreigner and bear no responsibilities. I was not a party to the conflict there. I financed neither side. I did not take sides. I did not vote. I was the benevolent foreigner who had come to help. I soon clearly realized how comfortable it was to assume that position.

Speaking of money, one of our principles was that people should earn money. We decided not to ask people who had nothing to volunteer only because we could. It was very clear that we needed to create a different kind of space in that project, as well as in our interactions with the town – and it worked. The same was with friendships – how do you form them? How do you establish relationships when you have everything and others have nothing? I get by in Spanish. I mean, I can't read a newspaper, but I can speak a little. Some of the women there don't. They have their local languages, so communicating with them involved hand gestures and plenty of physical contact and sitting together. People there welcomed me with super-open arms. When people feel transparent and no one sees them, and then someone comes along offering help, they ask no questions. They were in such a bad shape that they had no room to be judgmental and say – "Yes, I want what you're offering," or not. I am an Israeli, not an American, and there is plenty of antagonism against the USA there, in Mexico; justifiably, I think. Being an Israeli meant that I was closer to Jerusalem and Jesus. Every time I came back from Israel I brought them crosses and water bottles, which definitely made them appreciate me more. I gained from the sanctity.

Still, most of the relationships I formed cannot be called friendships, and where friendship did develop, it required plenty of courage and made me change myself. I could not ask an abused woman, "Why do you let him do that?" but only say things like: "What do you need now to feel better?" That was a lesson I learned. You don't take them out and buy them coffee. I went with them to their houses and ate the food they'd cooked because that was where they were comfortable and could do without my charity. I learned that I had to make appointments and meet when it was convenient for them because they looked after their children and worked. After all, most of them provided for themselves because their men were drunk all the time. I could not say to them "Well, your schedules are inconvenient." Why would I? Because I wanted to have a good time? I mean, I was in Mexico, on the Caribbean shores, so I should spend my time visiting those neighborhoods late in the evening? That was a lesson in making space, in not being judgmental. I once told my son Gal that it is easy to be generous when you have plenty. The trick is to be generous when you don't have much. He said: "Mom, what you are saying is not fair. Many people have plenty and are not generous. It is always hard to be generous, so perhaps it is harder when you have nothing." I agree with his wise observation; still, it is relatively easy to give when you have. Learning to give when you have nothing is a bit more complicated. I also had to learn not to judge these women or push them where I thought they should go. It was a lesson in feminism that we should all learn.

DANCING BETWEEN MY CHOICE OF PEOPLE AND MY FREEDOM

I loved my life in Mexico and did not intend to return to Israel. Then I went on home vacation. Friends of mine and Gil's [Shiri's spouse] had been meaning to introduce us for a while, but never managed to convince both of us at the same time. I told them to tell him that I was not interested in anything serious. "I live in Mexico and I'm not coming back, so if he feels like a summer fling, that's fine; if not, thanks a lot." He must have misunderstood them and heard that I was not going back to Mexico but staying in Israel, so he said OK too. A week after we met, we decided he was going to come to Mexico. When I left Israel, I was already pregnant.

I panicked. After Ram was killed, the entire family fell apart and I felt responsible and perhaps even hoped that if I returned to Israel, it would start something new in the family. Throughout the years, my friends had been trying to convince me to return to Israel. Suddenly I was pregnant and afraid of giving birth and raising a child on my own, with only Gil. What did I know about raising children? This is why, when I was six months pregnant, I returned and settled in Gil's town – Jerusalem.

The first years back in Israel were very hard. In New York and Mexico, I was alone in the sense that I knew no one when I arrived; I was an alien. There are many foreigners in both these places. On the one hand, you are free to be yourself, who and what you are. No one is judging you for what you are and you don't have to fall in line with anyone. You can be this, that, or the other. On the other hand, the people that you meet and connect with over there also left their familiar and orderly lives and went to seek something else in New York and Mexico. Connections made there are very strong and very real. The choice is very clean. These are not necessarily people you grew up with or befriended because your children attend the same pre-school. You choose them consciously, which made me very happy. I felt good dancing between my people and my freedom. It really allowed me to do things I wanted to and loved. Then I returned to Israel, to Jerusalem, and had a child, and felt lonely like I'd never felt before. All those friends who for years had badly wanted me to come back to Israel were now very busy raising their own children, and everyone around me expected me to be very happy. Now Gil is a Jerusalemite, a twenty-fourth generation here. He works in Jerusalem, where all of his friends reside. He would go out to work each morning, leaving me alone, and I did not know what to do with myself. It was time for me to do something. When I was still pregnant, I attended a meeting of women's organizations in Israel, using contacts I'd made in New York and when I had visited Israel.

I remember going to a conference of peace organizations, sitting there and weeping. I saw so much ego there, so much war, competition, and violence. I felt sad that of all places, in Israel there was a great gap between the talk and the walk. It really paralyzed me. Everywhere I went, I felt I was falling into that gap, and I could not understand it. Why did members of peace organizations act so aggressively and belligerently? How can feminist organizations be so violent and brutal? I could not find my place and felt lost. So I went to school.

I studied for an MA in conflict settlement at the Herzliyya Interdisciplinary Center. Gladly, Professor *Galia Golan* was my academic director and became my gift for life. I'd met Galia before, in an organization known as Inclusive Security Institute – an international organization for women, peace, and security issues. When they formed a group in Israel, I was invited and Galia was there, as well as other many fine and worthy women who are still there. My MA thesis was about *UNSC Resolution 1325*. Regardless of the subjects of the courses I attended – be it international law or globalization – I wrote all of my papers on Resolution 1325 and somehow managed to combine it with gender studies. It was fascinating.

IF I WANT TO MAKE A DIFFERENCE, I MUST INFLUENCE MY SOCIETY

At around the same time, Yael Shalem, a peace activist who worked for *IPCRI*, tried to initiate specific activities for women and asked me to join her. Together, we formed the Palestinian-Israeli International Women Group, where we worked for about a year. It was fascinating work that enabled me to make contacts with Palestinian women I'd not known or been able to reach before.

We formed a mothers' group of some six or eight of the more dominant women and initiated various projects: We did yoga together; formulated a shared curriculum; ran a joint course on non-violent communication that created closeness, and many other such activities. All the while, the mothers' group would meet and keep it all together. At the same time, the meetings made me see even better that there was a gap between feel-good and effective activities. I found out that though I felt good about myself, I made no difference in reality. So, I had some Palestinian friends and we hugged and we kissed, and all was great. In the real world, I'd go back to my air-conditioned car and drive home without being held up at the army roadblock. I went back to my comfy home (we rented a house in Beit Zayit then) while they went back to their very different lives – and nothing really changed.

I don't want this to sound like I'm thinking that we were doing something wrong. I am still doing that in other constellations, but that led me to WWP. I realized that if I wanted to change things and make a difference – [raising her voice] if I wanted to make a difference! – I had to make an impact on my side, on my society. I realized I had to go back and do the work here in Israel. After all, it was very easy for me to feel comfortable with the Palestinian women, to identify with them and be empathic, and it was very easy for me to let slide parts of my narrative that I was not too happy with, so I could easily ignore those. In reality, however, the most dominant parts of Israeli society, the parts that actually shape it, are precisely the things I ignored – and this is where work should be done. Then I started to form a decision: I had to stop my binational work and start working within Israeli society.

I felt that working inside Israel was the key for change; that if I was committed to these Palestinian women I'd met and really wanted something to change, I must use my energy working inward, into the Israeli society. I joined the first policy promoters' course of the Geneva Initiative for activists of various political parties. For a whole year, we heard lectures, went on tours, and studied the conflict. In the end, I offered to volunteer in the organization, recruit people, attend meetings, write minutes, manage, and lead. At the same time, the IPCRI asked me to lead a joint project for Israeli and Palestinian women. There, I met *Huda Abu Arqoub* and our friendship started. I concentrated on these two tracks over the four years that preceded the establishment of WWP. I kept working in programs for Palestinian and Israeli women, while convening meetings and groups of Israeli women. In the latter, we insisted on diversity of the groups. We did not want only leftists or Ashkenazi women to attend, making sure they included religious, rightist, old, and young women to keep everyone out of their comfort zones. In the meetings of the Israeli women, we started talking about political stands and discourse and security discourse among women, about how women view peace or what peace looks like to Israeli women. Dr. Meirav Moshe, director of the School of Social Work at the Sapir College, and Galia Golan, who was active in Inclusive Security, helped me come up with an idea that turned into the *Dvora Forum*. This project regrettably did not materialize – it was about starting a group of Israeli women who live in border settlements where we would learn how they view peace.

In addition, around 2010, I was involved in the Coalition for Action on 1325 when the *Itach-Maaki Association* received funds from the European Union to help them establish a coalition and a 'national action plan.' They initiated round-table meetings of feminist and political activists. I remember sitting with *Nurit Haghagh, Neomi Hazan*, and *Sari Aharoni*, sharing our frustrations. After all, we were able to bring together a group of amazing women, create a platform for transformation, and have them come out of the meetings with new insights and motivations, and then we left them alone. They went home and at dinner they heard: "What do you know about politics? What did you do in the army?" and all that militant talk that silenced all the other voices, and they were all alone. How could we do things with those amazing women? Then

I received the email concerning WWP and I remember telling Gil: "Baby, this is money time. That's it!"

WOMEN WAGE PEACE: NO ONE WAS LEFT OUT

When we established WWP, I repeatedly stated that peace was everyone's. I came away from Mexico with a different perspective. I believed that all Israeli women want peace. This was my starting point and from it I act. I know I have to reach them and ask them what they need to take part: What do they need to become peace activists? First of all, I was not afraid to approach anyone. In fact, my basic assumption was that they were interested, and it was my responsibility to show up and make suggestions. I believe that when you act from a caring place, not on your interests, people will want to do, talk, partake, and show up. Also, I always assume a personal approach. In my life, I have met very many people from all kind of places, so it was very easy for me to connect the dots when we launched WWP. Since I was skilled in that, I used the connections and was not afraid of possible rejection.

Michal and me, with a few other women, traveled to the Jewish settlements on the *West Bank*, and to Lod, *Ramla*, and *Ofakim*. There were some who did not like it. My answer was: We knocked on many doors and stayed wherever they opened. We went to Lod and Ramla, and two or three women would show up and talk about other things half the meeting. We just sat there patiently. It is a process. You don't just form partnerships. You cannot approach a person who does not know you, does not trust you, has never done anything with you before, and say: "Listen: That's how things are. This matters." It does not work this way, it just doesn't, but peace organizations refuse to acknowledge that and then they don't understand why their camps keep shrinking. They don't see why fewer are active and why doors are slammed in their faces. You cannot walk up to people and tell them what is right for them, what they need, and how they should act. Who are you, anyway? Why should they listen to you? What made you smarter? Why do you think you are more convincing than they are? I believe in Martin Buber's assertion: "If you want to make a change, you must be willing to change; it does not happen otherwise."

I believe that the power of WWP follows from the fact that we gave up on no one, and we knew this was a marathon right from the start. I did not think that I would just wave my magic wand and puff! – turn some woman into what I wanted her to be. I never said, I want you to be this or that. I only asked questions: What is your responsibility for the current situation? If you are responsible, what are you willing to do for it: come every other month, once in six months, write on Facebook, press 'like' – what are YOU willing to do? And whatever the answer was, there I aimed and created resources for it. That was my guide, not some vision I had or some cause and knowing how it should look. And it worked.

For example, a group of women was formed in Ofakim around Yahaloma Zchut, who had established NATAL's Stronger Together Center to support the local community. We became soul sisters. She opened the door for me there. For the past two years, I have been traveling every week or two to Ofakim and worked with the women there in a group where everyone could speak, no one shut them up, and their needs and desires were just as legitimate as mine. Presently, there is a group of women and a few men there who define themselves as peace activists. I interviewed a woman there who told me: "I am a peace activist. I want peace," but at the same time, she said: "When rockets are fired at us from Gaza, I close my heart. I don't care what happens in Gaza. I don't care about the women and children there, but I do care about our soldiers. This is why peace will come. They cannot keep selling us this bullshit. We must have peace." When the parents of *Oron Shaul* decided to celebrate his birthday on the Gaza border, that group went with them. They wrapped themselves in Israeli flags to show sympathy. Then, a barrage of mortars fell around them, so the group members started treating anxiety victims. I believe there will never be peace if it is not wrapped in an Israeli flag, which makes their activities more important than mine. I cannot do the things they can, which is why their activities are the key for change. I need them, not the other way around, and this instructs my activities.

Once I addressed a group of people in a private gathering. The accent of one woman gave away that she was from Russia. At the end of the meeting, I walked up to her: "Listen, you cannot leave. You must help me start a group now." She said: "Me? I am a rightist and my husband is a police officer." I said, "That's even better! Come on!" and we started forming a group of Russian-speaking women. I am speaking of hard-working women with no privileges, often single mothers without means. I've never seen any of them coming to a meeting in their private car, nor can any of them afford to lose a workday for political activities. Yet, their work succeeded and gathered momentum and impacted on the Russian-speaking community and media, where they received plenty of items, met with trendsetters, and formed many caucuses.

Take the settlers, for example. In Hebrew, there is a distinction between settlers as 'colonizers' or as 'pioneers.' Now, I would not want to own anybody's self-definition, but for me, they are colonizers. When I talk with my friends who reside on the West Bank, I always speak of this or that 'colony' while they live in a 'settlement,' but I always use their term – 'settler.' Now people could not stomach that and kept asking me how I could forgo my truth and ideology. Between you and me, I am far more leftist than anyone who ever joined this movement. I am far more radical [laughing]. Everyone knows that. I support the *Breaking the Silence* organization, and if I attend memorial ceremonies, it is always joint Israeli-Palestinian ones. No one believes that I am something I am not. I have not budged an inch from my beliefs and opinions, nor have I concealed anything to make someone like me. People cannot grasp that. The idea is not to give up on your own identity, but to make room for others, to realize others' views are as legitimate as yours.

I have a friend who lives in Ofakim today, after being evacuated from *Neve Dekalim*. She is not happy there and feels that her soul is still in the old settlement and speaks her mind. I asked her: "You do remember I was for the Israeli Disengagement from the Gaza Strip, right?" and she said: "Sure, but it does not matter. Listen …" Just last week, I told her: "I am happy that you moved out of there. I believe you should have." And she said: "No problem. Never mind, but listen to me." You see? She did not need me to agree with her, but she needed me to listen to her.

Ariella Ginegar, currently one of the movement's steering coordinators who joined us quite early, was the woman who opened the door for the settlers/colonizers. For several years, she was a member of *Sharon Leshem's Talking Peace Project* and became friends with settlers she'd met at work. She organized the first meeting that took place in Ofra on the West Bank that some 12 women attended. I remember wondering what to do with that meeting. I searched for a text we could work with and luckily found one by *Rabbi Kook* that speaks of the territories near Temple Mount. As the story goes, several Jews wanted to buy Arabs' houses around Temple Mount to form a safe passage for the Jews, but the Arabs would not sell them. The Jews pressured, but the Arabs said it could not be done because these were Waqf lands (lands under religious custody) and could not be sold. The would-be buyers asked Rabbi Kook to rule on the matter. They told him: "They would not sell." He said: "Make them a better offer." They said: "Nothing works. Should we take it by force?" and the rabbi said: "God forbid! The parties must always find a solution, through honorable agreement, that both sides accept."

We started with a round of introductions in which I thanked them for having us and for coming because I was sure it was scary. It was scary for me, I told them, and I had to swallow hard before I came here. I have family living in the occupied territories that I have never visited and never will, but I came here because I feel personally responsible. Then I said I'd like to read something and when I did, the room fell silent and tense: Who is she to show us that Rabbi Kook is on her side? I told them: "Listen, I did not bring this text to convince you that Rabbi Kook is on my side, but to show you that when you believe in something, you'll always find the facts that support it. Since I believe we must make an agreement [with the Palestinians], I will find proof even in Rabbi Kook's texts, just like you will find proof that this is your land in the words of David Ben-Gurion, the first Israeli prime minister, or whoever. I believe it is important that we understand that we are not here to discuss the facts – they forever depend on our beliefs – but to ask you, as Jewish-Israeli women: Where is your responsibility for creating peace here? That is all!"

That meeting indeed opened things up and more meetings were held. After the third such meeting, several women called, asking to meet and study, and became very active in the movement. These settlers have a declared interest to maintain ties with locations inside the *Green Line* (pre-*1967* border). It is part of their strategy, but also part of their true belief that the people of Israel must be united. They feel there is a rift in the nation and mending it is a most important mission. The fact that they can sit with leftist women such as myself and talk and work together is very meaningful. Incidentally, most of them wanted to meet with Palestinian women, but we were ambivalent. Is it appropriate, given the existing colonialism and occupied-occupier ratio? On the practical level, we wondered how we could form a meeting between settlers and Palestinians. What song could they possibly sing together? I hate to say it, but the women of WWP get along better with settler women than with other groups because the differences are ideological, but not social. They all drive their cars, live in houses with gardens as we do, they are academics and we have the same professions and work for the same companies. It is easier.

We wanted WWP to be a movement of a variety of women, not in separate compartments but actually working together. When we established it and said it would be a flat movement, we also said work teams were important. You can't have everyone doing everything. People need rotation and change. When people volunteer, you cannot dictate to them what they do. You need to offer them a variety of choices for them to choose what they find convenient, and you need to know that's what will happen: They'll choose what's convenient for them and when they can't, you can only hope someone else is there who can. We formed about 12 working teams and in the end, they set the tone and are the engine that gets much of our activities going.

We also wanted men involved. At first, some 10 percent of us were men, but one of the 10 principles is that women will always lead the movement and there will be no men in decision-making positions. I am very much at peace with that. Several attempts were made to alter that principle, but I believe that if it does change, that would be the end of the project. I strongly believe in that principle, for several reasons. First, it is because women don't have a safe space to speak for themselves. I don't know a single woman, as opinionated as she may be, who can freely speak about peace and security at a dinner party with men and women. The militaristic discourse in Israel and other countries leaves no legitimate space for women to talk about peace and security. So first of all, women need safe spaces where they can even begin to think about their stands and views, and collect information. That safe space must be for women only so that no one can ask: "Where did you serve in the army? When did you hold a gun? What do you even understand?"

The second reason is the fact that women are so accustomed to the power balance in which they are considered to be the ones who do not understand, but they are in fact the utility workers. This is the familiar structure of our society, so if you want to make a change, you need to break this structure. We have met so many men since we established the movement – businessmen, politicians, you name it – who invited us to their place and told us: "What you're doing is great, but here's what you gotta do: Let me just put this small bag on your back and run. I'll give you money. I'll cheer for you and tell you 'bravo!' and you will be ambassadors for my ideas." I hardly met men in high positions who told us: "Maybe, I don't know. Perhaps you know what you're doing."

I remember meetings – and will name no one, but they were veteran peace activists, sitting in their fancy offices – where they told me: "We want to talk to your leader." And I replied: "We have no leader; I am that today, another one is tomorrow, and you'll talk to her." "But you must have one!" they said, and I replied: "No, we don't. You'll talk to the women who are present here and to others who may show up tomorrow." It made them mad, crazy, angry, but this is how we work. One time, we were several friends having lunch and chatting, and this guy walked up to us and said: "I believe that what you, WWP, are doing is wonderful, but you understand nothing, so here's what you have to say." I cannot imagine the situation being reversed, where a group of men are having lunch and a discussion, and a woman who just happens to be there steps in and explains to them what they need to do. So this is the second reason: Breaking down the current social structure and allowing for the creation of alternatives.

Another reason is that there are many studies on gender and conflict these days that show that women represent the various population groups and speak on the everyday level. Since women are not at the top or in decision-making positions, the experiences they bring to the dialogues speak for daily life affairs. Let us consider the current situation with the fires and Ofakim. Decision makers sit together and tell the media: "We need to relax. There are no fires." Yet, when you visit there, you see that mothers cannot take their children out to playgrounds because they start coughing and contract asthma because of the soot in the air. This is the reality. This is what people experience and what the women speak of.

Another reason is, of course, the legitimate right of 51 percent of the population to speak for themselves. A feminine (feminist) management and leadership style allows for a multitude of voices to be heard, giving more room to more population groups. That's why it is important to keep it feminine, and men are welcome to support as much as possible. It is like in the Sephardi struggle: I am 100 percent Ashkenazi, and I work with a group comprising very few Ashkenazis and a majority of Sephardis. I will never lead their struggle. I will never speak to the media or decide on activities on their behalf, but

I'll always be there to support whichever path they choose. In the same way, I don't think that men can lead a women's movement. There is plenty of room for them to support, but they don't have to make the decisions. You can see how men fight and try to join the decision makers. What's wrong with being on the sidelines? I believe these spaces are very important.

WOMEN WAGE PEACE – MY GREATEST SUCCESS AND BIGGEST FAILURE

The group of Russian-speaking women also exemplify the things that work in WWP as well as the things that don't. On the one hand, it is a success story: We had a group of some 40 Russian-speaking women that were mentioned often in Israel's Russian media, including clips and interviews they produced, insisting they included not only Russians. I used to sit in on their meetings and let me tell you: If you listen very hard even to a language you don't speak, you understand! So, as a rule, I understood most of the things they said, and they translated the rest for me. It was really important for them not to be segregated, not to include only Russian-speaking women, so they made sure Hebrew speakers attended every meeting they had. We also wanted to include them in our working teams. As a feminist organization, we follow the 30 percent quota rule. Many studies have shown that minorities cannot produce significant impact if they are less than 30 percent of the whole. We really wanted that, but failed because we did not have enough Russian-speaking women, and the places and times of their meetings did not work. That integration was very hard, except for very few teams or certain, very dominant women.

Initially, we found room for the variety of groups and women. It was balanced. At a certain point, however, with 30,000 women who joined in, the movement lost its balance and we could not keep doing this work. Now, work is in whatever is convenient for the women, whatever comes easy for them. This is crucial and significant and I believe that it is very important that some 30,000 women got out of their comfort zones and did things, regardless if it matched my agenda or not. This, however, was not the direction I believe we should have followed.

This is why WWP was my biggest success and greatest failure at the same time. The first 18 months were amazing, full of hope, and we did create something new. We started the movement in August and the founding-members nucleus included rightist, Arab, Russian-speaking, and settler/colonialist women. In November, we launched it at the Sapir College. Michal Shamir, who was in the original group, had a brilliant idea of a peace train that would travel from Kiriat Shemona in the north to Sederot in the south. As head of the Arts School at Sapir, she managed to organize a session at a social conference in Sederot. Just think about this: We held our first meeting in August, and in November we already had 1,000 women on that train. Now, these 1,000 women were mostly middle-class Ashkenazi leftists, and that shaped the trajectory of the movement. Naturally, in the second year-and-a-half, that group of women could not move because it was too big. Looking back, if we launched such a movement again, I'd do it completely differently.

I believe that WWP deviated from its original course. Its DNA no longer shapes its activities. I believe we were mainly responsible for that: We were not alert enough and did not stop where we should have when we still could. We should have insisted on maintaining the DNA and not surrendering to the multitudes who joined. It was very tempting to have tens of thousands wishing to join, but we paid a price that I found too dear.

So where do we go from here? *Shirley Kantor* – who was with WWP from the start and served as the *Four Mothers* coordinator at the time – showed up with plenty of experience and a very tight agenda. She kept telling me: Shiri, we need commando squads, not huge battleships. I agreed, but the beginning was so intense that we did not have time to stop and think. Michal Barak and I did nothing for 18 months but work for the movement – 24 hours a day, women came to my place or hers every Sabbath, we traveled all over the country to train women to speak at caucuses. We registered WWP as an association only after we had some 5,000 members. We really were too busy and couldn't manage to stop and think.

Members of the first group of speakers we trained started asking: Why are you making this one or that one a speaker? I told them: Listen, if it were my private company, none of you would be a speaker before you were fully trained and tested, but it is not my movement; it belongs to anyone who wants to join, and we reject no one. We never say "no" to anyone. At first, it was amazing and the women that joined felt they each had a voice, but the voices eventually became very similar – all the same voice.

I believe our concept was correct and even if we failed to attain our goal, we did attain a lot. WWP played a key role in bringing the word 'peace' back to public discourse and it is no longer an outcast. In the end, it is both a great success and a failure, but I feel it made serious waves and opened a door. When I decided to quit WWP, I did not know what I wanted to do next. I am working with Huda on joint projects of Israeli and Palestinian women. I believe that if I start something today, it would be an organization, not a movement, precisely because of the privileges. Today, I understand that if I want a Russian-speaking woman to coordinate our activities in Petah Tikva, for example, I want to pay her half a salary and not ask her to hold two jobs and then volunteer. If I started a new organization today, I would build it differently so as to allow populations that are kept outside peace activities to take part. I hate to admit it, but I believe that the peace camp kept large segments of the Israeli population away from their activities, and we all pay a price for that. I am speaking of immigrants from Russia and Ethiopia, young people, residents of development towns, and Arabs. There is certainly room and respect for Arabs in the peace movements, but what about those who don't go? I am looking for people who hear WWP and say, I am not going. This is what I care about and where my attention is, and I keep discovering amazing things there every time, so I don't know if it will be more or less institutionalized, or part of something that already exists.

Meanwhile, I am working on my doctorate thesis on, in general terms, gender and conflict management/resolution. I examine narratives of women from Ofakim to study how the conflict shapes their daily experiences, and I learn things I was not aware of. For example, the gaps between groups of immigrants from Arab countries. I interviewed a family that emigrated from Egypt, and the woman there told me about the deportation, how she was deported from Egypt, where her life was good. To this day, she only watches television programs in Arabic, and told me: "When we came to Israel, we did not speak the language." I said: "But you do speak Hebrew"; she said: "Not Moroccan Hebrew; everyone spoke Moroccan." She told me that in the *Sinai War* of 1956, her husband served as a police officer. They went to tour Gaza and she found an identification card strewn on the street and saw that it belonged to her neighbor from Alexandria. She went to the police station and it turned out that her neighbor had fought in the war and was a prisoner-of-war, held there in custody. They let her talk to him. The description of the discourse fascinated me: you have friendship and closeness, but you also fought against us, and also expelled us.

At the same time, I hear stories from Moroccan immigrants about how they had to flee because the Moroccans did not want them to leave and threatened to harm them if they tried. And I see amazing examples of the fact that security has nothing to do with tanks or rockets. The way they describe things, security means economic security, employment security, looking to the future – do we have a future here or not? Their perception of what makes up security is very different from the mainstream view. Tanks have no power in their stories, and yet – where does the state spend its resources?

SOCIAL ENTREPRENEURSHIP

What does it mean to be a social entrepreneur? First, it means saying "yes" to opportunities, without fear. Many of the things I did just happened. If there is a tip or quality associated with entrepreneurship – promoting peace or other things – it is knowing how to spot opportunities and saying "yes." I believe we all encounter very many opportunities, but most of us say "no" to them. My ability to say "yes" – at least in my experience and life story – changed my life.

The other thing is connections, connections, connections. When I was a child and people asked me, "What would you take to a desert island?" I'd always say: "people." "What do you mean, people?" They asked. I said: "People draw pictures, make music, write books – people. Get me people and I'd have everything and need nothing else." My girlfriends would get annoyed, asking: "Why do we have to be friends of your friends?" Thinking about where things connect, or how to connect things, makes you realize that connections are power. That's where knowledge is. That's the multiplier. After all, how much can I do alone? Even if I never sleep, there's only so much I can do. The ability to make the connections and form collaborations is the true ability to do significant things.

On the personal level, I always want to know the origins of my activities and the source of my authority to act. When I sat in women's circles and we held rounds of introduction, women would say their name and add, "mother of ..." I was a mother myself and it never occurred to me to mention that in the circles. It does not define my identity. I believe that I don't mention my motherhood first because I want to be true to myself. I was an activist long before I became a mother, and if I had not had children, my activism would remain at the same level. Motherhood did not create my activism. I believe that it could, but it was never like that for me. I am certainly familiar with the power of motherhood to motivate action, but I wish to remain honest and maintain the alternative. Women's activism does not have to follow from motherhood. I do things not for the sake of my children or because I don't want my son to serve in the army. No. I believe the conflict could and should be resolved, but not because of my children, regardless of my children. I don't mean to rule out women who are really motivated by motherhood, but I want to keep other alternatives.

The same holds for my brother, Ram. I was an activist before he was killed. I loathed the attempt to change my status into Captain Ram Levinas' sister. Of course, he was wonderful and amazing and loved, and I miss him every day, but I am certainly not defined by him. I could not stand the honor bestowed upon me and the way his death became an elevator that took me up to the fifth floor of honor in Israeli society. I could not stand the fact that when I spoke against the occupation, some said: "You are a woman, so you know nothing and shut up"; and as soon as I said that I was a bereaved sister, they would say: "Well, OK. She lost a brother. She paid the price." If I had to lose a brother to earn the right to speak up, then I have no right to speak. I have nothing but respect for the Bereaved Families Forum. I even worked with the women there professionally, but there was no way I could turn Ram's death into something political. It felt like a sin and, as a feminist, I felt it was pulling the rug from under my own feet. This is why I conceal my motherhood and bereavement. They are not the sources of authority in my social activism.

AGAINST ALL ODDS

One very important question in the context of my social activism is: "How can we go on, against all odds?" I believe that as an activist and peace entrepreneur, I have to ask myself this question, and if there's one thing I believe I should pass on, it is this answer. I do what I do because I believe it should be done, not because of the impact it may have or for the sake of my own success; and not because I did not succeed; and not because when I succeed, this and that will happen. I just have to do that! I believe that I am committed to having the changes in my life and in my surroundings as valuable as possible. I want them to better my society. If I succeed, great, and if I don't, that's just the way it is, but I don't have the privilege of not doing it. I know that leftist women are often depressed by the way things are, and I say that for me, my activity is like a candle. I am holding up a candle. It may seem very small here, but if there is someone standing up on the hill there, that candle could show him the way home. I don't know where the light from my small candle travels or who sees it. All I know is that my job is to hold that candle up and hope for the best.

10. A life of peace is not whole: peace is not whole – it is broken

Yakir Englander
Interviewed by Tammy Rubel-Lifschitz

Yakir and I met when we both studied for our doctorate degree, partaking in the Harry and Sylvia *Hoffman Leadership and Responsibility Program* at the Hebrew University of Jerusalem. All the students in this program engaged in social activity, and met biweekly to hear lectures and participate in discussions about various social issues. I remember Yakir as a person of silent and intriguing presence. He did not say much, but when he did speak, his words were meaningful, profound, and poetic.

I knew he used to be ultra-Orthodox and a founder of an impressive peace and religion enterprise named Kids4Peace, but I did not know him personally. When the opportunity to interview him for this book presented itself, I was delighted to hear his unique life story. The interview was very open and meaningful for me, even though it was held while he was in the United States and I was in Israel, over a computer screen, and though we are very different in terms of gender, religion, and lifestyle.

HOME: BETWEEN ULTRA-ORTHODOXY AND MODERNITY

I was born to a modern Hassidic home, a term that is familiar inside the Ultra-Orthodox jargon. I grew up in the *Vizhnitz Hassidic Court*, which comprises farmers and landlords, and is known for its simplicity, naiveté, and great warmth. My father was born in Romania during the *Holocaust*, but in a region that was not occupied by Nazis but by the Romanian government. Thus, Jews suffered relatively less there. My grandfather worked on labor camps but was never sent to a concentration camp. My father arrived in Israel when he was still young and was educated in a poor neighborhood of *Bnei Brak*. When he wanted to praise someone, he would say "*a sheyne yid*" – which literally means "a beautiful Jew," but actually means that this Jew is naïve in the good sense of the word. The *Rebbe*, *Admor*, the master and teacher of our Bnei Brak Vizhnitz community, lived in our city, and I remember mainly warmth, physical warmth, and many long walks on Sabbath from home to the Rebbe's court, while Dad recounted Hassidic tales. I remember the pleasant physical sensation of the crowded bodies during prayer or while watching Hassidic events of song and storytelling, known as Tish. To this day, storytelling is one of my favorite tools for getting to know people – hug and tell.

Unlike Dad, Mom hailed from the Polish Hassidic dynasty of Aleksander, which took pride in its members' sharp minds. The entire community and their Rebbe perished in Auschwitz. Her father, who survived, became a wealthy man in Belgium and, in his last years in Paris, served as a Rebbe who engaged in practical Kabbalah. My grandparents lost their firstborn, family, and community in Auschwitz, which created a complicated existence, characterized by silence and lack of human touch. Growing up in Belgium, my mother was raised by a very wise man in a post-Holocaust society that simultaneously experienced wealth, lack of contact, and silence over the years of war. Mom spoke with me more about her childhood and shared how non-Jewish maids actually raised her and her friends and even took them to church on Sundays. In Belgium, reading secular literature and going to the movies was not a rarity in the Hassidic world. Then, from a silver-spoon life, she came to Bnei Brak, a city of Torah and modest living, of spiritual aesthetics and struggles against Western culture. Both my parents came from Hassidic homes – Dad gave me a love of Hassidism, and Mom endowed me with a desire for modernity and the sharp sense of rebellion of Polish Hassidim.

Our home was an isolated conservatory in Bnei Brak. I played the violin, for example, while some of my brothers played the piano, violin, and cello. We read secular books such as *The Three Musketeers* and Israeli children's books by *Dvora Omer*, but not *Hasamba*, because Mom was averse to Israel's Sabra culture that was foreign to her. I was not familiar with Israel's secular world, except for very few people, but I was familiar with Beethoven and Mozart. Like other ultra-Orthodox (Haredi) children, we studied at ultra-Orthodox institutions that provided us with the confusing non-Zionist ideology of objecting to practical materiality in the spirit of "the hands are the hands of Esau" and, while holding Israel Defense Forces (IDF) soldiers in high esteem, resenting the kibbutz, Tel Aviv, and materialism.

MY TEENS: YEARS OF STRUGGLE

At 13, I joined the grown-ups' world. In the ultra-Orthodox community, there is this passage from childhood, which is dominated by mothers, to a masculine-yeshiva world. My parents sent me to a very special yeshiva – to *Rabbi Amiel's Yeshiva*. This ultra-Orthodox yeshiva was one of only two

Torah schools that included two-and-a-half daily hours of 'secular studies,' like language and mathematics. Dad, who studied there too, agreed even though he knew how difficult it was. This particular yeshiva is known for its graduates – some of the sharpest minds in the community: several heads of ultra-Orthodox yeshivas and figures that all Israelis know, such as the late attorney and counsel to prime minister *Benjamin Netanyahu*, Jacob Weinroth, as well as *Yigal Amir*, who assassinated prime minister *Yitzhak Rabin*. The yeshiva is known for being tough to the point of mentally abusing young students. Like my friends, I too spent five complicated years there. I am fully aware of the consequences of these years and work on healing the wounds, including through community work. Those five years at the yeshiva and until I left the ultra-Orthodox world at the age of 22 were a period of struggle with life.

Luckily, it was not a Hassidic but an ultra-Orthodox Lithuanian yeshiva, so I could always find some refuge in Hassidism, my safe space. For me, Dad's Hassidism was a warm and loving place when compared with the cerebral, ultra-Orthodox Lithuanian world, which I perceived as one-dimensional and associated with the Talmud's tort law and abuse.

I suffered in those years, which impacted on my body. I was always in bodily pain while struggling and attempting to hold on to life. Today I believe that my body consented to bear mental pain to help me survive the yeshiva. Furthermore, my body wanted to live, which was expressed in auto-sexuality, pleasuring myself. At the time, I believed it was a sin, but today I know that sexuality was my hold on life. And so, transgression and passion, sin and gratitude towards my body coexisted in confusion inside me.

When I turned 14, parts of me started rebelling against the ultra-Orthodox world. For example, I started secretly listening to secular radio stations, even though I was told they existed in an impure space. *Aviv Geffen* is one of the people to whom I am grateful for his music, which had an impact during that period. A classmate played Geffen's music for me, and though I did not understand every nuance of the lyrics, not to mention their context, something in it spoke to me – he demanded life. I realized then I was not the only one struggling where there was no room for talk of hardship. For me and many others in the ultra-Orthodox community, he and Ayn Rand, whose books found their way into the world of yeshivas, created a language.

As noted, I started struggling for my own voice early on. I dreamt of becoming a physician. At 14, I made a deal with my parents that when on holiday from the yeshiva, the period called *bein hazmanim*, I would volunteer at the Laniado Hospital of the *Sanz Hassidic Court*. That was my way of getting acquainted with the non-Haredi world. Though Hassidim owned it, like any hospital, Laniado employed secular doctors and nurses, and some of them were Arabs. Thus I got to meet with the non-Haredi world. While on holiday, I'd rise at 6 AM and take the bus to *Netanya*. Being an ultra-Orthodox hospital, they did not know what to do with a 14 year old, so they assigned me with feeding people who needed nursing in the internal wards. Thus death and I became friends early on as I sat with people until they died, fed them, and prayed with and next to them. When I turned 15, I worked at the hospice with dying cancer patients, but at 16, the staff must have realized that I knew how to help medical teams, so they gave me janitorial duties. Through this, I was exposed to naked human bodies, albeit sick ones. It was interesting for a young man to learn about the naked body through illness, through the eyes of those who suffer but must let us touch them. I had plenty of physical contact with men and women. I encountered the naked bodies of women who were ashamed of their old, ill, and broken shapes. Since I was a Haredi boy, coming from a world of theological questions, this naturally interested me even then: How to observe a sick body? What does it mean to look?

I struggled hard mentally in those days because between holidays, most of the year actually, I suffered at the yeshiva. I worked to save my soul, not to die inside, while maintaining direct contact with the broken world in hospitals and wanting that to be part of my life's voyage.

At 19, I completed five years of study at the Amiel Yeshiva and moved to a Jerusalem yeshiva, which in our dialect is known as 'a big yeshiva' where lads stay until they marry. At the time, I was a Vizhnitz Hassid, but also a fan of Aviv Geffen. I knew I was an ultra-Orthodox man, but I was certain I wanted to serve in the army. That is, I knew for sure that I would not find my place in Haredi life, though Hassidic lore is still my favorite. It was introduced to me through stories about generations of gentle and sensitive righteous men, and through Hassidic prayer, song, and dance. Of course, there is God, who has always been Hassidic for me and who has always been part of every moment of my life. "I have placed the Lord always before me" is a verse that became my tangible reality for many years, up until my 30s, when God became something different for me, but I'm getting ahead of myself.

At the time, my only outlet was to start going on matchmaking dates, but I soon realized that I had nothing to talk about with young ultra-Orthodox women. The system was attempting to get us married so that we officially remained 'inside' the Haredi world forever. At the time, I did study in an ultra-Orthodox yeshiva, but already I was looking sideways at other worlds. That is, I completed my secular matriculation duties during my time at the yeshiva rather quietly, and I also attended weekly sessions at a *Zionist yeshiva* in a settlement, where I was exposed to different and exciting theologies and Judaism. I studied the writings of *Rabbi Kook*, Zionism, and Kabbalah. I learned that our connection with the land is no less important than Halakah, the Jewish law, and cerebral Talmudic debates. At the time, it was all theory and no practice because I did not know anything about nature, but the seeds were sown. I stayed in the Haredi world for another three years until I mustered enough courage to leave and join the IDF at the age of 22. I did not rebel against God when I made that choice. I just wanted to preserve His image as I wanted to believe God wanted to be.

MILITARY SERVICE: A NON-ULTRA-ORTHODOX HAREDI

When I joined the IDF at 22, I only wanted some peace and quiet around me as I tried to create a life for myself outside the Haredi space. That choice obligated three years of full military service, which in itself was a rebellion against the ultra-Orthodox, for which one pays dearly in the social realm.

In the army, I attempted to get to know myself, the non-ultra-Orthodox world, and to survive. I now understand it was a period of great confusion as I was hurting because I had offended my family by leaving their world. At some level, I lost my family and had to reestablish ties with it while, very slowly, recreating myself. Suddenly, I did not look like a Haredi. I served with the IDF and had no idea who I was. I was in a cultural vacuum, but also incredibly curious about anything I encountered. That was before virtual space had been created, so I did not know others who had left the Haredi world or the *Hillel Association – the Right to Choose*, a fantastic group that helps people who leave religion. I was a Haredi soldier, looking for God in a world without language.

During my *army service* I also had my first encounters with women, and through them I realized that I really was a Haredi man – my body could not respond to touch. I had a Haredi mind, and a body that did not know how to act. With time, I found several women who adopted me, so my view of the non-Haredi, Western world was formed while living among women. For example, I learned about the world of Western men through their eyes.

I also remember how little I knew of the State of Israel. In the army, I traveled between locations that I had never seen before. I did not know the state or its Arab 'enemy.' I remember myself hitchhiking with my M16 while, in my mind, every Arab who drove by wanted to eliminate me. At the same time, I did not even know where I was.

Luckily, I met this amazing religious-Zionist man in the army who I still feel was a little like an angel sent to me from heaven. He and his family adopted me. Thanks to them, in the army and after ending my tour, I got to know Israeli life. When we had nights off duty, he used to take me to a *secular yeshiva*, and suddenly I discovered things such as secular philosophy or a literary genre named poetry. I remember the first time they let me read a poem by *Rachel the Poetess*. I was shocked. I did not even know that a thing such as poetry existed. The secular people I met were of the highest quality. I realized that there were beautiful people who were relaxed and calm, walking, and breathing in this world without struggling with the *Sitra Achra* (Satan) all the time. I could not grasp the fact that people could go easily through life. After all, we the ultra-Orthodox are always engaged in struggle. We struggle to save the world from Satan because our role is to amend the world.

UNIVERSITY YEARS: INSIGHTS ABOUT PEACE AND CONFLICT

After I had completed my military service, I joined that friend at the Hebrew University of Jerusalem. I started my love affair with philosophy that is now a decade old, and I thank him for it. There, I studied psychology and Jewish thought. Next, I had my first significant other, a girl who taught me that life was complicated and that she was bisexual. I was like, what's that? What a fantastic idea! Women can be with women. All at once, I understood the men from the yeshiva, who had to deal with hardships during their matchmaking period because they had to spend time with women, not men. Some of them would talk to me, using broken language because none of us truly knew what homosexuality was. I remember telling them, "What you feel is God," as if I had words I could not explain. Suddenly, along came this girl and put everything in order: some people are homosexuals, lesbians, bisexuals, and so on and on. So we raised each other – she, a secular woman with humanistic ethics from *Haifa*, with a nose-ring and painted hair; and I, a nice Jewish boy from Bnei Brak. We studied philosophy together, and thanks to her I also took courses in feminism. It was a fascinating time for me. I discovered issues such as gender, essentialism, and cultural impact. I told myself: you are not a real man because Israeli men grow up as macho men while I was raised as a Haredi, where, to no small extent, masculinity is feminine. I used to ask myself what I wanted to be, a man or a woman. I knew I did not desire men, only women, but I felt like I didn't belong to the Israeli masculine world. Luckily, I summoned some courage and decided to join a transgender group in Jerusalem. Arriving for my first meeting, I told them: "I am no transgender. I don't know what that is. I know, however, that like you, I am not 'normal' and I want to be with you." It was a special group, with a psychotherapist who accompanied us with great sensitivity. They let me join them, and I am thankful to this day for the right to be present in their sensitivity and their courageous struggles.

That was an exciting time for me, yet other significant events were happening. Those were the years of the Second *Intifada*.

Now, an important piece of information about me: As soon as I completed my three-year service term, the army asked if I would volunteer with the Disaster Victim Identification Unit as a reservist. Assuming that post was a very serious decision for me, and I am still searching for ways of coping with its consequences. I took an army course and then started studying at the Hebrew University. Halfway through my first month, a terror attack was perpetrated at the *Mount Scopus* Campus Mensa. I was in the adjacent library, and soon afterwards I was on-site, giving first aid and later identifying bodies of international students.

As the Second Intifada advanced, life introduced me to some of the worst terror attacks. I found myself collecting body parts. This changed and traumatized me long before I found words to describe it. I was suddenly exposed to the horrors of the Israeli-Palestinian conflict. Collecting pieces of mutilated bodies is disgusting, sacred work – yes, both. I remember entering scorched buses even before the first ambulance arrived, hearing the screams of the living. I administered first aid, and then I was left with the corpses.

I remember a voice inside me saying: "Yakir, these men who blew themselves up are very religious. You, too, are very religious. Go talk to them!" It is further necessary to remember that I was not raised on the Zionist narrative that all Israelis know, so in a way, I found it easier to understand Palestinians: After all, on some level, they are anti-Zionist like the ultra-Orthodox. Unlike other students, I did not live the differences that are so obvious to the Israeli society (true or not) – such as the difference between 1948 and 1967. My Haredi narrative was that secular people who did not believe in the Bible and Judaism decided, because of anti-Semitism, to return to this place, which the Bible – in which they did not believe – speaks of, and build a state here. Only they forgot to explain that to the locals and, at the same time, they ridiculed every Biblical and Halakhic condition upon which residing in the Holy Land was meaningful. Somehow, that fit the questions Palestinians posed: Stop playing between 48 and 67, why did you even come here? These are fundamental questions, and, as noted, I did not have the Zionist narrative then.

KIDS4PEACE

I started attending peace encounters at the Hebrew University. I met very secular people from both sides who were very angry at both religions, blaming the fanatics on the other side for every problem in the Middle East. I looked like one of those fanatics, but though I donned a yarmulke, I had an earring too. Still, I could not understand why they were all so critical of religion when I loved religion so much.

One day, a good friend called me and said: "Yakir, there is a group of religious Muslim, Christian, and Jewish children who need to travel to the United States, and they need someone Jewish to accompany them. Feel like flying to the States?" I've never been there, nor did I ever speak with religious Palestinians, so I immediately said "Very much," mainly because I knew that this was not an Israeli-Palestinian thing, but a Muslim, Christian, and Jewish encounter, which appealed to me. That is how I got to know Kids4Peace, a program created some 18 months before I joined it. It started with 12 children led by an American who I believed was a Christian. His tall and thin figure was what we recognized as foreign or, in Haredi lingo, *a goy* [gentile]. That was Dr. Henry Ralph Carse, who had lived in Israel and Palestine for 40 years since he was 18 when he fell in love with the land, the desert, the place where history repeats itself over and over. He experienced Jerusalem during the Second Intifada and started thinking of ways he could take children away from it, if only for a few weeks, just to breathe and deal with their trauma. Having been raised on deep Christian spirituality and feeling a connection with the desert, where the *fathers and mothers of the desert* lived, he knew that while religion was his tool for peace, it was also part of the problem and, thus, part of the solution. He decided to use religion as a tool for a dialogue of faiths in this region, where people need faith to keep pursuing peace and dialogue.

I flew with them to the USA and underwent a significant change on camp. Suddenly, there I was: on an American summer camp, in the middle of the south Georgia wilderness, and the people I felt most associated with were the Christian and Muslim counselors – both Palestinians – and the American clergy that accompanied us. They were priests who served as community youth leaders. Some were LGBTQ, and their proximity to God only helped them open up to others. Quite suddenly, I was in a place where I did not worry about exploding buses. The calm camp and powerful nature engulfed me, making me realize just how deep was the trauma we all carried, and how deep the military and the Haredi ways of thinking were still embedded in me. I feared the great outdoors because I did not know it. Haredi people rarely spend time in nature. Indeed, the founder of Hassidism roamed the wild, but Jews generally fear it, feeling that *shul* is their safe home. I knew nature mainly from the army as the place where I must carry a weapon. Suddenly, I was in the great outdoors of the Deep South and felt alienated from it, but from myself too. Questions started emerging: Is living without wars possible? Will my life still have meaning if I do not have to continually try to create a *tikkun* for war or the ultra-Orthodox world? Can I simply 'be'? The seeds of the fruit that would appear a decade later were sown there.

When we returned to Jerusalem, I met Henry, and I remember telling him: "It was lovely, but farewell. I am not here to take a dozen kids on holiday, but if you want to do it properly, I'd like to do it with you." Henry's answer was affirmative, and so we started a 10-year journey that changed every year because the more we aged, the more we dared to address the roots of the conflict and the ways it appeared on the streets.

Palestinian and Israeli women joined our organization in its second year. In the early years, I believed that we should all volunteer and receive only a small stipend just to prove that we were there for Kids4Peace. Henry led the program for several years, and when he left Jerusalem to go back to the USA, in 2008, the group asked me to manage what was by then an official association.

In those years, we needed to establish trust in the Palestinian and Jewish streets of Jerusalem. We needed to convince parents to send their 12-year-old children to summer camps and meetings. That required that we all become part of the Jerusalem streets, with all their diversity of perspectives. As we progressed, we wanted to see children of all walks of society among us, not only those who spoke perfect English and had Anglo-Saxon parents. We wanted the street level itself. Every such choice – to bring in children who spoke no or merely broken English, children from families who found it complicated to explain to friends and family why they chose to send their children to Kids4Peace – every such step required hard work by the staff behind the scenes. It necessitated hours upon hours of sharing our lives to create trust and a deep understanding of the various parties. That included meetings with principals at schools and illegal trips to villages outside *Ramallah, Bethlehem,* and refugee camps. All of that time was spent on forming trust, trust, and more trust. Then children started coming, and we started growing in depth and width. Luckily for me, I had Henry to take me with him for the first time, as we crossed on foot the barriers between Israeli Jerusalem and the villages on the outside. He taught us how to live between the walls, in a no man's land, where not many dare to live.

Slowly, we became an association. Here, the Hoffman Leadership and Responsibility Program at the Hebrew University of Jerusalem helped me a great deal. They connected me with *Shatil*, who took us by the hand, offered consultations with Amalya (Oliver) and Avner (De Shalit) (then the co-heads of the Hoffman program), and gave me a scholarship that helped me focus on my doctorate and peacemaking. Amalya was like a mother to me in this process of personal growth in the Hoffman program.

Before I turned 30, I had no personal life, rarely dated, and worked on my academic and non-academic fields of study in which I learned to speak Israeli and Palestinian. The first field was my BA, MA, and doctorate, and I succeeded in them thanks to the sensible teachers who accompanied me. The Hebrew University was a home for me, and I spent more time there than anywhere else. As a former Haredi, I was privileged to attend the Hebrew University. In this respect, the university helped me grow up, mainly thanks to the Hoffman Leadership Program, which was a space of personal and community studies for me. Amalya Oliver and Avner de-Shalit groomed me, and I cannot express enough how grateful I am for the scholarship I was given. At the same time, I studied education at the Kerem Institute and had the honor of being at home at the *Hartman Institute* as well. At the Hartman Institute, I met a different kind of Judaism. Institute founder David Hartman showed me a lot of love and raised me on pluralistic Judaism. I wrote my doctorate thesis under the supervision of *Orit Kamir* and *Avinoam Rosenak*, two advisers who invested in me ceaselessly. I worked with other scholars as well, such as *Avi Sagi*, who established a department for hermeneutics and cultural studies and asked me to write a book with him. Jonathan (Yoni) Garb connected me with the world of the Orient and gave me the courage to return to the mysticism I had known since childhood. I am privileged to have teachers who groom me to this day.

During this period, between the ages of 30 and 35, I was also very active with Kids4Peace, which grew and evolved. I learned to speak Palestinian and Israeli. After all, my Hebrew was Haredi. I learned more and more narratives because, in Kids4Peace, we had children from Russian homes, religious-Zionist settlements, traditional families, Sephardim, and of course secular homes – and I learned to speak their languages. The team and I learned to speak the Palestinian languages of Muslims from *Beit Safafa* and of Muslim villages across the *Green Line*. We studied the cultural language of Christians in Jerusalem – Catholics, Anglican, and Armenian – their inner struggles and narratives. We experienced *1948* and the War of Independence, and now I understand it, the Holocaust, and the *Nakba*. I do not compare or choose. The team's and my role is to breathe the various, conflicting types of life, and to allow them to spend time together because, otherwise, we would not be able to lead the organization.

In Jerusalem, Kids4Peace evolved mainly as a women-led organization – women found independent and leading positions there. We learned to breathe in the feminist struggles of the women who grow with and next to us in Kids4Peace, their ideas and values. I have learned that up until several years ago, wearing a *hijab* was a feminist act, and now I study why it is changing today.

Every step of the organization required making choices, and we did not always know what was right. We simply tried things. For example, because we wanted children and youths that didn't speak English to join us, we chose not to run our program in English as a common language. Rather, we decided it would be conducted in Hebrew and Arabic, with translations, teaching the children to listen patiently. The US summer camps, where our kids met American youths, were conducted in English. In the early years, all we had was the summer camp and meetings that preceded it. As the program gained success, its graduates started complaining that we were taking them back to life in Jerusalem, where they did not have the space to digest everything that happened to them on camp and in the program. "How can you just dump me in an Israeli school where everyone yells 'Death to the Arabs!' after I spent a summer with Kids4Peace. What am I supposed to do with that?" Thus, though she had no preparation, one of our instructors, Naomi Sullum Rouach, took it upon herself to create an annual program without funds or plans, but with a big heart and great courage.

Thanks to those years and the relentless staff, Kids4Peace today is different. It is a youth movement. We started with 12 children in a summer camp, and today we have a six-year program that engages some 300 youths of various ages. It grew so much, I believe, because its leadership was local right from the start and deeply connected with the street level. Whenever we encountered a problem we did not know how to handle, I would tell the team: "Every problem we have in the organization reflects a problem of the conflict for us. Once we find a solution to this problem, we could use it as a model for living together."

Today I can cite studies of youth encounters that were held in Bosnia, Serbia, South Africa, and Ireland seven years later, which show that change does not appear after partaking in a peace program for a year or two, but only after intensive three–four-year programs. These studies cannot be ignored, which is why Kids4Peace is a youth movement: Children join when they are in sixth grade and stay until they graduate from high school. That's plenty. This means that we could engage many more kids, but we prefer to invest in smaller groups of kids and their families for six years. We believe in that, Kids4Peace is a Jerusalem-based youth movement because we want to see change on the ground. Our staff see that schools change, and principals and teachers say that when their students attend Kids4Peace, the discourse between students at school changes. This, for us, is proof that we are making a difference on the ground. So Kids4Peace operates in Jerusalem and is an interfaith program. That means that we do not work with traditional political concepts, we are not Israelis and Palestinians, but a Muslim-Jewish-Christian organization. This is important because Israeli-Palestinian meetings are attended by a particular population segment that already belongs to the left-wing camp. Alternatively, we at Kids4Peace have always dreamt that it could be attended by kids from Jewish-religious families who wear their tassels hanging outside their trousers and girls that wear hijabs. Does this bring extreme rightists? Of course not, but settler families send their children to us because they too want peace. Not all of them, but not everyone in Tel Aviv is pro-peace either. Still, there are enough people who wish for change and a better future for their children. They want their children not to grow up hating others or viewing the entire other side as enemies if no peace agreement is made. This is precisely why we in Kids4Peace do not speak of the future, but only about the present. A question every child in the organization asks is: "How do I choose to behave today, and am I doing that more ethically?" That is: "How can I change my school, my class, my family, and mainly myself?" We are not talking about the future nor political solutions of one or two states. I have this saying that I came up with when we visited the White House: "When heads of states get together, they eventually need to present their political plan to the people. Then, they must not only ask whether their plan is good or not, but whether their nation will accept it." It is my role to make sure that Jerusalem is ready to accept any plan that allows for life with dignity.

We speak much about religion, understanding that though it is not the whole problem, it is part of the problem. By nature, religion is not logical but requires a leap of faith. It requires that we look at reality, in which many do not experience the mystery – whereas faith is the choice to believe that mystery exists, and live by that belief. This is precisely why religion carries considerable potential for both violence and peace. Violence emerges when, in the name of that illogical faith, people might perpetuate the worst of crimes and justify them too. At the same time, believers must also believe in the chance of peace when reality screams that there is no realistic chance for peace. Religious people pray daily for something that is not yet there. I remember that we held meetings even during the harshest times in Jerusalem when members of other political organizations held no meetings because times were too sensitive. Speaking at a staff meeting, one of our directors asked: "What will we do in our meetings when the street is on fire?" Another member answered: "We will just gather the children and the parents, and pray." In difficult times, we in the organization pray for faith in humankind, in us, believing we can change reality and be together here even when our brothers and cousins are fighting each other out there.

Now, because we deal with religion, we feel it is essential that we not only discuss it in theory but shine our faith into daily, practical things. In Kids4Peace, we work at being honest and try to avoid big words. In our first year at summer camp, we sang: "We can see that peace is coming." Two years later, youths from our movement came to us and asked, why did you lie to us? So we are cautious. We work with children who are innocent and have not yet experienced what adults have. I have seen scorched corpses. Other adults have suffered humiliation. So as adults, we are very pragmatic and should not use the children's innocence and naiveté as tools that serve our purposes. At the same time, I believe that our faith lets us see how joining us now will change, in five years, the kids and the schools from which they are coming. This is peace for me – not agreements between prime ministers, but the change that will take place in that school.

I genuinely admire this organization because it understands that it is impossible to make peace as long as the organization leaders do not know how peace is made. I am humbled by and sincerely thank the leaders I have had the privilege to work with, some of whom are still active.

There are some things that Kids4Peace has not done in the past because we were not ready. I could not do them, and I believe it is beautiful that we had to grow up first to organize correctly, with our unique sensitivities, including in gender and political terms. For example, the fact is that for many years, a woman who is also a priest has served as our president. It was no accident as the organization knew exactly what that meant. The fact that she is a priest is of enormous significance for the Christian Palestinians, for the Jewish and Muslim populations of Jerusalem, and for the Americans we work with. Our chief executive officer (CEO) is Fr. Josh Thomas – a gay American priest. I believe that the fact that our CEO is openly gay and the Palestinians and the Jews like him as he is and invite him to their homes is an outstanding success. The fact that since 2012 we have had professional managers, one Palestinian and one Israeli, shows our success, too: Rebbeca and Muhammad collaborate, proving to the community that change is possible.

To me, the most important thing has been staying in touch with the ground level. Peace cannot be made above the ground, away from the street. One of the greatest gifts I have been given in life is the fact that, from a relatively early age, I knew deep inside that the mysteries of the world are much greater than what is known, and that I profoundly don't know what is right. I was raised as a Haredi who believed he knew the world but discovered I did not. I was raised as a Jew and realized I didn't know. Lack of knowledge might lead to anarchy, but it can also be a great gift: On the one hand, you don't know; on the other, you never stop trying to heal, with humility and attention. The unknowing forces us to remember that what we believe to be peace work might possibly be wrong, that doing it might cause more harm than good. At the same time, I believe I am trying wholeheartedly.

Let me tell you an anecdote that I remember from Kids4Peace's first years. We threw a *Ramadan* party. It was September, and the children had just returned from summer camp. One Israeli parent was an army officer. He showed up for the party, held in the middle of a Palestinian village, wearing a uniform and carrying his M16. The fact was that the Palestinian parents did not tell him to leave, and he could not leave his gun in the car, could he? So carrying it with him at a Ramadan party, did he insult the other parents, or was he making a significant correction? No one knows. This world is mad, but when you are motivated by love and know it, you can step outside the boundaries of reality and do complicated things.

FROM DIALOGUE TO ACTION

In 2012, I received my doctorate and started a post-doc. I moved for three years, all by myself, to Chicago and Boston. Suddenly I was lonely, knew no one, and was without the conflict that had me meet dozens every week, and no one on the street saw me as an ultra-Orthodox man. I lacked a narrative. At the same time, I was engulfed in silence, which made me shed another layer off, and so I discovered that the image of God I had believed in simply faded away. Deeply, I lost the God who had been with me all my life. I cannot explain that, but the figure that had accompanied me for years, to which I had prayed, and in which I had believed existed though I had never met it – just died. I guess my maturation stage ended, so the image of God that had worked for me for 35 years simply ceased to exist. It was the worst crisis I had ever experienced. For the first time, I did not want to be. Thanks to my psychotherapist – and I say it most candidly – I did not take a road with no return. At the same time, God's death – and I cannot stress enough the importance of the crisis – helped me know myself in an even more straightforward way as a human being who is part of the entire universe. I mean, not just saying the words, but feeling that fully.

In Chicago, I lost the Hassidic narrative upon which I was raised. I mean, it has turned into yet another layer in me but is no longer the main thing that determines my current choices. In Chicago, I realized that I wanted to be a human being, simply, not in any sophisticated way. Gradually, I met with the mystery of life. I learned that one can walk this world with nothing but questions and a desire for answers, yet without an answer. This enabled me to experience the secret of life in the most banal places, by looking in the mirror, at others, at nature. Every person – when you observe them and their breath – is a secret that even he or she doesn't understand.

In those years, I found my passion for being a human being, to purge myself and be clean and simple. You need to understand that when I left for the USA, it was the first time I had left the conflict in which I was involved to my bones. Suddenly, I decided I wanted to be a human being and find my place in this world in the simplest way possible. I started hearing about remarkable teachers. We never heard of them in Israel, where we mainly heard of persons such as the Dalai Lama, but not about the dozens of righteous men and women who live in our world and teach how to touch life. It did not happen in a day or even a year. It is a process that started in 2012, and I hope it will continue until I die.

My post-doc led to another year at Harvard, where I learned about *Marshall B. Rosenberg* and the life and works of Martin Luther King. I met rabbis of various currents who try to understand the meaning of Judaism for our generation, as well as priests and imams who attempt to do the same for their religions. From them, I learned to shed layers while at the same time honing in on my peace work. I understood what I wanted and what I did not want to do. I understood that peace work as it was conducted until then in Israel and Palestine was of a very particular kind, and that I was ready and willing to do some different peace work. In those three years, I served as Kids4Peace vice president, which allowed me to hold in-depth dialogues with Muslim, Jewish, and Christian communities in the USA, discuss the [Middle East] conflict, and learn about the place it takes in the American narrative. Our CEO Josh Thomas was an amazing *Havruta* for this growth and many of the gifts I got in these years happened in dialogue with him and with other members of the Kids4Peace board members. During my third year, I was fortunate enough to meet Annika, and we fell in love, but I'd rather not talk about her. All I can say is that not a day goes by in which I am not grateful for the miracle of being intimate with Annika.

Then, I returned to Jerusalem. It was my choice because I wanted to offer a different kind of peace, and to see if it would have a purchase in the Jerusalem streets. In the USA, I realized that a dialogue between rivals might turn into a tool that allowed both parties to talk, but also might *not* change reality. I mean, if Israelis believe that partaking in dialogues with Palestinians or having Palestinian friends is enough, it might make them feel good enough about themselves, so they do not need to change reality or the status quo of the conflict. Clearly, when a person conducts a dialogue with an 'enemy,' that in itself could change their disposition towards life. At the same time, the reality of life does not change, and the parties keep hurting each other.

When I returned from my post-doc, the Kids4Peace team and I underwent an in-depth maturation process. We realized that maintaining organizations and dialogue was not enough. We needed things done. Upon my return to Jerusalem, I was fortunate enough to manage an experimental program in Kids4Peace, designed for young men and women aged 25–30. We named that experimental project From Dialogue to Action, met on rooftops and in monasteries in the Old City of Jerusalem, and trained in acting as 'peace people' who operate on the streets, and in what to do if anyone tried to harm us. Each time, we chose a different location. Among other spaces, we chose Palestinian buses in Jerusalem. Very few people know that, but there are two transportation systems in Jerusalem: One for the Israelis, and one for the Palestinians. We chose the Palestinian bus lines because there are no Israeli soldiers there, and we wanted to interact with the Palestinians where they ruled. We boarded those buses together, Israelis and Palestinians, and started speaking with Palestinian people on the buses. Now, working on those buses on the Old City streets was dangerous for us. We practically were in the hands of 'the other side' as there were no Israeli soldiers to protect us. This took place in 2015, the peak of the so-called Knives Intifada, so we knew something might happen to us. We held Hanukkah (A Jewish holiday) events in *Damascus Gate*. The army and the police were informed. Once, a police intelligence officer warned: "Yakir, one of your people will be stabbed, you know." They realized, however, that we did not mean to antagonize anyone, but meant to show that Jerusalem is all of ours in every way. We wanted to demonstrate to both parties that we must live differently. The From Dialogue to Action project created many things, including much pain to its participants, because we felt that we pushed too hard. We felt that our young participants were paying too dearly, including persecution on the Palestinian side. The Palestinian Authority feared they might form a new Palestinian leadership and started abusing them. Nevertheless, though we chose to close the project after 15 months, its very existence changed Kids4Peace because the teenagers wanted to follow those young men and women, and our entire staff had a change of heart and went from dialogue to action. Every sixth grader wanted to change his or her class, which turned Kids4Peace from a dialogue-oriented program into an action-oriented organization.

The program was formed as a year-long trial, and after 15 months, the organization management (including myself) felt that the street was not ready for it. I prayed a lot and held serious and poignant discussions with leaders on both sides, which made me realize that I was pushing something that the street could not tolerate. When we realized that, I remembered that the Talmud says: "As I was rewarded for preaching, I am rewarded for quitting." The decision to discontinue the From Dialogue to Action project was one of the simplest choices I had made. I want to believe that it had to do with the fact that the fracture I felt inside me had already fused, which is why I was tender with myself and thus with the street. I realized that an internal change is a complicated and lengthy process that requires patience. At the same time, the realization that the peace work I was conducting in my journey did not work in Jerusalem made it clear to me that just as I tried and failed to live in the ultra-Orthodox world, which I chose to leave with some pain but also with love and without frustration, I needed to leave Jerusalem, too. I decided to leave my beloved city and start a new chapter in my life, with Annika in the USA. Thus ended 15 years of military service and peace work, with great love, but also knowing that the next chapter of my life began elsewhere.

Henry and I had been inseparable ever since we established Kids4Peace. He was my mentor in the mystical sense. Today, he is almost 70 and went back to his father's land in Vermont, USA. He was raised in monasteries as a religious Catholic, and I owe him so much because he raised me and still does. He taught me so much about life, about accepting the beauty hidden inside me, and gave me tools I did not have. Thanks to him, I spent some time in a Catholic monastery for the first time and have since been trying to do that every year. He taught me how to live in nature, how to speak with trees, how to feel whole with the broken parts inside me. He understood me, just as he understood the DNA of many of us in Israel and Palestine, and still does. Thanks to him, I currently try not to identify with reference groups. When they ask me where I am from, I say Jerusalem. I am 'Yakir,' which is complicated, yet it is simple for me. I love the Zionist narrative and other Israeli narratives that I learned from those hundreds of youths and their family members. At the same time, I also love the Palestinian narrative and Sufi Islamic mysticism. During the two years I lived in New York City, I attended Sufi prayers every Thursday and went each Friday evening to a Hassidic synagogue near my house in Brooklyn. For me, this was simple and uncomplicated. I currently work on enriching the languages of life I want to use. I engage in contact through dance and karate.

I spent two years in a community of dancers in Brooklyn, and sexuality issues still touch my most tender and gentle spaces of life. I was lucky enough to marry a woman who grew in nature, so with her, with Henry, and years of psychotherapy, which is no less important, I make the ever so simple connection with life even deeper.

SOCIAL PEACE AND PERSONAL PEACE

There are two types of peace, political and interpersonal. They run alongside each other, almost touching, but they are different, and each is important. Interpersonal peace requires that every man and woman among us make sure that we live in dignity. I believe that nothing justifies harming others' dignity, and thus nothing could justify hurting Israelis or Palestinians. When Palestinian children see their fathers humiliated at an IDF roadblock, it harms dignity. When Israeli children see their father fearing for his life and running to hide in a bomb shelter because missiles are fired from Gaza, it harms dignity. We may understand that roadblocks are necessary (without even going into security issues), but that does not mean we should man those roadblocks with 18-years-old soldiers who are dead scared and would rather be home with their mother, or with their girlfriend on the beach. Such soldiers have a hard time observing others' dignity when they deal with thousands of Palestinians who have work problems and a very complicated daily life. Dignity is a daily issue in our region. Both the Israeli and Palestinian societies need to decide how they minimize harming dignity. These issues are all interconnected, but their resolution does not depend on the political solution of the conflict.

At the same time, a political solution is needed because political definitions and their consequences are important for both populations. I fully understand that having experienced the Holocaust and generations of anti-Semitic attacks, the Jewish people must maintain its security independently and cannot give this up. I feel it in my bones because it is in my DNA. I must have a state for the Jews. At the same time, the other side too needs to be acknowledged politically to end the narrative of harm and provide a sense of independence.

I believe that preventing harm to dignity is daily peace work, and no one is exempt from it. It is valid for Jerusalem, Israel, and Palestine. It is true everywhere in the world. Yet, it is hard to impose political peace on communities, and it is currently impossible for both the Israeli and the Palestinian street. Thus, communities may choose to live without political solutions.

I choose to believe that life brought me to this world to serve as a bridge between worlds and cultures. Life has given me gifts of which I am often not aware. I think of the journey that my Haredi family and I made together, and I admire their ability to open up and accommodate me, and the fact that I never stopped trying to be in dialogue with each one of them and to share our lives.

I choose to believe that we should speak about a 'life of peace' and not about peace agreements. Kids4Peace did not address the future but spoke of the present. A life of peace is what happens to individuals within their bodies – primarily the ability to accommodate ourselves as we are. A life of peace is not whole. Peace is not whole at all. It is broken. In our *Kaddish* prayer, we say, "He who makes peace in His heavens," as even God must create peace in the sky – not in the past, but every day and every hour.

11. I am me because Arik was Arik

Yitzhak Frankenthal
Interviewed by Einat Walter

Coming from a bereaved family – I lost my brother Boaz in the bloody War of Lebanon of 1982 – I was raised in a home where emotions were rarely uttered. How can anyone expect people who built a kibbutz in the Negev under constant *Fedayeen* attacks to speak of feelings? Dad was among the founders of Kibbutz Sde Boker, Mom arrived on the kibbutz as a soldier-teacher, and I was the kibbutz's second child. And yes, I got to meet Ben Gurion.

In the present – carrying the wound, the emptiness of no-brother, no Boaz – and being a peace seeker, I encountered the Parents Circle Families Forum (PCFF). I attended a few meetings and quit – I am too individualistic. When I was asked to contribute to this book, I was greatly honored, and right away, I knew that I wanted to interview the founder, though I did not know who he was. I started asking around and found he was Yitzhak Frankenthal. I sure can move things, but he was hard to find. I pulled some strings, tried harder, and found myself sitting in his unique and beautiful Jerusalem home. We had good chemistry right from the start and spent some five and a half hours together. He was interested in me, and it was very natural for me to share my story. During the interview, I felt like I had found a lost brother, not a replacement. I asked, I listened, we laughed, I cried too. I had the honor of meeting Yitzhak Frankenthal, a humanist who religiously implements his motto: "To achieve the possible, we must attempt the impossible again and again" (Hermann Hesse). As an evolving person, I could identify with this motto. We also shared the grief. Aware of the difference between losing a child and losing a sibling, and as one who does not speak of her pain, I interviewed the first person who promoted peace politics in the name of grief and dedicated his life to making peace. Which of those allowed two strangers like us to be relatively open?

When the meeting ended, we were both elated. It was a kind of voyage that we each embarked on separately and then weaved together in time, beyond present and future – a time of peace? Inshallah.

A WASTED CHILDHOOD

I was raised in *Bnei Brak*, which was then very different from its current shape. Some of the population was religious, national-religious or ultra-Orthodox Zionists. In terms of political orientation, many were Zionist and religious, like the Hapoel HaMizrahi Movement. Yet there were also many seculars. I can't even recognize the place today. My family belonged to Poalei Agudat Yisrael – somewhere between the ultra-Orthodox Agudat Yisrael and the religious-Zionist HaMizrahi. My father donned a black yarmulke, but was a knitted-yarmulke man in his heart. We, his children, all wore knitted yarmulkes, the boys went to the army, and the girls did national service.

I was always into giving and love of humankind, but my parents could not handle me. When I was in second grade in Bnei Brak, we were tested on four verses from the Bible, and their interpretation by *Rashi*, and I got an F. The teacher summoned my dad and said: "Look, your son did the test and cited interpretations by *Maimonides*, *Rashbam*, and *Ibn Ezra*, but nothing from Rashi. That is why he failed." As a result, I took two slaps in the face from Dad. Usually, when I came home from school with a letter of complaint, I had to shove a towel down my trousers so that Dad's belt did not hurt my behind. They did not know how to deal with me. Then they decided to check and see what the problem with this crazy kid was. I was subjected to what was known as an IQ test at the time and scored very high. My parents were at a loss with the result, so they decided to stick to their path and make me study their way, not mine. It all failed totally, which is why I say I had a wasted childhood. Still, I do not hold it against my parents, they did not know how to deal with me.

I am an entrepreneur by nature. I was graded 'gifted' in entrepreneurship tests I had. My military service, where they gave me free rein, was my golden era. I arrived in Sharm el-Sheikh in the Sinai desert. My commander was a *Holocaust* survivor, and so was his wife, who suffered much abuse. He spent most of his time in Tel Aviv, not on base, so I was the de facto unit commander. Some 18 months later, I moved with him to El Arish in the *Gaza Strip*. They had all kinds of pilot training facilities, and I developed various time-saving methods so that instead of training for two months, they needed two–three weeks. I had my way of doing things and I got results. The army wanted me to stay on as a career soldier and made me countless promises, but Dad wanted me to start managing our family's ice-cream factory, called Snowcrest. So I completed my *army service* but did not begin as a manager. I started at the bottom, cleaning toilets and sewage pipes. I was very close to Dad, but he did not know how to behave with me. One day, after I came up with a blue popsicle, Dad exploded: "Why on earth did you produce a blue popsicle? It is not normal!" I said: "Dad, it is going to be a hit with children" – and it was!

Later, after I made some changes to a production and freezing system that was built for a 150–180 ton factory, we started producing more than 1,000 tons and had to relocate the plant. We built a new factory in Petah Tikva's Kiryat Arye Industrial Zone that we later sold to *Tnuva*. Their chief executive officer insisted that I become the CEO of the new plant. We argued about the factory's profitability: I wanted to show that Snowcrest was a separate and lucrative unit, while he rightfully saw it as part of Tnuva as a whole. He understood me and even brought his men along to watch me, a 31-year-old little me, running a directorate meeting. Still, he was right too. I had to resign three times before he said: "Yitzhak, I can't do it anymore." That was the end of the road for me, and I moved on to some private ventures. We settled in *Moshav Gimzo* in 1978 and I started raising geese. I developed new methods in goose husbandry and made incredible profits until struggles with the Ministry of Agriculture made it unprofitable.

WHEN ARIK DID NOT COME HOME

I got married for the first time in 1974, as soon as the *Yom Kippur War* ended. Arik, my eldest, was born a year later. He made me a father. His brother Hananel, may he live a long and prosperous life, was born two years later. We moved to Gimzo when Arik was four. I made them a two-acre garden with a swimming pool and everything. We got divorced in 1981, and Arik and Hananel stayed with me. Believing the children must keep in touch with their mother and her parents in England, I made sure they did. After the 1982 *Operation Peace for the Galilee*, I married Hani, a war widow whose late husband was an Armored Corps battalion commander and whose sister lived on our moshav. She had a five-year-old girl and a one-year-old boy when she was widowed, and three years later, we had our son, my little one. When he was 15, we divorced. My divorcees and me are terrific friends to this day.

Arik joined the army and, some 100 days into his service, he did not come home one day. My wife Hani went crazy: "Why is he not back yet? He was supposed to be home." I was in Eilat then, working, when she called and frantically said: "Arik has not returned." I said: "What's the problem? He must have gone to see a friend. Why are you hysterical?" She replied: "No. Something happened. Arik is serious and responsible enough to let me know if he was not coming, and if he did not – something must have happened." I said: "You are just hysterical." The next morning, she woke me up at 6 am and cried: "Yitzhak, something has happened. Arik never called." Later I learned that she had called *Dan (Danny) Yatom*, then Yitzhak Rabin's military secretary, and told him: "Start a kidnapped-soldier procedure! Arik is missing." She pressured him and the Israel Defense Forces (IDF) chief of personnel, calling them every other hour. They answered her at first, but then stopped and she could not understand what was going on, feeling like a nag.

I returned home from Eilat at around 6 pm that evening. Soon, a taxi arrived and from it emerged a delegation of *angels of destruction*. My wife fainted as soon as she saw them, reliving her first husband's death in Lebanon in 1982. They walked up to me and said: "We regret to tell you that Arik has been killed." As it turned out, at the entrance to our house – some 60 meters from the road – there already were several dozen Gimzo residents who knew that Arik was dead. Two of them – my brother-in-law and another man – had been taken to identify the body. The only one who didn't know was me. A young man from the moshav came over, asking, "What is going on? Where is Arik?" and I said: "I don't know where he is. I am waiting for his return." As soon as he left, some 16–17-year-old girl called: "Is it true that Arik was murdered?" I said, "What are you talking about?" and hung up on her. Next, my wife's sister came over and said: "Prepare for the worst." I said: "If you know something, tell me. If you don't, shut up!" Her husband told her that he had identified Arik's body, and about an hour later came that delegation of angels of destruction and gave me the news.

Then I remembered what *Rabbi Akiva* said: "May I worship the Lord Almighty when my soul departs," and I said the traditional Jewish blessing: "Blessed be the True Judge. God has given and God has taken. May God's name be forever blessed." In those moments, I felt totally connected with the Almighty. It was a moment of indescribable connection. Naturally, dozens and hundreds of friends soon came to sit with us. They erected a tent in the garden, between the porch and the pool, and we sat there with friends until 3:30 am. That night, my wife Hani and I were alone in our bedroom when she started throwing pillows to the ceiling and cursing God for killing Arik after killing her first husband and after she had raised Arik for 12 years. I told her: "Listen, I want us to agree on three things tonight, and it is important that we reach these agreements tonight. First, we do not settle scores with God. We do not know what God's considerations were and we keep no score. Second, we thank God for having Arik's funeral in some six hours. Some parents do not even know where their sons are buried, but we will have Arik's grave. Third, we will be a sensible, not a bereaved family, because our children should not lose their brother and their parents too." She agreed only with the third thing. When the *Shiv'a* ended, we held a memorial service, and upon our return home, I turned on the television and told the children: "Sit down, watch some TV, come back to life." That has been my motto ever since. I don't even tell people when we hold our annual memorials for Arik because I want people to live their lives. I only need 10 men to attend so that I have a *minyan* and say the *Kaddish*. Beyond that, never mind.

Several weeks after Arik had been killed, I decided I would dedicate my life to two issues. One, creating an Israeli-Jewish ethos for the second millennium because it pained me to see what was happening in the Jewish Nation and the Israeli public. And two, make peace with the Islamic world. I know that I would fail with the former if I did not resolve the latter – which meant that I must first address the issue of peace and, after it was attained, I could dedicate my time to the first issue because many Israelis, mainly the religious, have lost the basic set of values concerning loving all humans – including the Palestinians, who were created in His image – and are willing to kill and sacrifice their children for Greater Israel, having totally lost their moral and humane path. That approach of many of the Zionist-religious and ultra-Orthodox Jews has resulted in a rift between the Jews of Israel and the Diaspora. If we attain peace, this alone will help eliminate that alienation amongst brethren.

FIRST TO SPEAK UP FOR PEACE AND RECONCILIATION

Already in 1993, a year before he was killed, Arik told me there was a religious-Zionist movement named *Oz veShalom – Netivot Shalom*, saying: "Dad, that movement fits you like a glove." I said: "You know what? Send me some material. I'll read it and see." Indeed, I joined the movement. After Arik died, movement members came to me: "Look," they said, "Arik was a member, but tragedy happened. We would like you to serve as the movement's secretary-general." I said I had a condition: I wanted general elections to be held; if the movement members elected me, I would serve, and if not, then I wouldn't. I was elected unanimously and headed the movement. At the time, that religious-Zionist movement comprised 350 members. Having done things my way, we grew to 3,000–3,500 members within 12 to 18 months. The movement's chairman *Moshe Halbertal* – a good heart-and-soul friend of mine – gave me free rein. "Do as you see fit. I trust you," he said, and when I made mistakes, he was never brutal about them. He would say: "Listen, I believe this is best done this way and that." When we analyzed things and I realized he was right, I made the necessary corrections and changes; and when I felt he was wrong, we argued and he would say, "OK, just go on as you feel," even if he did not agree with me. This is how the movement evolved.

When the Shiv'a ended, I wrote to then prime minister *Yitzhak Rabin*, foreign minister *Shimon Peres*, and IDF chief of staff *Ehud Barak*. Rabin came for a visit with cabinet secretary *Eitan Haber* and Danny Yatom, then the prime minister's military secretary. We had excellent chemistry and have been very close ever since. Several days later, Ehud Barak came to our house and we had unique chemistry too.

One day in 1994, I heard on the radio that bereaved parents were demon-strating outside Rabin's office, demanding that all negotiations with the *Palestinian Liberation Organization* be terminated because that produced terrorism – as if there were no terror attacks during *Menachem Begin*'s and Yitzhak Shamir's terms and it had all started after Rabin began talking to the Palestinians. I called Eitan Haber and said: "Please tell Yitzhak that they do not represent me," and he said: "Why don't you tell him yourself?" I arrived at the Prime Minister's Office an hour later, asked him for a list of all terror victims ever since Menachem Begin had been in power, and told him: "I will find a group of 10–15 bereaved parents who will support you as prime minister in your efforts to attain peace." Rabin looked at me and said: "If you find another one or two, it would be a miracle." At the time, all bereaved parents kept silent. I was the first to speak up for peace and reconciliation. I told him: "Look, Yitzhak, if I fail to find at least 10 or 15 people like me, it would mean I am weird, and you don't need weird people to back you up." He replied: "You are not weird. You just see things differently than most." I asked for a list of terror victims dating back to Menachem Begin's time in power, but was turned down since it might violate people's right to privacy.

At the time, I served as secretary-general of Oz veShalom – Netivot Shalom. I took a student and we went to the Beit Ariella Library, where we spent every day of three months examining newspaper microfiches. It was very hard. We actually got sick and had to stop every 10 or 15 minutes, but we compiled a full list of terror victims between 1977, when Menachem Begin had come to power, and 1994. We uploaded this information neatly onto a computer and found 422 families of terror victims. We sent letters to 350 of them. The remaining 72 families either bluntly spoke against any progress, like those demonstrators, or it was too soon after disaster had struck for me to send them such letters. Writing to everybody else, I mentioned each family name and their son or daughter who were killed and how it happened. I wrote that I too had lost a son some five months before, and I suggested forming a group and together supporting the establishment of a Palestinian state and the prime minister's efforts to attain peace. Some 100 letters came back with "address unknown" stamps. We were true detectives who even checked where funeral processions started to find family addresses, but it was only natural for people to change addresses. Two responses were nasty, but 44 agreed with me. That's how I started PCFF with parents of terror victims. The army called, asking how I had got that list. I told them I had found the information in the library, and they were astonished that I had come up with that technique to collect data.

The first meeting of the bereaved group members I organized was held in late 1994. I told them that I would like to go to Gaza and the *West Bank* to meet with bereaved Palestinian parents and see if they too were interested in peace and reconciliation, or was it just us, Israelis, who lost children and still wanted peace while the Palestinians did not care. They told me: "Go. We are behind you." That is how I started visiting Gaza. I went there some 200 times and toured the West Bank countless times while working for Oz veShalom – Netivot Shalom. I also organized a meeting between Rabin and the movement members in the Agron Guest House in Jerusalem. Since then, whenever anyone is regrettably killed in a terror attack, I have been to speak with the bereaved family. Some said they wanted to join, while others said it was not for them. I managed the PCFF through Oz veShalom – Netivot Shalom for some two years until in 1997–1998, we decided to establish an association and I was appointed as its CEO. The committee supported me and accepted everything I said or decided. We conducted numerous activities that featured in the media. It was vital for me to show the Israeli public that if bereaved parents could reconcile and make peace with the Palestinians, everyone could and must do it too. I made sure that the Palestinians did the same.

Our movement was small, with only 44 members. The Almagor Terror Victims Association had more than 1,500 members. I realized that I needed to expand the group no matter what, so I contacted everyone who had lost a child in the army to suicide, accidents, or illness – as long as these parents could be defined as 'bereaved.' I further told them that since they had not lost a child in a terror attack or military operation, they could not represent the movement, but would be movement members. I said: "You cannot speak in the media because they will ask you what does your son's death by suicide or disease have to do with reconciliation. Regrettably, you lost a child and your pain is equivalent to ours, but what special standing do you have on the issue of reconciliation?" That is how I brought some 200 people into the movement and we went from 44 to some 250 members. Next, the new members started arguing that they wanted seats on the steering committee, that they were the majority, and they too wanted to address the media, so disputes started.

I was always flying out to Europe and the USA to raise funds for our activities: lectures in schools by bereaved parents; a presentation of coffins in Israel; a presentation of figures outside the Tel Aviv City Hall; and many more activities on the Israeli media. We also staged a display outside the United Nations Secretariat Building, filling the entire avenue across from the building with 1,050 coffins, of which 250 were wrapped in Israeli flags and 800 in Palestinian flags. Just think of what it takes to organize such an operation. I had to fly out a dozen times, often leaving in the evening and returning the next day. That presentation resonated with the international media, including the *New York Times Magazine* and thousands of articles worldwide. Regrettably, I felt like I was spending increasingly more time and energy on arguing with other members about how, what, and who should do things, restricting myself.

PARENTS CIRCLE FAMILIES FORUM: A BEACON FOR ISRAELI SOCIETY

I established PCFF to serve as a beacon for Israeli society, a ray of light that shows that we can reconcile and attain peace. Right from the start, I determined an agenda geared at convincing the Israeli public that if bereaved parents can reconcile, everybody can and should. The movement's steering committee members wanted to set other goals, which were followed by numerous debates and unnecessary tension. What I believed was a mission to end the conflict had suddenly turned into in-house squabbles. As long as they let me lead and supported my decisions, I felt great vitality and creativity, but when I was told that we had a board that made decisions that I must follow, I lost my energy and creativity. It became clear to me that we had lost our way when a member returned from abroad with a donation of several hundred dollars. I wanted the money earmarked for a particular activity, but she wanted it to pay for another. I told her: "Excuse me, but you did not go as a private person. You raised those funds as a PCFF representative, where I make the calls." That started a debate among board members and they told me: "She is right." I said: "She is? Fine. Run the PCFF without me. Here are the keys. Farewell." I went into my office, collected my things, and left. That was the end of the story. I will remain a movement member, but I no longer want to be involved in managing it.

They turned the PCFF into two things that disappointed me greatly: First, they turned it into an Israeli-Palestinian forum, which I believe is a fatal mistake. If you want to influence Israeli society, you cannot address it as an Israeli-Palestinian entity, but only as an Israeli one because when you speak as an Israeli-Palestinian entity, you are considered to be the extreme left and cannot influence the right. After all, the purpose of peace organizations is to impact on right-wingers, and if you fail to do that, you are merely cuddling your own ego and nothing else. For example, we have the *Israeli-Palestinian Memorial Day Ceremony*. This is a sexy and wonderful event in the eyes of the Israeli left. What could be more amazing, more respectable, than Israelis and Palestinians weeping together on Memorial Day? Well, the idea is correct and wonderful, but the timing was pitiful. They could hold it on the International Day of Peace. Why do it on the Memorial Day for IDF Fallen and Terror Victims? Why not respect the IDF fallen? It is our army. How are the two issues even connected? That move greatly angered the Israeli right, and Israeli society as a whole could not accept that Israelis and Palestinians marked Memorial Day together. Try to step away, momentarily, from the approach of the classic Israeli left. Are we in the same conflict? Of course we are. That is why we can do it together on International Peace Day. I used to attend these events regularly. The PCFF had a wonderful impact on the Israeli left, but that was not its purpose. The second disappointment was that PCFF members started holding joint sessions abroad. Nothing is sexier than having a bereaved Israeli mother and a bereaved Palestinian mother or a bereaved Israeli father and a bereaved Palestinian father mourning together. It is the Second Coming for people abroad, but it has no impact on Israel; and the idea was to work here, not abroad. This is why I feel that the PCFF had lost its way, straying from the path I had marked early on.

My biggest mistake was bringing in families that had nothing to do with the Israeli-Palestinian conflict, families that had lost children during their military service to traffic accidents, disease, suicide, or friendly fire. I believe now that these families cannot promote reconciliation with the Palestinians. I paid the price for this. The fact is that I am currently not a PCFF member. The PCFF is not an end, it is a means to an end, and as such, I believe it missed its goal because it cannot reach the public it should have reached to promote peace. At the same time, the PCFF is an excellent project because its byproduct is a fantastic support group that never existed before, where people help each other to channel their pain in their shared direction.

I do not believe that the PCFF feels it failed. Its members believe it is successful, winning prizes all over the world when Israelis and Palestinians appear together. This is a huge success, but does it make any difference with the extreme Israelis? The *Breaking the Silence* organization made the same mistake. They launched activities in 2009–2010 and for a long time had no money to pay salaries or for anything else. I personally funded them and made sure they had enough money for salaries. Furthermore, when Leonard Cohen gave us a grant, I asked them: "Why do you need money and why do you not receive any?" At the time, they had started fundraisers but, they said, "No one will fund our investigations." I said: "OK, we will give you $20,000 for that. We will give you what others do not." And so it was. I believed that their activities were vital because they spoke to the Israeli public. Then, they made the mistake of going abroad. I understand them – they receive their money from abroad and none in Israel. For the past 24 years, I have traveled extensively, mostly to the USA, even though flying hurts my back because I have four herniated discs. I addressed people at Harvard, Yale, Berkeley, Boca Raton, and many other universities worldwide but never besmirched Israel because I believe it is wrong. After all, we are victims just much as the Palestinians are, but the extreme left does not see it that way. They only have eyes for the Palestinians, which is a mistake, a big mistake! And doing it abroad is even worse.

When I quit the PCFF, members of the founding nucleus and close friends called to say I was crazy to leave. "You initiated and established it. You should stay and kick them out." I disagreed with this, saying I would hurt no one. They suggested that I establish a new organization to counter the PCFF, but

I refused. I am very honored by the fact that even though I left the PCFF some 15 years ago, it still exists and operates, which shows that I built it on strong foundations. I am never sorry for things I said, only for what I did not say, and I go on and say what I have to say.

"ARAFAT WOULD MAKE PEACE WITH YOU"

At the end of 1994, a few months after Arik fell, I had a coronary event. While in hospital, I received a call from Rabin's office inviting me to the Nobel Prize ceremony in Oslo. At first, I was not sure, wondering: Why Noble Peace Prize now? There is no peace or anything! Still, when I saw the onslaught of hatred against any progress on the peace issue, and particularly the hatred directed at Rabin and Peres, I decided to come along. In Oslo, I met with *Yasser Arafat* and met him after this several dozen times. Whenever I went to see him, though he knew he was talking to a religious-Zionist and I knew he was the Palestinian leader, we had an excellent rapport. One of his cabinet members once told me: "Arafat would make peace with you and we would lose because he resists you the least." We had amazing chemistry! Amazing! Now, why did I tell you this? When in 2000, Ehud Barak went to Camp David for peace talks with Arafat, I put up a tent on Rabin Square in Tel Aviv. No phones were allowed in Camp David and the only call Ehud Barak was allowed to make was to my tent, and I made sure it was held on open speaker and broadcast on Israeli radio.

I met Arafat on the Thursday before, and he told me: "I will go to Camp David, but I must have sovereignty on Temple Mount. You may have the Jewish Quarter and the Western Wall, but I must have Temple Mount and to resolve the right of return for it to refer to Palestine and not Israel." On the same day, they called me from Ehud Barak's office, saying that he wanted to and believed it was important to meet me before he went. On Friday, July 7, 2000, at 2 pm, I went to the Prime Minister's Office and repeated Arafat's remarks to Ehud Barak. I added: "I want you to know that I have spoken with *Rabbi Amital, Avi Ravitsky*, Moshe Halbertal, and *Michael Melchior* (who was a member of the Barak cabinet). They said they would be willing to stand by your side if you told them we had no choice, that we must compromise and give the Palestinians sovereignty on Temple Mount – giving them de facto what they have de jure. Arafat even told me that once he obtains sovereignty on Temple Mount, he will let us build a small synagogue on the compound, but he must have the sovereignty." I brought Ehud Barak a plastic bag in which I placed a white sheet of paper and a piece of branch from the cypress that grows on Arik's grave. "Ehud, today is July 7," I told him. "Seven years ago today, Arik was murdered. I visited his grave this morning and cut this little branch. Please, take it with you to Camp David and should a moment come when you have to give in, look at this and see the price we pay." On the next day, as Sabbath ended, friends called to say that, speaking on television on Saturday night, Ehud Barak showed what I had brought him and said that this was what he was taking to Camp David.

When the negotiations exploded, everyone blamed Arafat. The only one who wrote the truth was *Gilead Sher* in his book, *The Israeli-Palestinian Peace Negotiations 1999–2001: Within Reach.* He wrote that everything exploded over Temple Mount: Ehud Barak could not bring himself to let Arafat have sovereignty on Temple Mount. He lost his momentum and courage. Regrettably, there are a thousand and one versions whereby Ehud Barak gave him everything, but Arafat was not willing. I am not naïve or stupid, and it is hard to pull the wool over my eyes.

I had several close conversations with Arafat, who said: "Yitzhak, we need that peace much more than you do." I asked: "Why don't you do an *Altalena* as Ben Gurion did?" I did not have to explain what I meant. He answered right away: "Ben Gurion did Altalena when he had a state. When I have my state, I would not have to pull an Altalena because HAMAS will join me, and we will take care of whoever does not." I asked: "Why do you not educate your children to reconcile with Israel?" He replied: "If I taught them to make peace and reconcile with Israel while you keep up with your conduct and occupation, I'd have no soldiers." I posed him some hard questions. Two months before he passed away, I visited him for the last time and said: "I have just returned from abroad, where I talked about things I heard from you. They told me that this is how you speak in private. Would you have your guy put everything we say now on film?" He said: "Fine. Let's talk now and then eat together." We often had dinner or lunch together and he would tell me what was kosher and what was not: "You may eat this, but not that."

I interviewed Arafat and posed the toughest questions. Next, he told his camera operator: "Give Yitzhak the tape." And the man said: "What do you mean? Unedited?" Arafat said: "You don't have to edit for Yitzhak." The man said: "But we don't have a copy?" "Yitzhak will make one for us," Arafat replied. And so it was. We had that kind of relationship. Before Rosh Hashanah, he called to wish me a happy new year. I brought the videotape to Channels 1 and 2 of Israeli television and said: "Look, Arafat speaks of the right to return to the State of Palestine and about peace like they have in Europe. See for yourselves." No one was willing to watch it. After he died, they asked me for the tape and then aired short bits from it. I was involved in so many things over the years.

I FORESAW THE FUTURE

Arik fell in July. A year later, on *Memorial Day for the IDF Fallen*, ITV wished to interview me on things I had done since Arik had died, and wanted to shoot it at his grave. I told them that it was a red line for me. They shadowed me everywhere for two or three days, shot and interviewed me. I told them: "You spend hours on this interview and in the end, you will only air five–ten minutes. If you want to go with me to Arik's grave, I have one condition: Promise me that whatever I say over Arik's grave will not be edited or kept off the air." The show producer agreed. Standing at the grave, I looked right at the camera and said: "People think this is a sacred place, but it is the most impure place. There is nothing more vile than graveyards and the dead. From here, I beg the people of Israel: Do not raise your hand on a Jew because we are in a peace process. Let no Jew spill another Jew's blood." Sadly, they did not air this in the end.

The night Rabin was murdered, I spoke from the Tel Aviv stage. He hugged and kissed me, and Leah Rabin told my wife: "See how Yitzhak loves Yitzhak." I was on the committee that organized the event, together with *Shlomo Lahat (Cheech)*, *Jean Frydman*, *Dov Lautman*, *Amos Yaron*, and others. Later that night, at around 2 am, Cheech rang me up and said: "I murdered Rabin." I replied: "You gave him the best moments in life. It was not your fault. It was the responsibility of the Israeli Security Agency. Do not take this upon yourself." At 8 am, my phone rang again. It was that ITV producer, who said: "I am so sorry we did not air your remarks. You saw what was going to happen."

I foresaw the future, not exactly what would happen, but I saw a reality in which a Jew might be murdered by another. I could not name anyone, but I knew it would be peace talks-related. I went to see President Ezer Weizman and sat with rabbis and public leaders such as *Rabbi Drukman* and *Hanan Porat*. I told them that I had heard Rabbi Nahum Rabinovich, head of the *Birkat Moshe* Hesder Yeshiva in Maale Adumim, say: "If the government orders settlement evacuation, we should place landmines all around them and tell the IDF soldiers: 'Don't come any closer or you'll be killed.' If they do it anyway, their blood is on their hands because they are evil." I could not believe my ears, so I asked to see him again a week later and got it on tape, which I later played back to the Netivot Shalom board members. They were shocked.

I experienced that personally in my community. I moved to Gimzo when I was 27. As soon as I settled in, I built a synagogue there, complete with furniture, a Torah scroll, and an ark. I served as Local Committee head for a while and was one of the most popular men there. After Arik died and I started speaking about peace, I lost almost all of my friends. I still have two friends left, and another five or six people who kept good ties with me, but in secret. They did not want others to know. It came to the point that when I say Kaddish for Arik at the synagogue, two men would leave so that there would not be a *minyan* for me to pray for my son. All based on blind hatred of the political path for peace I was following.

THE PARADOXICAL WAY

On the Gimzo synagogue wall, there was a massive picture of Arafat and me so that they could all see who Frankenthal was. My youngest, a very clever and sharp boy, seemed kind of depressed when he was eight or so. He would say nothing when he came home, so I told him: "You are in pain. I can feel that on you. Share with me." He did not want to at first, but then he told me that his classmates were calling him names such as 'filthy leftist' because of me. I said to him: "Listen, son. Tomorrow, when they call you filthy leftist, tell them that you are not only a filthy leftist, but the father of all filthy leftists! Tell them: 'My mother is a filthy leftist, my grandmother is a filthy leftist, and everyone in my family is a filthy leftist. What are you going to do about this?'" He did as I suggested, and they stopped harassing him on the same day. Some two months ago, his son, who is three years and four months old, told me: "Grandpa, there is a boy in kindergarten who calls me Dumb Yotam." I said: "Look, Yotam. If he calls you dumb again, tell him: 'I am not just dumb, I am the father of all dumb people, as are my mom and dad.' This is called 'the paradoxical way.'" "What is that?" he asked. "It is an illogical way. What did that boy want? He wanted to upset you. But if you tell him that you are the father of all dumb people, what could he possibly do? His words would not upset you and it will all be over!" Last week, he told me that that boy called him dumb again, "and I told him I was the father of all dumb people, and he stopped at once." "Which way did you take?" I asked him. "The paradoxical way," said he.

Some people say that I take advantage of my grief. That is true! I did not lose Arik to an accident or disease. I lost him because there is no peace and I take advantage of my bereavement to attain peace. That shuts them up. Finito! What could they say to that? You think I take advantage of my bereavement? Sure I do, in that old paradoxical way. The most important thing is that I am entirely at peace with myself.

I SEEK MY BRETHREN: THE ESTABLISHMENT OF THE ARIK INSTITUTE

I had a talk show on the *Voice of Peace Radio*, an hour a day, five days a week, and I had to work for eight hours to prepare for each show. As part of the show, I interviewed right-wing activists. Sometimes, they would debate with leftists, but usually, I debated with them. I spoke to settlers, Yesha (Judaea, Samaria, and Gaza) people, and right-wing Parliament members, and we discussed respectfully. So much so, that *Yisrael Harel* once told me: "You are the only interviewer I enjoy talking to. I greatly appreciate and respect you even though we disagree. You let me say what is on my mind and when you counter me, you do it correctly, respectfully, and politely. We don't agree with each other, but we respect each other, and that's how things should be done." Regrettably, Israelis forgot how to debate.

I established the Arik Institute in 2005. One day, in 2009, my phone rang and a voice said in English: "Hi. My name is Robert Kory. I am the personal manager of Leonard Cohen, who is going to Israel for a peace and reconciliation concert." Being a *yeshive bucher*, I had no idea who this Leonard Cohen was, but I Googled him quickly and got an idea. Then he told me: "Look, we have conducted a thorough and deep inspection and concluded that you are the man who deserves to collect the concert proceeds. We know that you established the parents' cycle and quit it, and then established the Arik Institute. You are the man who will receive our proceeds. It is Thursday. On Sunday, Cohen performs at Radio City Music Hall in New York. A ticket will be waiting for you. Come and see him. We will talk later." I said: "I am very sorry, but I am supposed to meet a couple that is arriving from the USA, especially to see me. I can make it to New York on Monday." He called me back 10 minutes later and said: "Fine. Monday at 9 am. Soon I will send you an email with hotel information."

I arrived in the USA in the morning. We met for breakfast at 9 am and sat and talked together until 4:30 pm. I told them two things. "I want you to come to Israel for a peace and reconciliation concert. How about performing in *Ramallah*?" Leonard Cohen looked at his manager Robert and said: "If you can arrange it, I will come to Ramallah." Then I said: "It would be very nice if I received $2 million from this concert, but what will I do with the money? Two or three projects and it will all be spent, but there still would be no peace. What will we have achieved? Nothing! I suggest that we study why there is no peace. We'll set up an American fund and after we understand why there's no peace, we'll deal with that." He said: "Fine. We are with you." We sat until 4:30 pm and at 6 pm I was already back at the airport. I arrived in Ramallah the next day. That was four months before the concert, which is zero time for organizing anything. I met with a Palestinian minister who showed me the Faisal Husseini Hall, which seemed to me like an excellent venue. I called Robert and said: "I am in Ramallah now. They have a wonderful hall and we can have a concert here." "Fine," he said. "We'll arrive in Ramallah in two days, on Thursday. We will have a team to observe the location." A team of six soundmen arrived from Europe and the USA, and after they had inspected the hall, they said: "Excellent venue. Well done!" Next, the Palestinian media reported that Leonard Cohen was coming for a concert in the Palestinian Authority. Still, the *BDS* people in London pressured the Palestinians to boycott Cohen, and this is how that story ended.

In the meantime, we established the fund, and I set up more than 100 brain-storming groups on both the Israeli and the Palestinian sides to study why there was no peace. We sat with politicians, political science professors, journalists, and students, and talked with various groups. I set up a team of three young men – two of my sons and their rightist cousin – and presented them with the results of brainstorming sessions we had held, some of which they had attended. They said: "We suggest that you brand it." "Brand what?" I asked. "Peace, reconciliation, tolerance, what?" "Brand the conflict," they said. I said: "Are you mad? You want me to market the conflict?" And they said: "Listen, Dad. You think like a leftist. We have dissociated ourselves from the left and realized that if you want to change things, leave the left alone, and bring the right to the center – and there is only one way to do that: the paradoxical way. You should go even more right than they are and show them that we need the conflict, that it is in our DNA. That would make them think: 'Am I connected to that conflict? Do I really want it?'" I told them I did not like the idea and that I wanted to look into it. I then spoke to members of the fund board, Moshe Halbertal and *Ron Pundak*. They said: "Listen, we don't believe in it, but go with your instincts. We trust you."

Next, I went to see Professor *Eran Halperin*, who was then at the Herzliya Interdisciplinary Center (now at the Hebrew University), and told him: "I will make some clips that speak of associations with the conflict. Please check for reactions to them in your lab." Eran said: "Look Yitzhak, this runs contrary to the entire psychology of attitude change that we have learned for 80 years." He did not want to do that, but in the end, he said: "Fine. I'll run the test if you want me to. It is your time and your money. I don't mind, but I will eat my hat if it works." Some six weeks later, he called me and said: "I am not ashamed to admit that I should eat several hats now." In our study, we showed the clips to people who filled out questionnaires before and after watching them. We knew about their political stands. Some 59 percent of the subjects were right wing, but 30 percent of them changed their approach and now believed in ending the conflict.

I spent the next two years raising funds for my next project, which was to be held at *Giva't Shmuel*. I chose that town because some 80 percent of the residents were religious and rightists, and intended to run the project for six weeks. On the day we started, the so-called *Knives Intifada*, or the Third Intifada, broke out. The kids said, "Dad, stop this. It is the wrong time," but I said: "Sorry, this is the State of Israel and it is like that all the time. We go on." We conducted surveys before and after, with control groups and everything, and the results simply stunned us. In our Giva't Shmuel study, we divided the participants into three subgroups – center left, right, and extreme right – based on their questionnaire answers. Then we showed them clips bearing paradox-ical messages such as: "We probably need the conflict because, without it, we would be immoral," or "We probably need the conflict because, without it, we would not have the world's strongest army." Then we measured their readiness for reconciliation and voting patterns. (Incidentally, we put posters on billboards, but the municipality took them off. We sued in the district court and won; they appealed with the Supreme Court, and we won there, too.) We found that paradoxical messages improve readiness for reconciliation and that the extreme rightists made the more significant shift because their paradox was bigger. All of that was published in two articles about *paradoxical thinking and the conflict*, in the most important scientific journals in the USA. Now we knew we had an instrument with which we could influence the extremists, who were willing to forgo the conflict and choose peace.

What is the idea? When you get up in the morning, brush your teeth, wash your face, and go to the bathroom, you do that while thinking rapidly or even without thinking, almost automatically. When you go shopping for a shirt, a dress, glasses, or a car, you switch to complex thinking. When people encounter paradoxes, they turn to complex thinking; and when they are alone and unaffected by their surroundings, they are free of prejudices or stereotypes. They face a paradox and start thinking by themselves. The paradoxical way is effective with extremists. Currently, I am working on this with Professor *Dan Ariely*.

Let me tell you how I met him. It is an interesting story. Several months before at around 1 am, I heard noises coming from the house next to us, where there were two rented rooms. A woman was standing there with a little boy with side-locks and two suitcases. She told me they had rented the rooms, but could not get in. It was not the first time this had happened, and so I tried to open the door for them with a code that the landlord once gave me. But I failed. I went back home and told my wife: "There is a woman here – a divorcee or single parent – with her child outside. They flew in from South Africa and cannot enter their rooms, so let's prepare our spare room for them to sleep in." And so we did. They slept at our place, and in the morning I made them coffee, freshly squeezed orange juice, and breakfast. Then they rushed to the Western Wall for the Bar-Mitzvah of the boy's friend, which was the reason they had come to Israel. We left their suitcases on the terrace because we were out for the day, thinking that the boy would be able to climb up and get them. We returned at around 7 pm, but the suitcases were still there. An hour and a half later, they arrived with another young man. He was her driver whenever she visited Israel, and it turned out she was one of the richest women in South Africa. She owned the best-looking house in Johannesburg and every promi-nent Israeli who arrived in the city stayed at her place. She started crying when she saw Arik's picture and then said: "I want to talk with you at length. Let's make an appointment." We sat down together and I explained exactly what I was doing. She said: "Let me get you in touch with a man who I believe could greatly help you. His name is Dan Ariely." She emailed him and a connection was formed. Dan told me: "I am familiar with your project. I read the articles in the scientific journals. I feel connected to it." A week later, he invited me to speak at a meeting of 12 prominent scientists of all fields of knowledge that is held annually in Los Angeles. I went there, gave them a lecture on what I do, and have been working with Dan on this project ever since.

Dan recruited a million-dollar donor. I need $8 million to do my projects properly, but a million can get me going. I expect to duplicate the Giva't Shmuel project in southern towns. If that works, we would have a tool that could do two things: First, it would interest the right. I don't care about the left. If I succeed in changing the minds of only 10 percent self-proclaimed rightist – not 30 percent as in Giva't Shmuel – I will have done my part. Besides, I want to run the Despaired Paradox Project some two months before the elections. It will address all of those who believe they make no difference and despair, including Arabs. Should I manage to move five or six MKs from the right to the left-center bloc, it would be the end of the story. Bibi, as in *Benjamin Netanyahu*, may remain prime minister, as far as I am concerned. I'd like that. I believe it would be wonderful to have Bibi as prime minister while his cabinet urges him to make peace. Bibi can do that just like *Ariel Sharon* could push Israel out of Gaza and do other texts too. We need a reconciliation process for both nations, which will take time. But once a peace accord is signed, I could travel to Gaza just as I can fly to Egypt or go to Jordan in an hour. This is peace. There will be no love, and I am not looking for love. There is no love even among Israelis, but the parties need to accept each other.

Today, I am not as strong as I used to be, physically, I mean, not mentally. I am getting old, but I am still trying to launch this project and, once it starts, I will be working 18 hours a day. I am thinking of a huge project, but until it starts, I have plenty of free time that I use for writing. Incidentally, after Arik died, writing became my best friend. I wrote endlessly. Writing and learning – that's my therapy.

For the past 13 years, I have been writing a book I called *Pirkei Banim* (Chapters of the Sons), echoing the Talmudic Tractate of *Pirkei Avot* (Chapters of the Fathers). In the book, I discuss matters related to Judaism and peace, values, benevolence, and many other issues based on Judaism over the ages. It already contains many entries but is not done yet, and since I am not a half-done job person, I sit and study and write whenever I can. The book could serve as an important tool for understanding the roots of the conflict, advocate reconciliation, and mainly speak about the distortion of Judaism, which, in essence, is its "ways are pleasant ways, and all her paths are peace" (Proverbs 3, 17). To my chagrin, many Jews have forgotten that all of us, including the Palestinians, were created in the image of God. I am citing our sources, trying to prove that Greater Israel is far less important than living out of respect to others.

I AM ME BECAUSE ARIK WAS ARIK

Before Arik was killed, I was wild and somewhat crazy. I feared no one, but I had a kind heart. That has always been my motto. Arik, too, was a wild one, a wild beast with a golden heart. During the Shiv'a, people told me that when he was 15 and other children in his class were yelling "Death to the Arabs," he climbed on the desk and yelled: "Heil Hitler!" His friends cried: "What are you doing?" And he said: "This is how it started in Germany, with death to the Jews." Arik wrote tirelessly and I keep many poems and other texts he wrote. After the Shiv'a, they brought us two boxes with Arik's stuff, which included some two dozen books he had read during basic training. Arik had told me that in the evenings, he used to sit with Nitzan, his platoon commander who was his best friend, and discuss Tolstoy, Buber, and others.

At the funeral, Nitzan told me that it was his fault that Arik was murdered. I hugged and kissed him, and said: "Thank you on Arik's behalf. Arik loved you very much and had a friend in you even though you were his CO [commanding officer]. You only wanted what was best for him and sent him to a medical examination because he had four stress fractures. Arik wanted to keep training, and you made sure he did not sustain bodily damage for life." Arik was on his way home. He hitchhiked a ride with *Hamas* members dressed as Hassidim. When he identified them, they started fighting in the car. The Israeli security agency told me about this later. The Defense Ministry sent me a notice that his tomb would include the inscription "Fell in battle." I said: "What are you talking about? What battle? The kid was butchered!" They said: "No. Arik fought for his life. The driver took a bullet in the leg, but sadly Arik was shot four times in the head. We are going to publish a *Battle Heritage* in his name." Nitzan did not show up for the first annual memorial ceremony. Soldiers told me he was killed in Gaza a month before. I called his mother that same day and we visited Nitzan's grave.

What do I bring to my activities? Giving on the one hand and entrepreneurship on the other. I always look after others; always have. In times when money just slipped through my fingers, when I saw people in need or someone who had lost a job and made no living, I took care of them without them even knowing. I was always willing to pay for my principles and I did. My most significant fault is that I am a loner who operates solo. I hate mediocre people, but I am not a misanthrope; I only hate and have no patience for mediocracy. This is a huge flaw and I am aware of it. When I do something alone, I take it to unusual heights. Still, once other people start interfering, trying to steer me in different directions, I step aside, leave them the stage, and the whole project goes in another direction. The goal is to reach people, their hearts, and show them this is the way to go, without bragging or being just, but by presenting people with facts and reason. I always use simple words and sincerely speak my mind. Even when I sit with kings, leaders, the US vice president and US president, I always talk at eye level. I don't feel I am sitting with a president, but with a human being, always. And I always cry inside when I sit with that person – president, king, or whatever – because Arik is gone, and I sit with them not for me, but for Arik. I always say that I am me because Arik was Arik. He taught me a saying by the *Rabbi of Kotzk* that I did not know: "If I am me because I am me and you are you because you are you, then I am me and you are you; but if I am me because you are you, and you are you because I am me, then I am not me and you are not you."

Today, I am me because of Arik. I do not mean that I think about the boy every minute, but I do think of him every hour. You asked if I talk to Arik. Look, I sometimes say that if Arik wants to tell me something, let him do that. If he says nothing to me, I cannot converse with him. We will talk only when he comes over. At the same time, he is with me all the time. I know that what I do, including what we are doing right now, is Arik. He is the only son of mine who changed my status twice – first he made me a father, and then he made be a bereaved parent; two statuses – that was all Arik.

As you may have noticed, I do not have an Arik headshot around here, only full-body pictures. I have never accepted that Arik is a head. I visit bereaved parents and see they have headshots of their sons. Our neighbor took that picture of Arik in their garden the day he joined the army. I went to the studio to have it enlarged, and when this picture came out, I started crying and left the room. That is the picture I've been keeping since.

My life is divided into before and after, and I was given this 'gift' when I was 43. Usually, bereaved parents are in their 60s, but I became a bereaved parent in midlife. It is not even the middle; it is the end of the beginning of life. I met with and cared for hundreds of bereaved families. Bereavement makes people take off their masks and reveal deeper aspects. If you were a good person before, goodness comes bursting out; and if you were a piece of shit, that too bursts out. Masks fall off, leaving you naked. I have always known who I am, that I follow my truth and my head.

I feel like I failed. I brought a child to this world, and he is no longer alive – not because of some disease or accident, but because there is no peace. I am a peace fighter, not a peace entrepreneur. Peace entrepreneurship is about writing peace plans and proposals. In 1995, I published a peace plan that speaks of a Palestinian state with territorial contiguity between the West Bank and the Gaza Strip. No one else mentioned such a state before. The plan included territorial exchanges: Israel would annex some 7 percent of the West Bank territories, while creating territorial contiguity; and absorbing more than 90 percent of the settlers. In exchange, the Palestinians would receive 7 percent more in the Gaza Strip. As for Jerusalem, Arab neighborhoods would be under

Palestinian sovereignty, while the Jewish Quarter and neighborhoods would be under Israeli sovereignty. I showed it to Rabin, Peres, and Arafat, and they told me that in the end, that is how peace will look, changing a line here or there. At the time, Avi Ravnitzky told me: "This is the first time I see that peace is doable. You have proven, here on this map, that most of the settlers can be annexed to the State of Israel without starting a civil war. This is how it will be in the end." Today, I understand that drawing peace outlines is not my job. My duty today is to draw the extremists to the center so that they support the government that makes peace. This is one of the mistakes they make on the left: They keep initiating peace plans. Who are you to do that? With all due respect, you are not the government; it is the government's role.

PEACE AS REVENGE

When I write letters, I write Arik *HYD* [Hebrew acronym for "May the Lord revenge his blood"] because only God shall avenge his blood, for who knows what vengeance is? The Lord knows exactly who and why, and He will name the actual criminals whose fault it is that Arik is not alive. I blame the Israelis, not the Palestinians. People see that I write Arik HYD and ask: "What does he want? Is that a peace warrior?" They think I am out for revenge, but I want to take revenge from those who prevented peace. For me, the best revenge is peacemaking.

Most bereaved parents seek revenge, not reconciliation. They ask me: "What makes you so unique that you seek reconciliation?" Several universities around the world have studied this relatively unique phenomenon. I believe that generally speaking, the answer is the benevolence, love for humankind that I feel, that characterizes people who seek reconciliation, not revenge. At the same time, I believe I am more rational than emotional. Benevolence is affective, but I do it logically.

I thought the same when I sat Shiv'a for Arik. I lost him because of us, the Israelis. We forget that God made us all in his image, and that includes the Palestinians. To me, the Palestinians are the same as you and me. They are not beasts or animals. We failed to make peace with them. Loving humankind for me is rational, which impacts on emotions. But rationality is stronger. Peace is a technical thing. On top of it, we must do what is right – reconciliation. If I could be concise, I would not have written so much, but generally speaking, the secret is to deeply understand that there is no difference between me and the other, and if the other was not nice to me, something must have gone wrong and should be fixed. Before you can fix anything, you need first to understand that something is wrong and find ways to reconcile. Reconciliation is a critical stage on the road to peace, and the most critical stage in the reconciliation process is for each party to understand the mistakes it has made and own them.

I wish we will succeed in making peace, though I know that peace will knock me down because Arik – who talked and dreamt about peace – did not live to see it. At the same time, I have another four children and 11 grandchildren, so for them and for my beloved Nation in its homeland, for the Palestinian Nation, and for everyone else, we must attain peace.

12. Discussion: peace entrepreneurship – insights and reflections

Haneen Sameer Magadlah, Tammy Rubel-Lifschitz, Yosepha Tabib-Calif, Amalya Oliver-Lumerman, and Tammar B. Zilber

This book is a study of the lives and endeavors of 11 peace entrepreneurs – Israelis and Palestinians, women and men, religious and secular – whose efforts are geared towards promoting reconciliation, liberty, and dialogue. Each of these peace entrepreneurs' paths is unique, rooted in their personal life story, and reveals how they understand themselves and the reality within which they live. Each story echoes a singular voice of one peace entrepreneur, revealing unique strengths, pains, and actions that aim to influence the reality of the long-lasting Israeli-Palestinian conflict.

Although each story stands on its own merit, together they reflect a broader social context of the local conflict and efforts to bring peace. Here we focus on the similarities we found across these personal stories. Since this book includes only 11 stories, we do not intend to merge their accounts into a single conceptual framework or generalized theory about peace entrepreneurs. Similarly, our discussion does not intend to offer answers or solutions for the conflict, but rather to face the absence of precise answers, given the complexity of our interviewees' lives. However, we do point at recurrent themes and try to shed light on the ongoing efforts these peace entrepreneurs have made and are making to change the situation, efforts that often remain unknown despite their vast importance.

We employ Lieblich et al.'s (1998) content analysis method, which reveals recurrent themes found in the stories. The content analysis yielded six main themes: three relate to personal, familial, or social contexts that motivated the entrepreneurship actions; and three relate to the actual peace enterprises, challenges surpassed for their establishment, and success they may have had. Through our analysis, we attempt to understand the underlying conditions for the development of peace enterprises in a reality of ongoing conflict, diplomatic stalemate, and political uncertainty. We present these themes in the following pages, exemplifying them through quotations from the life stories of the peace entrepreneurs who feature in this book.

FROM PRIVATE PAIN TO SOCIETAL ACTION

Many of the peace entrepreneurs created a connection between events they experienced personally and the projects they developed. These events often took place in childhood, when the interview first revealed their activist identity, which evolved over the years and led to their later peace activities. In some cases, the peace entrepreneurs described situations in which they could not condone injustice or inequality and chose to rebel or struggle against it. In other cases, the entrepreneurs experienced some traumatic event that directly resulted from the conflict – such as the death of a person they had known or being exposed to violence, directly or indirectly. The entrepreneurs presented these events as life-defining moments that impacted their lives' trajectory. It seems that the hard feelings these incidents awoke served as motivations to work for peace, and many of them founded peace-related ventures that echoed their life stories. Below are three examples of such links that we found.

Gershon Baskin, the founder of the Israeli Palestinian Center for Research and Information (IPCRI), describes his childhood memories in the United States, of beginning to understand issues such as racism, injustice, and the struggle against war:

> As a child, I also discovered the world. When I was eight or nine, we took a trip to the southern United States, where I first witnessed American racism. Traveling through Virginia, I saw a sign in a restaurant that read: "Whites only." That was several months before discrimination was outlawed in the USA. My mother, a teacher, brought me a library book that greatly influenced me, a life-changing book, *Black Like Me*. It was written by a white journalist who injected some material into his body that turned his skin black. It describes his travels as a black man in the American South in the late 1950s and early 1960s. It was a best-seller and had a substantial impact on me. When I was 10, I was already active in the struggle against the Vietnam War and knew our local congressman, who was a prominent figure in this regard.

Baskin recalls the first time he heard of the 'Green Line' and learned of its meaning in the context of the conflict, realizing how little he had known before:

> When I returned to the USA, I worked in the movement's Zionist summer camp for Jews. I did not want to be an instructor because I needed time to process the one-year experience I had had in Israel, so I worked in the kitchen. I was the camp cook's assistant. In my room, I hung up a map of the Land of Israel – the Greater Israeli map, including the *Sinai Peninsula* and the *West Bank*, and marked the places

I'd visited with pins. One day, when I came back to my room, I discovered that someone had drawn the *Green Line* on my map.

My roommate Barak Berkowitz was the one who had drawn that Green Line. He was older than me and the founder of Choice (*Brera*), a movement established in 1975–1976 after the *Yom Kippur War*. This movement began asking questions such as: Do we really make certain decisions because we have no other choice? They concluded that there is always a choice. They were for establishing a dialogue with the Palestinians, acknowledging the PLO, and striving towards the two-state solution. These days, Berkowitz lives in San Francisco, a former Apple employee, still working in hi tech.

For me, the Green Line was a revelation. I looked at this map and saw Kibbutz Ein Harod and Highway 90, the Biqa Road, that I had taken so often. I realized then that though I'd spent a year of intensive study of the Zionist Movement, walked all over the Old City of Jerusalem, and was charmed by it, I had yet to have a single conversation with an Arab. Suddenly it hit me: There's a massive gap in my knowledge. In the following year, I started reading, covering some 100 books on the Israeli-Arab conflict, taking a few courses in university, and discussing it with other people.

Summarizing his activities with IPCRI, the main peace venture he established, Baskin has a sense of closure. He has a clear understanding of the main issues that need to be resolved by IPCRI, including the most needed expertise and a clear sense of direction:

> So this is the story. I established IPCRI and managed it for 25 years. I have mediated over 2,000 Israeli-Palestinian meetings and have overseen workgroups with experts in security, agriculture, tourism, antiquities, economy, water, and science. I have no doubts concerning how to achieve this peace. It is all known, written, thought of. Anyone who wants to, can. I don't doubt this.

A similar link between childhood experiences and peace venture is expressed by Shiri Levinas, co-founder of Women Wage Peace (WWP), as she refers to her early childhood memories, clarifying the roots of her feminist approach:

> The seeds of my involvement in the establishment of WWP were sown years ago, having to do with the development of my feminist awareness. My feminist activism started when I was a child … I was a reverse feminist, believing I was stronger and better than all of the boys. I refused all girly trappings and would not wear dresses or play with dolls. When I was six, visiting relatives from the city brought me a golden necklace. I was so insulted that right there and then, before their amazed eyes, I tossed it in the sewer [laughing]. I got into fights, joined bike races, played football … I understood intuitively how the power balance worked at a very young age and decided that if this was the game to play, I would be on the winning side.

Later in her story, when Levinas narrates what was important for her to do at that point, she finds a desired commitment, hoping to make a difference and an impact. She deliberately chooses to work with various Israeli women – including some who do not share her political views and come from diverse groups within Israeli society. She aims to act outside their comfort zone while talking about peace with the Palestinians:

> [T]hat led me to WWP. I realized that if I wanted to change things and make a difference – [raising her voice] if I wanted to make a difference! – I had to make an impact on my side, on my society. I realized I had to go back and do the work here in Israel. After all, it was very easy for me to feel comfortable with the Palestinian women, to identify with them and be empathic ... In reality, however, the most dominant parts of Israeli society, the parts that actually shape it, are precisely the things I ignored – and this is where work should be done. Then I started to form a decision: I had to stop my binational work and start working within Israeli society ... I kept working in programs for Palestinian and Israeli women, while convening meetings and groups of Israeli women. In the latter, we insisted on diversity of the groups. We did not want only leftists or Ashkenazi women to attend, making sure they included religious, rightist, old, and young women to keep everyone out of their comfort zones. In the meetings of the Israeli women, we started talking about political stands and discourse and security discourse among women, about how women view peace or what peace looks like to Israeli women.

Our third example comes from the narrative of Bassam Aramin. He was locked in an Israeli prison at 17, where he had an opportunity to learn from others, reflect on and form his life philosophy. Aramin recalls:

> I was 17 then ... I learned a lesson in jail that I would never forget: If you know your enemy, you can defeat or kill him; but if you just hate him, you are killing yourself. Honestly, if you hate someone all the time, it will only give you a heart attack. Hatred hurts no one but the hater. I seized the opportunities I had in prison and started learning Hebrew so that I could master the enemy's language and know how to kill him, destroy him, defeat him.

Although Hebrew was studied at first as 'the language of the enemy,' it also allowed Aramin to establish a dialogue with one of his Israeli-Jewish wardens. He described how this relationship encouraged him to learn more about the two sides in conflict, and consequently reshaped his perspective:

> One day, a guard who was just as tough as any noticed that I was a limping and silent man who could be nice, so he wanted to understand what I was doing in prison because I was not the terrorist type. We started arguing ... He encouraged me to learn about myself, who I was, what a Palestinian was, where we came from, and also about what Jews were, who was an Israeli, what was Zionism – so that I could argue with him better ... So I started educating myself. Like an excellent student, I began writing down specific questions for me to ask him the next time we spoke so I could convince him. We became good friends in just a few months and I started waiting for him to come on duty. He told me that he was telling his children and wife about me. We truly became personal friends and I felt like I won and convinced him that I was neither a terrorist nor a warrior or a murderer, that I was a child who became a warrior because the occupation turned me into one.

While in prison, Aramin also learned about the Holocaust, which has influenced his insights and activities since. Later on, he became involved in a few peace-related ventures where he advocated a better understanding of the other side. Although Aramin speaks in the first person, he refers to what his peace-related venture needs to do – understand the other side and become familiar with its past, history, and the way it fights in the conflict:

> Now, not everything you know about your enemy is the enemy. I realized that I must develop, learn about the Jews ... with insights I gained from it, I am seeking the most effective way to fight the conflict. I must change my reality from bad to better ... You evolve and make partnerships with the other side ... I believe that the Palestinians must be taught about the Holocaust. From their point of view, the Jews have been using the Holocaust to explain the occupation ... I then realized that it is important to educate about the Holocaust, not as a personal issue, but as a fact. On the Palestinian side, this is my mission – not for the Jews, but for my nation, for my side to be familiar with the enemy's past and history. We need to see how Jews accept their history, and how you find that Jews are very simple people. My mission was to truly understand that, first for myself and my children, and then for my society. That changed me and helped me, so I want to help them.

Having lost his daughter, Abir, who was killed by an Israeli soldier, Aramin related how this tragedy made him intensify his pro-peace activities:

> Personally, my thoughts are to promote peace ... I hate traveling, but have since traveled some 200 times, given hundreds of lectures, five–six a day sometimes. I don't know where I get the energy for it. I decided I am doing this for Abir.

Similarly, Yitzhak Frankenthal, who lost his son Arik in a terror attack and subsequently established the Parents Circle Families Forum (PCFF), describes how personal tragedy made him committed to pro-peace activities:

> I am me because Arik was Arik ... I became a bereaved parent in midlife ... I met with and cared for hundreds of bereaved families. Bereavement makes people take off their masks and reveal deeper aspects ... I have always known who I am, that I follow my truth ... I feel like I failed. I brought a child to this world, and he is no longer alive – not because of some disease or accident, but because there is no peace. I am a peace fighter.

Tragic incidents such as losing a family member or being exposed to violence, as described by the interviewees, may be analyzed and understood in several ways. Psychological literature, particularly Viktor Frankl (1970, 2011), suggests that one can deal with pain and suffering through meaningful activities. Frankl argued that the search for meaning can increase people's ability to endure hardship. He stressed that the stand a person takes when dealing with suffering may include associating personal hardship with existential issues, consequently leading one to take responsibility and act for the benefit of a greater cause, such as preventing such suffering in the future. Thus, finding meaning that transcends the personal into the existential is a way to deal with the situation despite their agony and grief. It seems that many peace entrepreneurs found meaning and order in their complex reality through their pro-peace activities. They converted their harrowing experiences into peace-seeking activities in their attempt to create a reality where such events do not recur. Recent studies indicate that acting towards other individuals' welfare or one's communities alleviates individual hardships (Vestergren et al., 2019). The assumption is that working for something greater than oneself is a fundamental human aspiration that could promote mental welfare even when facing extreme and traumatic events (Wong, 2014; Adler, 1964).

Similarly, sociological literature that originated from the narrative approach (Lieblich, 1987; Lomsky-Feder, 1995; Spector-Mersel, 2008b) seeks to define centrally significant moments that shape the subjects' lives and leave a long-lasting impact. Such events may occur in various locations and times, including marriage, divorce, or fighting in a war. In her book *Sabras Don't Age* (2008a), Spector-Mersel studied how partaking in combat action shaped her subjects' lives. Spector-Mersel collected life stories of former senior officers who had fought in the War of 1948, who were in their 70s in the interviews. She shows that they still boast about and glorify their war period – when they held important positions, had power, and were young and handsome – which delayed their aging process.

According to the narrative-constructivist approach, the officers chose specific memories and incidents they related when telling their life stories because they felt those had played a significant role in understanding their social activities later on. Aiken (2018), a British researcher and social activist, examined social activists' motivations through their biographies. He found that many described their experiences as children – in school, at home, or even in their dreams – as unforgettable and significantly affecting their activities. The peace entrepreneurs featured in this book also associated memories of early social activism with the nature of their peace projects as adults.

In summary, we found insightful links between the peace entrepreneurs' early experiences as they recalled them and the characteristics of the peace ventures they later established or joined. Those early memories and events partly explain later involvement in specific activities that aim at specific goals. Additionally, while all the peace entrepreneurs we interviewed actively benefit their communities, they view their work and the ventures they established as very personal affairs.

BEYOND THE DICHOTOMY OF VICTIMS AND AGGRESSORS

Our interviewees spoke of constructive work as an emotional and practical alternative to revenge. The wish to avenge the death or injury of a loved one often emerged in the stories. Waiving the urge to revenge was presented as a conscious choice that followed from an acknowledgment of the similarities between the two parties and the realization that revenge not only would not bring back their loved ones but would prolong and deepen hostilities and the conflict. Even while knowing the identity of the individuals who had harmed them, the peace entrepreneurs chose not to blame those persons as individuals. Instead, they highlighted the situation that made the perpetrators act the way they did. Despite their pain and loss, our interviewees stressed basic humanitarian similarities, arguing that people are often affected by their social and political environments, often becoming victims. Thus, they reject clear black-and-white dichotomies, as if they are the only victims and the other is the aggressor. Furthermore, they view individuals on both sides as nearly equal victims of the same situation, regardless of their personal activities.

Khaled Abu Awwad, whose brother Youssef was killed and who founded later on the Roots-Shorashim-Judur peace and conciliation initiative, made the following comment:

> [T]his was not only the story of Youssef and that soldier whose name I don't know. Youssef and the soldier represent the two nations. It was not personal. Youssef did not know the soldier, and the soldier did not know Youssef. They had no personal history between them or anything that would make one hate the other enough to kill him ... It was like watching a match and managing to stop yourself from seeing just your side, looking at the bigger picture, and trying to understand the situation anew. That started a new quest in my own and my family's life. I knew we had to stop this together.

The blurring of the dichotomy between victims and aggressors seems to be significant. It has helped our interviewees replace their desire for revenge with activities they perceive as beneficial and positive, wishing to change the entire situation and end the conflict between the nations. Following are some remarks by the PCFF co-founder Yitzhak Frankenthal about the 'peace revenge' concept:

> People see that I write Arik HYD and ask: "What does he want? Is that a peace warrior?" They think I am out for revenge, but I want to take revenge from those who prevented peace. For me, the best revenge is peacemaking ... To me, the Palestinians are the same as you and me. They are not beasts or animals. We failed to make peace with them. Loving humankind for me is rational, which impacts on

emotions. But rationality is stronger. Peace is a technical thing. On top of it, we must do what is right – reconciliation.

Frankenthal's words reveal a conscious effort to overcome the desire to take revenge (which he describes as emotional), advocating the rational solution of peace and reconciliation between the nations. The absence of peace is seen as a situational factor that feeds violence and harms both sides, which are described as human and quite similar. Thus, Frankenthal challenges the dichotomy between victims and aggressors, which he claims quickly leads to demonizing the other party and entertaining revenge wishes. His solution is to adopt an alternative view whereby both parties are essentially human and are victims of a situation, which must be changed. Later in his story, Frankenthal elaborates on how he translated these ideas into action. One of the first practices he introduced was holding condolence visits with Palestinian families that had lost their loved ones:

> The first meeting of the bereaved group members I organized was held in late 1994. I told them that I would like to go to Gaza and the West Bank to meet with bereaved Palestinian parents and see if they too were interested in peace and reconciliation … It was vital for me to show the Israeli public that if bereaved parents could reconcile and make peace with the Palestinians, everyone could and must do it too.

Khaled Abu Awwad recounts how his worldview changed after Frankenthal visited his home with several Israeli bereaved families to pay their respects after his brother, Youssef, was killed:

> They came, a full bus … These were Israeli families – Jews, Arabs, and Druze – and each had its story. I sat with them, listening, and could not believe my ears. So this is not only happening here! It is there too! What is going on here?! So I listened to the families and wondered: Why? Why did it happen to them? Why did it happen to us? Why is this happening at all? Before the meeting, there was that person. He was guilty and, as far as you are concerned, he should be punished and placed behind bars. And now, here, the party you have been blaming is a victim, too … These are not criminals, and we are not victims because there are victims on the side I believed was the criminal.

It appeared that the encounter with the Israeli bereaved families made Abu Awwad unsure about the 'good versus bad' dichotomy, gave rise to new questions about the reasons for the suffering on both sides, and thus connected his personal experience with the political reality.

Several peace entrepreneurs referred to the similarities between the two sides, stressing how political and social issues shape individual lives on both sides of any conflict. For example, Huda Abu Arqoub, a Hebron peace activist, describes her interest in collective traumas of both parties and other underprivileged groups worldwide as follows:

> We all suffer from trauma, whether it is trauma which emanates from the British Mandate, the Israeli occupation, or the Holocaust. I am always interested to hear the stories of marginalized people, either in Israel, in Palestine, or in other places in the world.

Perceiving the similarities between both sides to the conflict and their shared humanity may turn into partnerships. Parents Circle Family Forum, Peace Warriors, and other initiatives are based on specific resemblances between Palestinian and Israeli activists. The organizations' names accentuate the fact that there are bereaved families and warriors on both sides and that it is the connection between them that leads to peace enterprises. Other organizations are based on a broader identity that is not directly associated with the conflict. For example, Women Wage Peace builds on a general gender identification element, intending to establish a cross-national female aspiration for peace. Similarly, Kids4Peace signifies the desire to encourage children of all denominations to live in peace. Abu Arqoub describes her association with female peace activists on the Israeli side:

> Women Wage Peace is a great initiative that represents me. It encourages women to participate in political activism and combats the exclusion of the other ... Following the Oslo Accords, the establishment of the Palestinian Authority led to a great decline in the political role of women ... My main goal is to promote female political activists for change. I believe that Israeli society also needs this type of change.

Social activist Ghadeer Hani relates to how she accepted an invitation to assume a leading role at WWP. It was out of her disappointment after the introduction of the Israeli Basic Law: Israel as the Nation-State of the Jewish People, which she believes harms coexistence within Israel:

> When they were trying to pass the Nation-State Law, I stayed up until dawn to watch the news, the debates, and the modifications they were making to the law. At some point, I closed my eyes to rest them for a little. It was only a matter of seconds, and when I opened them, I saw that they had already voted for the law. I was shocked. I felt as if all that we do is for nothing ... Coexistence and joint work were over for me. Peace was not an option anymore, and regarding my Jewish colleagues, I'd do what I had to do, but nothing beyond, I was over it all. Many tried to speak with me. Others left me alone because they did not want to stress me out, but I was utterly devastated. On that same day, Women Wage Peace had a tent put up for the last day of the mothers' training program that ran that summer. The aim was to finish it with a demonstration near the presidential residence, and everyone asked me to join them to lead the group in Arabic. I ended up agreeing ... when I speak with my friend Liora who is from the *Alei Zahav* settlement. When we talk, we disagree about 90

percent of the things, but there is the other 10 percent where we agree, and I try to hold on to those 10 percent.

Yakir Englander, the founder of the Kids4Peace movement who was born and raised in an Orthodox Jewish community, explains how similarities between faiths motivated him to create a dialogue with religious Muslim communities while meeting with victims of terror attacks in Jerusalem:

> As the Second Intifada advanced, life introduced me to some of the worst terror attacks ... I was suddenly exposed to the horrors of the Israeli-Palestinian conflict ... I remember entering scorched buses even before the first ambulance arrived, hearing the screams of the living. I administered first aid, and then I was left with the corpses. I remember a voice inside me saying: "Yakir, these men who blew themselves up are very religious. You, too, are very religious. Go talk to them!"

In summary, peace entrepreneurs challenge the dichotomous divisions into victims and aggressors, good and bad, right and wrong, similar and different. According to psychological literature on processes of conflict escalation and demonization (e.g. Alon and Omer, 2006; Ben-David and Rubel-Lifschitz, 2018), these views represent a shift in the basic assumptions regarding the nature of the two sides in conflict. When destructive basic assumptions underline the perception of the conflict, the two sides are seen in homogeneous terms, as solely negative or positive, victims or aggressors, which leads to conflict escalation. When constructive basic assumptions underline the perception of the conflict, the two sides are seen as complex, heterogenous entities, composed of both good and bad elements, and of both victims and aggressors.

Consequently, similarities as well as differences are identified among the two sides, and there is more room for collaboration and dialogue. The nullification of those dichotomies helped the peace entrepreneurs discover connections with the other side and experience empathy for their pain and hardship. This shift may further effect the complex psychological experience of victimhood, which includes a need for acknowledgment of one's suffering, moral superiority, lack of empathy, and rumination over hopeful events (Gabay et al., 2020). Waiving the dichotomous distinctions between victims and perpetrators may be connected with letting go of moral superiority, and consequently the aspiration for revenge. At the same time, it calls for relinquishing the stand of weakness. Once these views are abandoned, people experience a strong sense of inner freedom that allows for going on quests that cross personal and societal boundaries within which peace initiatives are born. It appears that rejecting the dichotomies is a crucial part of creating an alternative story or giving a new meaning to the complex, harsh, and violent reality. Smashing through that binary perception seems almost necessary to envision a different future and nurture peace initiatives.

CHALLENGING PHYSICAL AND MENTAL BOUNDARIES

Many of the peace entrepreneurs who feature in this book describe how they attempted to push the boundaries of what is possible. Namely, looking for what could be done given the conflict and the complicated reality of both nations, they pushed and challenged the boundaries of each side's perception of the other. Moreover, they crossed physical, geographic, normative, and social boundaries. For example, Eliaz Cohen – poet, social worker, and co-founder of A Land for All, Two States, One Homeland – describes how he was willing to violate laws and take personal risks by visiting Bethlehem despite the existing security ban:

> We ask for no one's permission to attend. For us, this means that whenever we go there, we violate the regional commander's decree forbidding Israelis from entering the Palestinian territories, which is the civil cost we are willing to pay for future generations.

Khaled Abu Awwad describes his family's activism, crossing boundaries of gender and taking personal risks:

> My mother was a brave woman. She took part in our activities and made contacts, even reaching Yasser Arafat. My brother Jamil was like her. We used to hold conversations with Arafat even during the intifada. Once, we went to see him in *Bethlehem*. His office had a floor for receptions and another concealed floor, where there was a darkened room, with no lights or windows, a cordless phone on the desk, and a hidden staircase. We had to look around, make sure no one was there, and only then did we go upstairs. Even if the whole world came, they would not know there was someone upstairs. In that room, there was a phone to talk to Arafat ... People were more or less active, but we as a family – particularly my mother – were at the most involved end. Also, there were disputes and arguments, anger, and even dissociations, particularly among women. They used to fight each other a lot, and sometimes they would hug. There were many things, but all in all, that was the leadership – a strong and leading body of women. And those women could lead!

Yakir Englander, Kids4Peace co-founder, speaks of the personal risks he assumed to promote dialogue with Palestinian civilians:

> When I returned from my post-doc, the Kids4Peace team and I underwent an in-depth maturation process. We realized that maintaining organizations and dialogue was not enough. We needed things done... we chose Palestinian buses in Jerusalem ... boarded those buses together, Israelis and Palestinians, and started speaking with Palestinian people on the buses. Now, working on those buses on the Old City streets was dangerous for us. We practically were in the hands of 'the other side' ... Once, a police intelligence officer warned: "Yakir, one of your people will be stabbed, you know." They realized, however, that we did not mean to antagonize

anyone, but meant to show that Jerusalem is all of ours in every way. We wanted to demonstrate to both parties that we must live differently.

Pushing and crossing boundaries often required directly addressing decision makers on both sides. The peace entrepreneurs were sometimes able to do that due to their public standing and the legitimacy they gained within their communities mainly because they personally paid a price for the conflict.

Like Khaled Abu Awwad, who met with Yasser Arafat, the Palestinian leader, Frankenthal describes how he contacted Israel's senior decision makers, attempting to change policies:

> When the Shiv'a ended, I wrote to then prime minister *Yitzhak Rabin*, foreign minister *Shimon Peres*, and IDF chief of staff *Ehud Barak*. Rabin came for a visit with cabinet secretary *Eitan Haber* and [*Danny Yatom*], then the prime minister's military secretary. We had excellent chemistry ... One day in 1994, I heard on the radio that bereaved parents were demonstrating outside Rabin's office, demanding that all negotiations with the *Palestinian Liberation Organization* be terminated because that produced terrorism – as if there were no terror attacks during *Menachem Begin*'s and [*Yitzhak Shamir*'s] terms and it had all started after Rabin began talking to the Palestinians. I called Eitan Haber and said: "Please tell Yitzhak that they do not represent me," and he said: "Why don't you tell him yourself?" I arrived at the Prime Minister's Office an hour later.

Gershon Baskin, founder of IPCRI, describes how he pushed the boundaries in his attempts to communicate with the Palestinian leadership:

> It all happened because I had ties with the PLO. I had an office in East Jerusalem, across from *Damascus Gate*. I was the only Israeli there during the First Intifada. Every time I phoned a PLO office abroad from my office – I would call Tunis via the Palestinian phone service in Cyprus or the PLO ambassador in Holland – as soon as I hung up, my phone would ring. When I picked up, there was no one on the other end. It was a message for me: "We're listening. We can hear you. Be careful and cross no red lines."

Although all peace entrepreneurs practically push and cross existing boundaries, their practices seem to be related to the national and gender contexts wherein they operate. Specifically, reaching out to power figures features more in the Jewish males' stories than in the narratives of Palestinian men and of women on both sides, who described more careful and calculated conduct vis-à-vis their respective national power centers. For example, Huda Abu Arqoub, a Hebron peace activist and chairperson of the network of peace organizations in the Middle East, explained that she would rather avoid direct contact with Israeli government figures because the Palestinian Authority should represent her and the Palestinian people:

> I mainly meet ordinary citizens through my work, but I sometimes meet diplomats and Palestinian Authority representatives. I do not meet with Israeli officials because we are not ready to deal with them. The Palestinian Authority represents us and communicates with the Israeli side when needed.

Crossing and pushing boundaries seems to be part and parcel of peace activism, yet – like peace activism more generally – it is molded according to the activists' identity and requires sensitivity and adaptation to the unique circumstances, including their social positioning.

THE COST OF FOUNDING PEACE PROJECTS: SCARS, CRACKS, AND SOURCES OF STRENGTH

The peace entrepreneurs we interviewed paid a price for their activism. They described various hardships they endured from their own communities' resistance and opposition, and because they were often viewed as traitors or a threat to their societies. Some were attacked and criticized in social and traditional media. Others were excluded from circles of friends or denied interaction with the authorities. For example, Eliaz Cohen described his exposure to criticism:

> Harsh remarks were exchanged on the streets and on social media, and everything became very difficult … Some have treated me as a deserter, traitor, abandoner. It pops up now and then, certainly in extreme Facebook posts: "You love the Arabs more than you love us."

One of the harshest reactions, which made many peace entrepreneurs feel guilt and sorrow, were attacks on their children. Hadassah Froman, who promotes peace dialogue in Israeli settlements after partaking in similar efforts with her late husband Rabbi Menachem Froman, related how her husband's peace initiatives impacted their children:

> Everything became harder and harder, and he encountered a lot of resistance in the settlement and the whole world. Hardly anyone agreed with him, both in the left and the right wings. He was viewed as 'the crazy rabbi' or a traitor, or something. It was hard on the family, and our children grew up against a backdrop of 20 years of opposition to their father. They had to cope, but some of them did not and still carry the scars. It was not simple for them to watch him being humiliated at the synagogue, having stones thrown at their home, or reading abusive graffiti. When the children grew up and started hitching rides, they were asked: "Where are you from?" And they said: "Tekoa." "Aha, so this rabbi of yours is so and so." Before they got out of the car, they would say: "I'll have you know – he is my father!"

The peace entrepreneurs cite several sources of strength that help them cope with harsh criticism directed at them. Personal loss, such as bereavement, was mentioned by some peace entrepreneurs as a source of inner strength to repel criticism. Bassam Aramin, for example, said:

> Sometimes, others have a hard time accepting my way. A friend of mine once read in the paper that I was willing to be the first Palestinian who forgave his daughter's murderer for the sake of reconciliation between the two nations. He yelled at me angrily: "Did you say that? How could you? Have you no shame?" And I said: "Hush now. Take it easy … Why should I be ashamed? Come, read it again: I am willing to be the first to forgive my daughter's murderer. See? I said 'my daughter' – not *your* children. What is mine is mine and does not belong to the Palestinian nation" … I believe that people like me have no right to keep quiet. I have no right not to speak because I have no fear because the worst has already happened to me, so what do you fear more?!

It seems that bereavement can create both a deep inner commitment to take action and inner strength and immunity to social criticism. Dedication and strength enable peace entrepreneurs to work for peace, even amid hostility and opposition.

Frankenthal described how his son's death helped him face social reproach:

> If bereaved parents can reconcile, everybody can and should … Some people say that I take advantage of my grief. That is true! I did not lose Arik to an accident or disease. I lost him because there is no peace and I take advantage of my bereavement to attain peace. That shuts them up. Finito! What could they say to that? You think I take advantage of my bereavement? Sure I do.

Yet, certain peace entrepreneurs do not wish to associate their personal loss and their social activities for peace. Some of them even say they reject the social legitimacy that bereavement brings as they want to be judged by their own actions.

Shiri Levinas, a WWP co-founder, said:

> The same holds for my brother, Ram. I was an activist before he was killed. I loathed the attempt to change my status into Captain Ram Levinas' sister. Of course, he was wonderful and amazing and loved, and I miss him every day, but I am certainly not defined by him. I could not stand the honor bestowed upon me and the way his death became an elevator that took me up to the fifth floor of honor in Israeli society. I could not stand the fact that when I spoke against the occupation, some said: "You are a woman, so you know nothing and shut up"; and as soon as I said that I was a bereaved sister, they would say: "Well, OK. She lost a brother. She paid the price."

The Palestinian peace entrepreneurs refer to another source of social legitimacy that gives them strength – being held in an Israeli prison. Bassam Aramin describes how he attempted to legitimize Warriors for Peace in Palestinian society:

> The Palestinian prisoners are the warriors of the Palestinian nation, and the Palestinian society greatly respects and believes in us.

Our interviewees also paid tribute to family and community as sources of support. Eliaz Cohen, for example, stressed that the family context in which he operated was most important and described how belonging to a strong and respectable family with social and political achievements validated and helped legitimize his peace projects:

> I have been known as a reputed second-generation settler whose father established the settlement movement before Gush Emunim was even founded.

Huda Abu Arqoub describes how her family and community supported her in her persistent pro-peace efforts:

> I receive generous support from my family, neighbors, and community, as well as the Palestinian Authority. I have no fear because I do not have a hidden agenda. I do not want to become a prime minister or part of the upper-class elite. I am just an ordinary person who likes to sit with her mother at the end of the day and watch television.

Finally, another source of peace entrepreneurs' strength lies in the connection between their activities and their long-term impact on children and future generations. Ghadeer Hani, a social activist, and Standing Together management member, describes her motivations:

> For me, any child in the world is a child of mine. There is nothing I would wish for my little nephew that I would not want for any child.

AN ACTIVIST'S JOURNEY

The peace entrepreneurs whose stories appear in the book describe their long road of diverse social activities and involvement with various initiatives. Each such experience of promoting social justice and correcting wrongs makes them wonder, think, and learn. Most of them see their activism as part of their daily lives, including in small acts that may appear marginal at first, but through which they attain knowledge and skills that feature in their later activities and foster their ability to initiate, promote, and lead changes.

Amin Khalaf, the founder of the Hand in Hand bilingual school chain, described junctures in his life where he developed the will and the desire to be an activist:

> At 26, I was active on the Jewish-Arab issue, but mainly with Arab students. I was also a journalist. Then the first *intifada* started, and things became more difficult. Later, I took a group facilitator's course at *Neve Shalom*, or *Wahat al-Salam* in Arabic, where I learned how to facilitate Jewish-Arab dialogue meetings. I also met my wife there. We're both educators. After the course, I served as a grammar school teacher at Neve Shalom. It is an extraordinary school that gave me plenty of knowledge relevant to things I did later, and I became involved in education. For me, the two great things that happened during that period were that I became increasingly involved in Jewish-Arab dialogue meetings, and I started instructing teachers at the School for Peace and then worked with *Peace Child YMCA Israel*.

Shiri Levinas spoke about the time she spent in Mexico as formative years for her pro-peace activities in Israel:

> I believe Mexico was an excellent cocoon for my butterfly to spring from. The two years I spent there and things I did in Mexico actually for the first time combined gender with conflict. Being away from everything I had known or belonged to, being absolutely detached, created the potential for things I realized later, when I returned to Israel. I believe that without that period, I would not have been able to act at all.

Khaled Abu Awwad described how he formed his path after six years of action and experience:

> I decided to establish the *Al-Tariq* Movement, The Way, the Palestinian Institution for Development and Democracy. I chose that name because after six years of experience going in the direction I had been following since that meeting at our house, I had become confident that there was no other way, and that was the only way, so I simply named it The Way. I kept thinking, this is the way. We should not deviate from it left or right and must stay on its course. We did quite a lot before we established Roots.

Gershon Baskin, at the same time, related how failure in activism was a learning experience for him:

> During these years, I taught on a Jewish-Arab course for young instructors, following the example I learned in the Young Judaea youth movement. We even received a budget from the Ministry of Education, but it was a colossal flop, and I certainly did some damage. I am sure that the kids who attended the course learned to hate the other side because we did not know what we were doing. That experience taught me that goodwill is not enough. Dialogue between groups in conflict is a job for professionals and has to be studied. We should have a strategy, a methodology, and a pedagogy.

Thus, peace projects were not a starting point for our interviewees but rather were entwined with more extensive activism, viewed as an ongoing way of life. These journeys are combined with the speakers' identity and include many diverse operations. They often describe their paths as a trial-and-error process where each experience enriches and feeds the one that follows. It would seem that this process of continuous learning is entwined with daily life so that even the simplest of acts could motivate a reexamination of basic assumptions. Hadassah Froman, for example, describes how she and her husband, Rabbi Menachem Froman, changed their ideas about ownership of land after considering the meaning of a sticker:

> [W]e were invited to see the house assigned to us in Migdal Oz. On the door, there was this sticker: "The Land of Israel belongs to the Nation of Israel." As I was about to enter the house, all rejoicing and happy, Menachem told me: "Remove this. I will not enter a house that has this sticker." And I said: "What's wrong with that? We are settling the Land of Israel, are we not?" He said: "No! It should be the other way around: The Nation of Israel belongs to the Land of Israel." I remember this well because it was a mental turning point for me. I was under the influence of Rabbi Levinger, genuinely believing that the land was ours and that we were settling it because we had every right to do so, and it meant that the Arabs' right was not as real as ours. Menachem believed that we belonged (to the land of Israel), but there may be others who belonged too. Also, belonging to the land is nothing like owning the land, as if one is masculine and the other feminine. That's where he started believing that Zionism is a feminine movement. Originally, Zionism was a (feminine) movement of surrendering and dedication, not a (masculine) movement of penetration. Not a movement of occupation, but one of submission. You give in and try hard to make it yours, but you don't reject others for that purpose.

Thus, taking part in social movement activity is not seen as separate but rather as a part of the activists' daily life and experience. Roth (2016) showed in her study that such a combination of social and daily activities practically sustains the former over time. Ghadeer Hani explains that her desire for peace motivates numerous and various peace enterprises, which are inseparably intertwined with her daily life:

> Every day I wake up, I do it to make peace possible, break dogmas and stereotypes about us Palestinians, about us as Arabs, because this is how peace can become an option ... I started many different and small initiatives as well. No matter how small they might be, they have so much significance ... I rarely say no to requests to participate in such programs and initiatives, not that I have time, but I usually sleep three–four hours and sometimes even less. I sleep only because my body demands rest at some point and because I need to dream to go on and continue with what I do. Dreams fuel my efforts to make peace possible because if peace happens here, peace can happen everywhere.

Most of our interviewees are serial peace entrepreneurs. They have been involved with the initiation of multiple peace activities. Some of them realized with time that they were more radical than the organizations they had founded, and this for them was their cue to move on. Many of them related that after their organizations were institutionalized, they chose to leave them in the hands of others who could manage them and move on to further entrepreneurship.

Gershon Baskin, for example, explained why he left IPCRI, the research center he'd established:

> I was IPCRI's directorate chairman until a few months ago when I quit. Two young people run IPCRI today ... I quit because I wanted the Palestinian residents of East Jerusalem to run in the Jerusalem municipal elections, but the IPCRI team feared this ... the young people who presently run IPCRI were in disagreement over the Jerusalem issue, and I realized that I needed to step down because Jerusalem is more important to me than the organization.

Amin Khalaf explained why he quit the school chain he formed:

> I quit as Hand in Hand chairman after 14 years on the post. I felt I'd exhausted it. I wanted to grow with Hand in Hand and expand our influence and reach beyond the school, but the board and our donors were against it. Some argued that our only mission was to establish schools. Still, I believed we should go further, formulate and disseminate our knowhow and truly impact larger populations and policymakers.

In summary, it seems that peace entrepreneurs' journeys do not end after they have established an organization or launched an initiative. They promote the enterprises for as long as these match their values and dreams. Still, when innovative enterprises become too formalized or too conservative for them, they move on to the next project.

ACTIVISM IN MOTION: ON KNOWING AND THE UNKNOWN

One of the questions we raised in this book's introduction was: What gives peace entrepreneurs the strength to sustain hope and continue working for peace in a situation of political deadlock and constant violence? One of their key answers, it seems, was embracing the unknown. Many of our interviewees referred to their peace activities as ongoing learning processes. Instead of long-term plans, they highlighted daily activities. This preset time orientation allowed them to persevere even if the end of the process remained unknown. They believed that only time would judge their efforts. Many of them spoke of the existential experience of knowing and unknowing, relating how the unknown actually sparked an interest and a sense of adventure in them.

Yakir Englander directly distinguishes between the two:

> One of the greatest gifts I have been given in life is the fact that, from a relatively early age, I knew deep inside that the mysteries of the world are much greater than what is known, and that I profoundly don't know what is right. I was raised as a Haredi who believed he knew the world but discovered I did not. I was raised as a Jew and realized I didn't know. Lack of knowledge might lead to anarchy, but it can also be a great gift: On the one hand, you don't know; on the other, you never stop trying to heal, with humility and attention. The unknowing forces us to remember that what we believe to be peace work might possibly be wrong, that doing it might cause more harm than good. At the same time, I believe I am trying wholeheartedly.

Hadassah Froman spoke of her inner dialogue about combining action with unknowing:

> I said to myself that life brings you whatever you need, so I don't need a house or any other assets. I decided to believe that whatever I needed would be available, and I should not worry about it. That became my rule in life.

Indeed, our interviewees acknowledged that the very definition of peace was at times ambiguous, not clear, and ever changing. Eliaz Cohen related:

> Naturally, questions are being asked, and we don't have all the answers, not even I, but I am sure this is the way to go. I've grown up and realized that this is a mission for generations to come – not one, but many. I am optimistic, very optimistic given all that is happening, including the bad things that I am confident will not last forever. At some point, the hunger for change will bring about change.

Bassam Aramin spoke of his ever renewing personal vision that evolves through experiments, activities, and learning from the process:

> On a more general level, you kind of develop a new vision. We learn every day that there is no difference between Palestinians and Israelis. We have the same fears and expectations ... My duty is not to dwell on the past because it is over and gone, with the good and the bad in it. It is my job to look forward and say that reconciliation is possible.

While deeply committed to reconciliation between the two nations, the peace entrepreneurs we interviewed accept that they do not know the way there. Still, that vagueness does not stop them from acting. They have no clearly defined picture of the future, and they know that the end result might not be attained in their lifetime. Still, they are guided in their actions by a compass of inner values.

CONCLUSION

In accordance with the general definition of entrepreneurship (Shane and Venkataraman, 2000), the life stories of peace entrepreneurs that feature in this book portray peace entrepreneurship as resulting from the intersection between the nature and behavior of individuals with their environment and the opportunities it presents or that can be created from it. The analysis of these stories reveals several characteristics that are relevant to entrepreneurship in a specific context (Bruyat and Julien, 2001) – in this case, peace activism to resolve the Israeli-Palestinian conflict.

On a personal level, most peace entrepreneurs describe themselves as being social activists since they were very young men and women who demonstrated nonconformist behavior and rebelled against social standards. It further seems that, over the years, they developed an inner moral compass based on values, as well as inner strength, thanks to which they endured criticism and attacks. Additionally, they all seem to have embraced some tolerance for ambiguity, a desire to push and challenge boundaries, curiosity, and the courage to embark upon uncharted paths.

Most of the peace entrepreneurs that feature in this book were raised at the center of the Israeli-Palestinian conflict, and operate in it while focusing on issues that are dear to their hearts. Many of them have endured some trauma or injury that directly resulted from the conflict, and have personally experienced the negative and painful consequences of the Israeli-Palestinian conflict. Still, they chose to abandon their roles as victims and their desire to take revenge. Instead, those traumas made them take action, seeking reconciliation and facilitating change. Those significant life experiences (Morgeson et al., 2015) that were a direct result of the conflict served them as a substantial source of energy for action aimed toward ending the conflict. They have chosen to act in a specific entrepreneurial manner within a given reality (Weerawardena and Mort, 2006).

The initiatives they founded and their activism often encountered harsh criticism from their social circles. Our interviewees have been charged with treason and betrayal, among other things. Facing these sentiments, they have found strength in certain personal qualities, relying on their loyalty to inner commitments and the values they uphold. Additionally, some of them rely on the social legitimacy that comes from having lost close family members to the conflict, belonging to respectable families and, in the Palestinian case, spending time in Israeli prisons, which provided them with both the respect of their society and a deeper understanding of the conflict.

Finally, our analysis suggests that peace entrepreneurs' activity is embedded and pending on their position in the social order and the resources and limitations that derive from it. The stronger their connections to powerful others and their networks' diversity or connectivity, the higher their ability to make an impact.

Israelis and Palestinians live in a harsh and complicated reality. Some may argue that all hope is lost, that we have tried everything, and that no matter how hard peace activists work and how determined they may be, reality will not change. That is quite understandable. People who live in the shadow of such a prolonged conflict that creates cynicism and doubt might develop an acquired sense of helplessness, a feeling that there is no point in trying, and that things might only get even worse.

This book carries the voices of individuals who live in this very reality, in which their voices are easy to be obfuscated and even ignored. Still, the stories of the peace entrepreneurs we interviewed attest to individuals' amazing ability to initiate, promote, lead, and develop peace enterprises while keeping up hope in a painful and harsh reality. They leverage their personal pain to imagine a different reality and introduce possible change.

We end this book hoping that the stories we have recounted will encourage you, the reader, to imagine, believe, and act for a different reality. Through this book, we wish to make these hopeful voices heard and present. We want to promote more hope beyond hope. We hope that readers will share our optimistic sentiments, born out of our engagement with these peace entrepreneurs and their stories – the belief that change is indeed possible and that peace will come, eventually.

Glossary

This glossary includes terms, historical events, and names of persons or organizations mentioned in our interviewees' stories. Since many items appear in various narratives, we have compiled them to benefit readers who are not familiar with them.

The task of putting this glossary together was not easy. At first sight, this is a tool that organizes information and makes it accessible for readers' use. Yet, following the constructionist-narrative approach that guides us in this book, it is apparent that each entry's meaning is embedded in multiple social, economic, political, ideological, and cultural contexts. In other words, the definition of each item is rarely neutral nor objective but rather represents personal, cultural, and social perspectives and views.

Take, for example, the meaning of the 1948 war. For some, this is the War of Independence that led to the happy event of Israel's establishment. For others, this is the Nakba (Catastrophe), a traumatic event of loss and expulsion. This complexity also became evident when we sought to characterize cities and localities in the region. Should we note whether they are inside or outside the Green Line? Should we note whether these are 'Jewish' or 'Arab' localities? Some cities are mostly populated by Jews or Arabs, yet still include a small mixed population. How can we represent such complexity? Our definition of a city as Jewish or Arab can be read also as a political statement that may strengthen a clear-cut dichotomy. By so doing, it may prevent future change, and this is not our intention. Similarly, we debated what information we should present regarding wars and conflict events and how deep we should go into the details. Is it sufficient to offer the start and end dates? Should we address the context, the trigger, or the cause of the event? Do we need to provide information on the results in terms of casualties, the land occupied, or agreements achieved? The underlying problem is the diversity of historical narratives regarding each event. On which source should we build? There is no real way to separate the 'facts' from their interpretations, and these interpretations are multiple and debated between the various parties to the conflict.

As authors, we are not neutral either. The book is based on a collaborative work of five female authors, one Palestinian and four Jewish-Israelis, who come from different ages, ethnicities, religious affiliations, and backgrounds. As such, we hold different views. These affect what meaning we apply to various entries and how we define them.

We have coped with this complexity in several ways. First, we offer only a minimal explanation for each item. Our goal is to allow the reader to understand the term, event, person, or organization just enough to move on with the reading. We aim to provide a clear and reliable depiction of each item and minimize our interpretation of it by focusing on objective characteristics (like time and place). We present different meanings of an item when we feel they are crucial for its understanding. The readers wishing for a deeper and more contextual description of the glossary entries are invited to further inquire through other sources.

We composed the glossary through several stages. First, we listed all terms, events, and individual or organizational names mentioned that seemed to need clarification for the general reader. We then moved to define them based on different sources, including Wikipedia.[1] All five authors reviewed the definitions and suggested changes or additions. Finally, we conducted four long interactive sessions. We agreed on a consistent approach to the definition of entries, discussed each debated entry, added needed information, or deleted too-specific information until we reached full consensus for the most parsimonious description. We hope our readers benefit from our efforts to clarify the terms, names, and events needed to understand the narratives of the peace entrepreneurs we interviewed.

NOTE

1.   We deemed Wikipedia as a good source for our needs, as it struggles with the same complexity around debated entries through collaborative, crowd-based approach. Indeed, debated entries in Wikipedia go through a process of editions and revisions (e.g. Rosenzweig, 2006).

1948/War of Independence/Nakba	A war between Israel and several Arab countries, following the UN resolution (November 1947) to end the British Mandate and partition the land into two states. The war started when the mandate ended and Israel declared independence on May 14, 1948. The armistice agreements between the parties signed in March 1949 ended the war with a defeat for the invading Arab forces, leaving many casualties on both sides, Palestinian refugees, and the establishment of the Jewish state. While the State of Israel celebrates May 14 as its Independence Day, the Palestinians commemorate this date as a day of mourning (Nakba).
1967/Six Day War/Naksa	A war between Israel and neighboring Arab countries, during which Israel occupied or liberated, depending on the narrative, the Sinai Peninsula, the West Bank, the Golan Heights, and the Gaza Strip. The war lasted six days.
Abu Dis	A Palestinian village situated east of Jerusalem, hosting the Al-Quds University, Abu Dis campus.
Abu Mazen/ President Abbas	The nickname of Mahmoud Abbas, the president of the Palestinian Authority since 2005.
Acre	A port city in northern Israel.
ahalan and sahalan	'Welcome' in Arabic.
Ahmed Yassin, Sheikh	A Palestinian imam and politician, founder of Hamas. He headed the organization from its establishment in 1987 until he was killed by the Israeli army in 2004.
AJEEC-NISPED	Arab-Jewish Center for Empowerment, Equality, and Cooperation-Negev Institute for Strategies of Peace and Economic Development. Located in Beer Sheva.
Al-Aqsa Martyrs' Brigades	Known as Katā'ib Shuhadā' al-'Aqsā in Arabic, which is a coalition of Palestinian armed groups in the West Bank. Established by Fatah with the beginning of the Second Intifada in October 2000.
Al-Azaria	A Palestinian town in the West Bank located on the southeastern slope of Jerusalem.
Al-Hamishmar	An Israeli daily newspaper published between 1943 and 1995 by Hashomer Hatzair, a socialist-Zionist youth movement, reflecting the left-leaning ideology of social justice, activism, peace, and equality.
Al-Kabri	A Palestinian village in northern Israel destroyed during the war of 1948.
Al-Tariq Movement	A Palestinian non-governmental organization, established in 2006, operating in the areas of democracy and community development, gender, human rights, internation/cultural relations, youth and education in Palestinian society.
Al-Zeeb (Achziv after 1948)	A Palestinian village in northern Israel that was destroyed during the war of 1948.
Alei Zahav	A Jewish settlement in the southwest of the West Bank.

Ali Abu Awwad	A Palestinian pacifist and peace activist, founder of the Taghyeer movement for non-violent resistance. Brother of one of our interviewees, Khaled Abu Awwad.
Ali Yichya	An Israeli-Arab teacher and diplomat, served as the Israeli ambassador in Finland and Greece.
aliyah	A Hebrew word meaning moving to a higher plain, and referring to the immigration of Jews to Israel as part of the Zionist project.
ALLMEP	The Alliance for Middle East Peace, a group of over 90 leading non-governmental organizations working to foster reconciliation between Israelis and Palestinians and between Arabs and Jews in the Middle East.
Alon Tal	A researcher and professor of public health policy, focusing on environmental issues, a leader of the Israel Union for Environmental Defense, and active in the Green Movement.
Altalena	A ship carrying weapons, which was at the center of a violent confrontation that took place in June 1948 by the newly established Israeli army against one of the Jewish paramilitary groups – the Irgun (also known as IZL).
Amal Saleh	Palestinian social activist in the field of education.
Amos Yaron	Israeli army major general, served as director general of the Ministry of Defense.
Anata	A Palestinian town in the West Bank located northeast of Jerusalem.
angels of destruction	A term from the Bible (Psalms, 78: 59), referring to a delegation that brings bad news.
Ar'ara	A town in northern Israel.
Arbor Day	Celebration of trees all over the world.
Areas A, B, and C	In the second Oslo Accords between Israel and the Palestinian Authority, the Israeli-occupied West Bank was divided into three areas, each with a different governance arrangement. Area A is governed by the Palestinian Authority, Area B refers to the territories in which civilian control is in the hands of the Palestinian Authority while security control is in the hands of the State of Israel, and Area C is governed by Israel.
Ariel Sharon	An Israeli general and politician (1928–2014), who served as the 11th prime minister of Israel between 2001 and 2006.
army service/ conscription of ultra-Orthodox Jews in Israel	By law, Israelis have to serve in the Israeli army at the age of 18. Ultra-Orthodox Jews who study in yeshivot (institutes for religious Jewish studies) are exempt from military service, but some of them decide, individually, to join the army.
Avi Ravitsky	Professor Emeritus of Jewish Thought in the Hebrew University. Among the founders of the religious-Zionist peace movement (Oz Ve-Shalom).
Avi Sagi	Professor Emeritus of Philosophy, Bar Ilan University.

Avigdor Lieberman	An Israeli politician who held different positions in the Israeli government, as the foreign affairs minister and defense minister.
Avinoam Rosenak	Senior lecturer at the Department of Jewish Thought, the Hebrew University.
Aviv Geffen	An Israeli rock musician, who was highly popular with Israeli youth during the 1990s.
Awni al-Mashni	A Palestinian political commentator, a Palestinian Liberation Organization (PLO) Fatah activist, among the founders of the Two States One Homeland and A Land for All movement.
Bassam Shakaa	A Palestinian politician and leader (1930–2019), supporter of the PLO. In 1980, he was critically injured by the Jewish Underground.
Battle Heritage	A genre of military history, focused on heroic battles in the Israeli army.
BDS	A Palestinian-led global political movement promoting boycott, divestment, and sanctions against the occupation of the territories by Israel.
Be'eri	A kibbutz in southern Israel that borders the Gaza Strip.
Beer Sheva/Beersheba	The largest city in the Negev Desert of southern Israel. Often referred to as the 'capital of the Negev,' it is the eighth most populous Israeli city.
Beit Jala	A Palestinian town in the West Bank, close to Jerusalem.
Beit Safafa	A Palestinian town sharing its territory between East and West Jerusalem.
Beit Ummar	A Palestinian town located near Hebron.
Benei Akiva	A religious-Zionist youth movement established in 1929 in Mandatory Palestine, active in Israel and Jewish communities around the world.
Benjamin Netanyahu (Bibi)	An Israeli right-wing politician serving as the prime minister of Israel between 1996 and 1999, and since 2009 until 2021.
Bereaved Families Forum/ Bereaved Parents Circle	A group of Jewish and Arab bereaved family members, working together towards peace.
Bethlehem	A Palestinian city south of Jerusalem, in the West Bank.
Bnei Brak	A city located near Tel Aviv, a center of ultra-Orthodox Judaism.
Breaking the Silence	An organization of veteran combatants who have served in the Israeli military since the start of the Second Intifada, who have taken it upon themselves to expose their experiences during their military service in the occupied territories.
British Mandate	The British Mandate on Palestine, awarded by the UN, lasted between 1923 and 1948.
children's house	Early in the history of Israeli kibbutz, children were living, sleeping, and educated in separate communal houses following the founding principles and collectivist ethos of the kibbutz movement.
Combatants for Peace	An Israeli-Palestinian non-governmental organization formed in 2006 committed to non-violent action against the Israeli occupation of the Palestinian territories.

Courage to Refuse An organization established by a group of Israeli soldiers who refuse to serve in the occupied territories.

Dalia Rabin A former Israeli left-leaning politician, the daughter of late former prime minister Yitzhak Rabin.

Damascus Gate One of the main gates of the Old City of Jerusalem.

Dan Ariely An Israel professor of psychology and behavioral economics.

Dan (Danny) Yatom A former Israeli politician who was head of the Mossad security service.

Dar Al-Mu'allimat A teachers' seminary in Ramallah, the Palestine Authority.

Davar A Hebrew-language socialist daily newspaper, published 1925–1996.

Dheisheh Refugee Camp A refugee camp established in 1949 and located near Bethlehem in the West Bank.

Dov Lautman An Israeli philanthropist (1936–2013), past chairman of Delta Galil Industries and former president of the Manufacturers Association of Israel. Former executive chair of the Peres Center for Peace and a member of the board of the Yitzhak Rabin Center.

Dovrat Committee A national task force for the advancement of education in Israel (2005).

Dura A Palestinian town located near Hebron.

Dvora Forum Women in Foreign Policy and National Security – a non-profit non-governmental organization with an active network of professional women in an array of fields relating to Israel's national security and foreign policy.

Dvora Omer An Israeli author (1932–2013). Most of her books relate to Israel's history, are written for young adults, and are translated into many languages.

Efrat A Jewish-Israeli settlement established in 1983 in the West Bank.

Egypt-Israel Peace Treaty A peace agreement between Egypt and Israel signed in Washington in 1979.

Ehud Barak An Israeli army general and politician who was leader of the Labor Party and served as the prime minister between 1999 and 2001.

Ehud Olmert An Israeli politician, former mayor of Jerusalem and the leader of the Kadima Party, served as the prime minister of Israel between 2006 and 2009. Later, he was convicted of accepting a bribe and sentenced to a prison term.

Eilon Schwartz A founder of the Shaharit Institute, member of the Jewish School of Education at the Hebrew University of Jerusalem; founder and former chief executive officer of the Heschel Center for Sustainability.

Ein Harod Ihud A veteran kibbutz in northern Israel.

Eitan Haber An Israeli journalist and publicist (1940–2020), served as the director of the Office of the Prime Minister Yitzhak Rabin between 1992 and 1995.

Elkana A Jewish-Israeli settlement in the West Bank.

Eran Halperin An Israeli professor of social psychology and intergroup conflict and reconciliation at the Hebrew University.

Experimental School in Jerusalem	Jerusalem experimental school, established in 1971 as a democratic student-centered progressive learning environment.
Fatah	A Palestinian national liberation movement founded in 1959. Among the founders of the PLO.
fathers and mothers of the desert	Early Christian hermits, monks, and ascetics.
fedayeen	In Hebrew usage, refers to Arab guerrillas operating against Israel during the 1950s. In Arabic, refers to people who sacrifice themselves for their country.
Four Mothers	A protest movement formed in 1997 after two IDF helicopters that carried soldiers to Lebanon collided in mid-air, killing 73 soldiers. The original co-founders, named after the Biblical four mothers, lived in the north and had children who served in Lebanon. They initiated the movement to encourage the IDF pullout from the Security Zone in southern Lebanon. The Israeli Army withdrew from Lebanon unilaterally in 2000.
Fulbright scholarship	One of several United States cultural exchange programs whose goal is to improve intercultural relations, cultural diplomacy, and intercultural competence between the people of the United States and other countries through exchange.
Galia Golan	A feminist left-wing activist and professor of political science.
Gamal Abdel Nasser	An Egyptian politician (1918–1970) who served as the second president of Egypt during 1954–1970. Was president during the 1967 Six Day War.
Gaza Strip	A Palestinian territory between Israel and Egypt.
Gemara	A component of the Talmud, comprising rabbinical analyses and commentary of the Mishna.
Geneva Initiative/ Organization	A non-profit organization that promotes a permanent agreement between Israel and the Palestinians.
Gershon Baskin	A founder and former co-chair of IPCRI, dedicated to the resolution of the Israel-Palestinian conflict based on a 'two states for two people' solution. He is interviewed in this book.
Gilad Shalit	An Israeli soldier who was kidnapped in 2006 and held in captivity by Hamas for five years. He was released after a public campaign led by his parents in exchange for over 1,000 Palestinian prisoners.
Gilead Sher	An Israeli attorney who served as chief of staff to Israeli prime minister Ehud Barak.
Givat Gonen school	A secular school in Jerusalem, aiming to integrate children from well-to-do and run-down neighborhoods of Jerusalem. While most of the students are Jewish, the student body includes some Arab children as well.
Giv'at Shmuel	A city in the Central District of Israel.
Green Line	The truce line based on the 1949 Armistice Agreements between Israel and its surrounding neighbors, drawn in green on the maps. The line marks the borders prior to 1967.

Gush Emunim	An Israeli Jewish right-wing activist movement, founded in 1974, committed to establishing Jewish settlements in the West Bank, the Gaza Strip, and the Golan Heights.
Gush Etzion Junction	A junction at the heart of Gush Etzion, a central roadway in the West Bank.
Gush Etzion Regional Council	A cluster of Jewish settlements located in the West Bank south of Bethlehem.
Haaretz	An Israeli newspaper with leftist orientation. Founded in 1918, making it the longest running newspaper in Israel.
Hadassah Froman	A religious peace activist who resides in the West Bank. The widow of Rabi Menachem Froman who was well known for his efforts with Palestinian leaders to seek peace between Israel and Palestine. She is interviewed in this book.
Haifa	A northern Israeli port city.
Hajar School	The Hajar organization was established in 2006 by Jewish and Palestinian parents and political activists who are residents of the Naqab/Negev.
Hamas	A Palestinian Islamist and nationalist organization, with social and military wings. It has been the de facto governing authority of the Gaza Strip since 2007.
Hanan Porat	An Israeli Orthodox rabbi and politician (1943–2011) who served as a member of the Knesset. One of the founders of Gush Emunim.
Hartman Institute	A research and education institute based in Jerusalem that offers pluralistic education in Jewish thought.
Hasamba	A series of Hebrew children's adventure novels.
Hasidim	A Jewish Orthodox group that arose as a spiritual revival movement in Eastern Europe during the eighteenth century.
Havruta	A traditional approach for Talmudic studies in which small groups of students analyze and discuss a shared text.
Hebron	A Palestinian city in the southern West Bank.
Hefer Valley	Agricultural valley in the center of Israel.
Herut Party	Was the major right-wing nationalist political party in Israel from 1948 until its formal merger into Likud in 1988.
hijab	A headscarf worn by women in Arab and Islamic circles.
Hillel Association – the Right to Choose	An Israeli non-profit organization dedicated to helping young adults who have left the ultra-Orthodox world.
Hoffman Leadership and Responsibility Program	An interdisciplinary program for top doctoral students at the Hebrew University dedicated to developing leadership capabilities and social responsibility activities.
Holocaust/Shoah	The genocide of six million Jews by the Nazis during World War II, between 1941 and 1945.

honor killings	Acts of vengeance, usually death, committed by family members against female members, who are perceived to have brought dishonor upon the family.
Huda Abu Arqoub	A Palestinian feminist and peace builder, ALLMEP regional director. She is interviewed in this book.
Hura	A Bedouin town in the Southern District of Israel.
Ibn Ezra	One of the most distinguished Jewish biblical commentators and philosophers of the Middle Ages.
intifada (in Arabic: Palestinian Uprising)	The Palestinian Uprising against the Israeli occupation of the West Bank and Gaza.The First Intifada started in 1987 and ended in 1993, with the Oslo Accords. The Second Intifada, known as the Al-Aqsa Intifada,was in 2000–2005. The Third Intifada, also known as the Knives Intifada and Silent Intifada, was in 2015–2016.
IPCRI	Israel-Palestine: Creative Ideas is a research and information center established in 1988 to promote a solution for the Israeli-Palestinian conflict. See the chapter on Gershon Baskin.
Islamic Jihad movement	Known also as Palestinian Islamic Jihad. A Damascus-based Islamic organization formed in 1981 in Gaza. The movement rejects the Oslo Accords and strives towards the establishment of an Islamic Palestinian State. Promotes the military destruction of Israel.
Islamic Movement (in Israel)	Established in 1971, advocating for Islam in Israel.
Ismail Haniyeh	A senior political leader of Hamas, served as de facto prime minister in Gaza between 2006 and 2014, and on 2017 was elected as Hamas' political chief.
Israel Prize	An award handed out by the State of Israel and regarded as the state's highest cultural honor. Awarded annually on Independence Day to Israeli citizens or organizations who have displayed excellence in their field(s) or who have made special contributions to Israeli culture.
Israel Social TV	A non-profit independent media organization for social change.
Israeli Communist Party (*Rakah*)	Rakah was established in 1965 when the Israeli Communist Party (Maki) split. Most of the Jewish members remained in Maki while most of the Arab members (and a few Jewish members) joined the new party.
Israeli-Palestinian Memorial Day Ceremony	A memorial ceremony for all victims of the Israeli-Palestinian conflict, organized by Combatants for Peace and Bereaved Parents Circle. Takes place on the evening of the Israeli Memorial Day for the Israeli fallen soldiers and victims of terrorism. Offered as an alternative to the formal National Memorial Day in Israel.
Israeli President Hope Prize	A prize for the creation of partnerships in social and economic fields representing all sectors of Israeli society. Launched in 2015 by the Israeli president Reuven Rivlin.

Itach-Maaki Association	In Hebrew and Arabic, 'with you'. This is an association of women lawyers for social justice in Israel that extends legal aid to women in need, promotes women leaders, organizes discussions on various topics in various communities, and runs a lobby.
Jaffa (Yafo)	The southern and oldest part of the integrated city Tel Aviv-Yafo, an ancient port city in Israel.
Jean Frydman	A French businessman who was part of the French Resistance. He became involved in the highest level of negotiations between Israel and Palestine including being instrumental in starting the Oslo Peace Accords.
Jenin	A Palestinian city in the northern West Bank.
Jeremy Benstein	Together with Alon Tal established the Arava Institute for Environmental Studies, the Israel Union for Environmental Defense, and the Heschel Center for Sustainability.
Jerusalem Fund	The Jerusalem Fund for Education and Community Development is a non-profit organization. It focuses on the education and humanitarian work of Palestinians. Founded in 1977 by Hisham Sharabi.
Jewish Underground	A radical right-wing militant organization that operated between 1979 and 1984.
Jezreel Valley	A large agriculture plain and inland valley in the Northern District of Israel.
Jibril Rajoub	A Palestinian political leader and formal militant. Was head of the preventive security force in the West Bank until 2002.
Kaddish	Mourner's Kaddish is a Jewish prayer that mourners recite during the bereavement period and to mark the anniversary of the death of a loved one.
Kafr Qara	A town in northern Israel.
Kalashnikov (AK-47)	Assault rifle developed in the Soviet Union during World War II. It has remained the most popular assault rifle in the world.
Karim Khalaf	A Palestinian politician and leader (1937–1985). In 1980, members of the Jewish Underground placed a bomb in his car. In the explosion, he was critically injured and lost his right foot.
Katamon	A neighborhood in Jerusalem. During the 1948 war, the local Palestinian population fled the neighborhood and it was repopulated by Jews.
keffiyeh	A traditional Arab headdress, a symbol of Palestinian identity.
Kfar HaRoeh Yeshiva	A religious village in central Israel, established by Rabbi Moshe-Zvi Neria. The yeshiva was founded in 1939 and is one of the leading Jewish biblical studies high schools in Israel that integrates secular studies as well.
Kfar Hasidim	A village in northern Israel.
Kibbutz Barkai	A kibbutz in the center of Israel founded in 1949.
Kibbutz Kfar Etzion	A religious kibbutz settlement located in the southern West Bank. Established in 1927, depopulated in 1948 and re-established in 1967.
Kibbutz Lavi	A religious kibbutz in northern Israel.

kidnapped boys	Three Israeli teenagers were kidnapped near one of the Israeli settlements in the West Bank and murdered by members of the militant Palestinian group Hamas. The event intensified the tension around the Gaza Strip, which brought about Operation Protective Edge or the Gaza War, in July–August 2014.
Kiryat Shmona	A city in northern Israel close to the Lebanese border.
KKL (JNF)/Keren Kayemet LeIsrael/ Jewish National Fund	The Jewish National Fund is a non-profit Zionist organization, founded in 1901 by Theodor Herzl to buy and develop land in Ottoman Palestine for Jewish settlements.
Knesset	The Israeli Parliament.
kosher	Food permitted to be eaten and prepared by a set of rules according to Jewish religious law.
Labor Movement in Israel	An umbrella term, referring to Zionist and socialist parties and movements, active before and after the establishment of the State of Israel.
Land Day	A day of remembrance and protest, marked each year to commemorate the March 30, 1976 strike and demonstrations against the confiscation of Arab lands by the State. In the events, six unarmed Arab citizens were killed and 100 were wounded.
Madrid Conference	A peace conference between Israelis and Palestinians, with the participation of some Arab countries, hosted in Spain and co-sponsored by the UN and the Soviet Union in late 1991.
Mahmoud Darwish	An internationally known Palestinian poet and author who was regarded as the national poet of Palestine.
Maimonides	A Jewish philosopher and Torah scholar, active in the Mediterranean region during the twelfth century. His work and teaching are still followed and studied to this day.
Mandel School for Educational Leadership	A joint venture of the Mandel Foundation and Israel's Ministry of Education, aimed at training Israel's future generations of educational leaders.
Mapay/Mapainiks	A labor, left-leaning Israeli party, which governed the State of Israel for 29 years until 1977 and was a symbol of the establishment of the state of Israel.
Marshall B. Rosenberg	An American psychologist who developed a model of non-violent communication, used around the world in various kinds of conflict.
Mashiv HaRuach	A literary journal and publishing house, dedicated to enriching Jewish Israeli culture.
matriculation exams	Taken at the end of high school, and used to assess a student's academic achievements. Used by Israeli universities to determine acceptance.
Melachim u Milhamot (Hebrew: Kings and Wars)	Rules of war, written by Rabbi Moshe Ben Maimon, known as Maimonides (1138–1204) in his book *Mishne Torah*.

Memorial/Remembrance Day for IDF Fallen Soldiers and Terror Victims	Israel's national day of commemoration of all Israeli military personnel who have lost their lives in active duty as well as civilian victims of terror.
Menachem Begin	Former prime minister of Israel, leader of the right-leaning Likud Party. Before the establishment of Israel, he was the leader of one of the Zionist militant groups that fought for Israel's independence.
Merkaz Harav Yeshiva	A prominent national-religious yeshiva located in Jerusalem.
Meron Rapoport	An Israeli journalist and writer, serves as the president of the peace initiative A Land for All.
Michael Melchior	Former leader of Meimad, a Zionist-religious political party leaning to the left, member of the Israeli Parliament, and a minister.
Michal Barak	A lawyer by training, serving as the director of the Center for the Study of Multiculturalism and Diversity in the Hebrew University, Jerusalem.
Moshav Gimzo	A Jewish religious village at the foot of the Judean Mountains in central Israel.
Moshe Halbertal	A professor of Jewish thought and philosophy at the Hebrew University.
Mossad	The Israeli national intelligence agency.
Mount Scopus terror attack	The Mount Scopus campus is one of three campuses of the Hebrew University in Jerusalem. Palestinian militants planted a bomb in one of the cafeterias on campus on July 31, 2002, killing nine people and injuring around 100 (among them staff, Israeli and international exchange students).
Muhammad Ali Taha	A Palestinian novelist, playwright, and satirical essayist (1941–2011).
Muslim Quarter	The biggest of the four quarters in the Old City of Jerusalem, along with the Jewish, Armenian, and Christian Quarters.
Naftali Bennett	Israeli's prime minister since 2021, representing Jewish-Zionist parties. Served as a member of Parliament and as a minister.
Naftali Rothenberg	An Israeli rabbi and scholar. Served as head of an army leadership institute 1986–1989 and initiated a high school program for democratic and peace education.
Nahal Brigade/Nahal Core groups	A military program in which youth movement groups are drafted together as a core group, combining military and community service.
Nakba/Nakba Day	Literally translates as 'The Catastrophe.' It refers to the mass exodus of about 750,000 Arabs from Palestine during the 1984 war.
Natan Alterman	A notable Israeli poet, playwright, and translator, 1910–1970.
Nation-State Law	An Israeli basic law emphasizing the Jewish nature of the Israeli State. The bill passed in 2018.
National Religious Party	An Israeli political party representing the religious Zionist movement. The party was active between 1956 and 2008, most of the time as part of the ruling coalition.

National Scouts Movement	The Israeli chapter of the Scouts, established in 1919 and still active all around Israel.
Naval Commando (*Shayetet*) **Disaster**	A unit from the Israeli Navy's special forces, on a mission in South Lebanon in 1997, was ambushed by Islamic guerillas, killing 12 Israeli soldiers. Captain Ram Levinas (brother of our interviewee Shiri Levinas) was killed during this commando operation on September 5, 1997. He was 22 years old.
Nazareth	A city in northern Israel. According to the New Testament, the childhood home of Jesus.
Neomi Hazan	Professor of political science and African studies, leftist, and human rights activist, former Meretz member of Parliament (1992–2003) and president of the New Israel Fund (2008–2012).
Netanya	A city in the center of Israel, on the coast of the Mediterranean Sea.
Neve Dekalim	One of the Jewish settlements in the Gaza Strip that Israel evacuated unilaterally as part of the disengagement in 2005.
Neve Shalom/Wahat al-Salam	A Jewish-Arab village in central Israel, dedicated to educational work for peace.
Noam Shalit	Father of Gilad Shalit (see above). Together with his wife, Aviva Shalit, orchestrated a long public campaign for Gilad's release, in both Israel and abroad.
November 29, 1947	On this day the United Nations (UN) General Assembly voted in favor of a resolution, which adopted the plan for the partition of Palestine between Jews and Arabs into two states.
Nurit Haghagh	An Israeli feminist peace activist.
October 2000 events	A series of violent protests in Arab cities in northern Israel, starting on October 1 with the beginning of the Second Intifada, in support of the Palestinians. The protest escalated, 12 Arab citizens of Israel and one Palestinian were killed by Israeli police and one Jewish citizen was killed by the demonstrators. The events were investigated by the Orr Commission.
Ofakim/fires in Ofakim	A town in the southern periphery of Israel, populated mainly by Jews (92 percent). In the summer of 2018, as part of their protests, Gaza Palestinians started flying kites and balloons across the border, to which they attached flammable material that started fires on the Israeli side.
Operation Cast Lead	Also known as the Gaza War, and in the Muslim world as the Gaza Massacre. A three-week armed conflict during December 2018 and January 2019 between Hamas and the Israeli Army. Resulted in more than 1,000 Palestinian and 13 Israeli deaths.
Operation Peace for the Galilee	Also known in Israel as the First Lebanon War. Lasted between June and September 1982. It ended with a ceasefire, the PLO and Yasser Arafat were expelled from Lebanon, and Israel forces stayed in southern Lebanon until 2000.

Operation Protective Edge	In Hebrew known as Tzuk Eitan, or as the Gaza War 2014. An Israeli military operation in the Hamas-ruled Gaza Strip. The operation lasted seven weeks during July and August 2014 and resulted in thousands of deaths, most of them Palestinians from Gaza.
Or Etzion Yeshiva	A Jewish religious high school that prepares students for army service, located in southern Israel.
Orit Kamir	An Israeli feminist, legal scholar, and activist.
Oron Shaul	A soldier who fell in battle between the IDF and Hamas in the Shaja'iya Neighborhood in July 2014. His body is held by Hamas.
Oslo Accords	Agreements between Israel and the PLO, negotiated in Oslo and signed in two parts, in 1993 and 1995. The agreements reflected mutual recognition between the parties, and the creation of the Palestinian Authority. The Oslo agreement was debated and criticized on both sides.
Other Voice	A grassroots organization comprised of people living near the Gaza border that works for a peaceful, non-military solution to the Israel–Gaza ongoing armed conflicts.
Oz veShalom – Netivot Shalom	A religious Zionist movement and peace organization, founded in 1975.
Palestinian diaspora	Palestinians who live outside of historical Palestine (the land on which the British had a mandate by the League of Nations). The majority of the Palestinian diaspora is comprised of Palestinians who were displaced, became refugees, or migrated overseas during and after the 1948 war and the 1967 war.
Palestinian Liberation Organization (PLO)	Founded in 1964 to liberate Palestine through armed struggle. In 1993, Israel and the PLO mutually recognized the other's right to exist in peace. The conflict, however, ensued, and the PLO retracted its recognition of Israel in 2018.
Palestinian National Authority	A self-governing body, established in 1994 following the Oslo Accords, over Gaza and Areas A and B of the West Bank.
paradoxical thinking and the conflict	See the research by Hameiri et al. (2014).
Paulo Freire	A Brazilian educator who had several important theories in the field of education.
Peace Child YMCA Israel	An educational organization, teaching coexistence, tolerance, and mutual respect through joint artistic projects by Jewish and Arab teens.
Peace Index	Monthly survey of public sentiments on the Israeli-Palestinian conflict, as part of the research activity at the Israel Democracy Institute.
Peace Now	A non-governmental left-leaning Zionist organization promoting peace through the two states solution since 1978.
pilots' letter	A public letter, published in 2003 by Israel Air Force pilots, opposing unlawful and unethical orders to attack targets in the occupied territories.

Popular Front for the Liberation of Palestine (PFLP)	Together with Fatah, PFLP formed the majority of the PLO. PFLP was a secular Palestinian, Marxist-leaning organization founded in 1967.
Project Wadi Attir	An initiative of a Bedouin community in the Negev Desert, establishing a model sustainable farm that leverages Bedouin traditional values.
Prophet Mosque, Al-Masjid an-Nabawī	A mosque built by the prophet Muhammad in Medina, Saudi Arabia.
Rabbi Akiva	A Jewish scholar who lived from the mid-first to the early second century and contributed significantly to Jewish thought and central texts.
Rabbi Amiel's Yeshiva	Also known as the New Yishuv Yeshiva, one of the first high school ultra-Orthodox institutions to be established in the early twentieth century in Israel before the State of Israel was established.
Rabbi Amital	Yehuda Amital (1944–2010) was an Orthodox rabbi who founded a known yeshiva and a left-leaning religious party, Meimad. Served as a Parliament member and a minister.
Rabbi Cooperman	Yehuda Cooperman (1930–2016) was a pioneer in women's Torah study, and established a college for women to study the Torah and achieve an academic degree in education.
Rabbi Drukman	Haim Drukman is an Israeli Orthodox rabbi and former politician.
Rabbi Kook	Abraham Isaac Kook (1865–1935) was an Orthodox Rabbi, one of the fathers of religious Zionism. Among his most known writings is a series of books entitled *Orot Kodesh* (*Lights of Holiness*).
Rabbi of Kotzk	Menachem Mendel Morgensztern of Kotzk (1787–1859) was a Hasidic rabbi.
Rabbi Levinger	Moshe Levinger (1935–2015) was an Israeli religious Zionist and Orthodox rabbi, leader in the Jewish settlement movement in the occupied territories.
Rabbi Menachem Froman	(1945–2013), an Israeli Orthodox rabbi, a founding member of Gush Emunim, the religious settlement movement in the occupied territories. He had close ties with neighboring Palestinian religious leaders in their joint quest for peace and was married to Hadassah Froman, interviewed in this book.
Rachel the Poetess	Rachel Bluwstein (1890–1931) was a famous Hebrew-language poet, who immigrated to Palestine from Russia.
Ramadan	The ninth month in the Islamic calendar, during which Muslims fast during the day and break the daily fast with prayer and community and family gathering.
Ramallah	A Palestinian city in the central West Bank.
Ramallah lynching of 2000	On October 12, 2000, two Israeli soldiers accidently entered the city governed by the Palestinian Authority. The two soldiers were taken to a police station. A Palestinian crowd broke into the building, killed the soldiers, and mutilated their bodies.
Ramat Aviv	A northern neighborhood of Tel Aviv.

Rami Elhanan, Smadar Elhanan	A Jewish Israeli who lost his 14-year-old daughter, Smadar, in a terror attack by two Palestinian suicide bombers in the center of Jerusalem. Elhanan joined the Israel-Palestinian Bereaved Families for Peace organization and has been active in it ever since.
Ramla	A city in the center of Israel.
Rashbam	Rabbi Samuel Ben Meir (1085–1158) was a Jewish French scholar, grandson of Rashi.
Rashi	Rabbi Shalomo Yitzchaki (1040–1105) was a medieval Jewish French scholar.
Rebbe, Admor	In Jewish Hasidic circles, the title of a spiritual leader.
Revisionist Zionism	A stream within the Zionist movement in the 1920s, calling to renew the goals and activity of the World Zionist Organization.
Ron Pundak	A Jewish Israeli historian, journalist, and peace activist (1955–2014) who had a central role in initiating the Oslo peace process in 1993.
Roots-Shorashim-Judur Center	A Palestinian-Israeli initiative for promoting non-violence and understanding between the two people through face-to-face meetings on a regional basis.
S.Y. Agnon	Shamuel Yosef Agnon (1887–1970) was a notable Jewish Hebrew author and Nobel Prize Laureate in Literature in 1966.
Sabra and Shatila Massacre	The killing of hundreds of Palestinians living in these two refugee camps near Beirut, Lebanon, by militant Christian paramilitary units, in an area controlled by the Israeli Army in 1982. In 1983 a formal Israeli commission found that Israeli military personnel, aware that a massacre was in progress, had failed to take steps to stop it.
Sami Michael Prize	A prize under the name of a Jewish Israeli Hebrew author. Michael is active for peace, and has served as president of the Association for Civil Rights in Israel since 2001.
Samih al-Qasim	A contemporary Palestinian writer and poet who frequently wrote about resistance and revolting against colonialism.
Sanz Hassidic Court	A Hasidic dynasty that originated in the city of Sanz in Galicia. The dynasty has been divided into separate courts, many of which perished during the Holocaust. Active to this day in both Israel and the United States.
Sari Aharoni	A researcher at the Gender Studies Program at Ben Gurion University, studying public policy and gender, and a peace activist.
Sayeret Matkal	A special forces unit of the Israeli Army.
secular yeshiva	Modeled on religious schools (yeshiva), a secular yeshiva integrates the study of various texts, extending beyond religious texts to include philosophical, artistic, and social thought.

Sharon Leshem's Talking Peace Project	Leshem is a member of Kibbutz Urim, director of the group guidance school of the Negev Voices Association at the Sapir College, and professor at the Ben-Gurion University. The Talking Peace Project she established offers a new Jewish understanding of peace, based on religious and metaphysical principles.
Shatil	A support organization, established by the New Israel Fund to support activists and organizations working to promote a just, democratic, and equal society in Israel.
Shimon Peres	An Israeli politician (1923–2016) who served as Israel's prime minister and later president. Together with Yitzhak Rabin and Yasser Arafat, won the 1994 Nobel Peace Prize for the Oslo Accords.
Shirley Kantor	An Israeli consultant on corporate responsibility processes, social impact, and marketing.
Shiv'a	A Jewish ritual, in which the first-degree relative of the dead mourn for seven days after the burial, and members of the community visit and console them.
Shlomo Lahat	Nicknamed Cheech (1927–2014), a major general in the IDF and a right-leaning politician, four times mayor of Tel Aviv.
Sinai Peninsula	A large peninsula in Egypt. Israel conquered it in the Six Day War of 1967. In 1978 Egypt and Israel signed a peace accord in which Israel agreed to return the territory and completed its evacuation in 1982.
Sinai War	Also known as the Suez Crisis. An armed conflict between Israel and Egypt, as part of a military operation initiated by the United Kingdom and France aiming to secure their interests in the Suez Canal in 1956.
Sitra Achra	In Aramaic, The Evil Other Side/Way. The representation of evil or impure spiritual forces in Jewish mysticism.
Sota Tractate	The sixth tractate in the order of Nahism in the Mishna, one of the holiest Jewish texts, formalizing in text the Jewish oral tradition, dated to the third century.
Standing Together	An organization founded by a group of Arab and Jewish activists striving for equality, dignity, and social justice.
state of all of its citizens	The state of Israel is defined as the Nation State of the Jewish people. Some suggest it should be a state of all its citizens, regardless of ethnicity or religion.
Taghyeer, Positive Community	An independent Palestinian organization working towards creating innovative and safe spaces, where Palestinian youth and adults are inspired to take action to create positive change and confront negativity.
Tamra	A city in northern Israel.
Tekoa	A Jewish Israeli settlement in the West Bank, established in the mid 1970s.
terrorist attack at Dizengoff Center	The Dizengoff Center is a large shopping mall in the center of Tel Aviv. During the holiday of Purim, in 1996, a Palestinian suicide bomber blew himself up in a crowd, killing 13 Israelis and wounding 130.

Tiberias	A city in northern Israel, near the Sea of Galilee. Established around the year 20 CE.
Tnuva	An Israeli food-processing cooperative owned by farmers in kibbutzim and villages, specializing in dairy products. It was bought by private investors in 2006 and later sold to a Chinese food conglomerate.
Tulkarm	A Palestinian city in the West Bank.
Umm al-Fahm	A city in northern Israel.
Umrah	An Islamic pilgrimage to Mecca, the holiest city for Muslims, located in Saudi Arabia.
UNESCO	The United Nations Educational, Scientific and Cultural Organization, aiming to bring peace through international cooperation in educational, scientific, and cultural activities.
Unified National Leadership of the Uprising	A coalition of local Palestinian leaders that mobilized the first Palestinian uprising against Israel (intifada) in 1987.
UNRWA	The United Nations Relief and Works Agency for Palestine Refugees in the Near East. A relief and human development agency, founded in 1949. As of 2019, more than five million Palestinians (people directly displaced due to the conflict, as well as their descendants) are registered with the agency.
UNSC Resolution 1325	Made in October 2000, the UN Security Council Resolution 1325 includes a UNSC pledge to guarantee women representation in conflict-settling processes, peace arrangements, and violence-prevention acts, particularly gender violence.
Uri Elitzur	A Jewish Israeli right-wing publicist (1956–2014).
Uri Zvi Greenberg	A known Jewish Israeli poet (1896–1981) and right-wing political activist.
Vizhnitz Hassidic Court	Originated in the city of Vyzhnytsia (present-day Ukraine), the dynasty is still active to this day in both Israel and the United States.
Voice of Peace Radio	A radio station established by Abie Nathan that promoted peace between Israel and the Palestinians. To bypass the restrictions set out by Israeli law at the time (1973–1993), the station operated from a ship traveling offshore, just outside Israeli territorial waters.
West Bank	A territory bordered by Jordan to the east and by Israel to the west, south, and north. Its name was given to the territory after it was captured by Jordan in the 1948 war because it sits on the west side of the Jordan River. Jordan annexed the territory in 1950 and held it until 1967 when it was occupied by Israel during the 1967 Six Day War.
Women Wage Peace	A civil society non-partisan grassroots movement established by women to pressure the Israeli government into ending the Israeli-Palestinian conflict through peace negotiations.
Yad LaBanim	An organization supporting the families of fallen Israeli soldiers.

Yamit	A Jewish Israeli town, established on the Sinai Peninsula after Israel occupied it in the 1967 war. Following the peace agreement with Egypt, Israel returned the Sinai Peninsula and evacuated all its settlements there in 1982. The agreement, and the struggle over Yamit, with inhabitants and supporters aiming to halt the evacuation, were hotly debated.
Yarmouk University	A Jordanian public university located in Irbid in the northern part of Jordan.
Yasser Arafat	A Palestinian political leader, chairman of the PLO (1969–2004), and president of the Palestinian National Authority (1994–2004). Won the 1994 Nobel Peace Prize together with Yitzhak Rabin and Shimon Peres for the peace negotiations at Oslo.
Yehuda Shaul	A Jewish Israeli human rights activist, co-founder of Breaking the Silence – an organization voicing testimonies of Israeli soldiers about their service in the occupied territories.
Yehuda Shenhav	A professor of sociology at Tel Aviv University, author, and translator.
yeshive bucher	Student at an institution for studying holy Jewish texts.
Yigal Amir	A right-wing extremist who assassinated Israel's prime minister Yitzhak Rabin in November 1995.
Yisrael Harel	A Jewish religious Zionist publicist and activist.
Yitzhak Frankenthal	An Israeli peace activist who founded the Bereaved Parents Circle bringing bereaved Israeli and Palestinian families together. He is interviewed in this book.
Yitzhak Rabin	A Jewish Israeli politician (1922–1995). Served as chief of the general staff, and as Israel's prime minister. Oversaw the Oslo peace process between Israel and the Palestinians. Won the 1994 Nobel Peace Prize with Shimon Peres and Yasser Arafat. Was assassinated on November 5, 1995 by Yigal Amir.
Yitzhak Shamir	A Jewish Israeli right-wing politician (1915–2012). Leader of the right-wing Likud Party, member of Parliament, and Israel's prime minister.
YMCA kindergarten	As part of the Jerusalem chapter of the YMCA, located at the heart of the city, this is a mixed Jewish-Arab multilingual kindergarten. The kindergarten follows the overall mission of the organization to promote equality, tolerance, and multicultural sensibilities.
Yoav Sorek	A Jewish Israeli editor-in-chief of the *Shiloach Journal of Policy and Thought*.
Yom Kippur War/ Ramadan War/ October War/1973 War	A war between Israel and a coalition of Arab neighboring countries, started on Yom Kippur, the holiest day in the Jewish calendar. From an early surprise and near defeat, the Israeli army eventually managed to win the war.
Yonatan Shapira	A former career soldier in the Israeli Air Force, who became a peace activist and was among the pilots who wrote the pilots' letter opposing orders to attack targets in the occupied territories.

Yossi Sarid	A Jewish Israeli left-wing politician (1940–2015), served as member of the Israeli Parliament and minister.
Yuval Rabin	An Israeli businessman, Yitzhak Rabin's son.
Ze'ev Jabotinsky	A Jewish Revisionist Zionist leader and author (1880–1940). His activity and writings laid the ideological and organizational ground for the right-wing Likud Party, which has dominated Israeli politics since 1977.
Zion Square/rally at Zion Square	Zion Square in central Jerusalem has hosted many rallies and demonstrations. In October 1995, during the bitter debate around the Oslo Accords, right-wing political leaders and demonstrators called for the rebuke of the Oslo Accords. Printed-out images of Rabin in SS uniform were distributed, and calls to kill him were heard. A month later, Rabin was assassinated by Yigal Amir.
Zionist ultra-Orthodox, Hardal	A faction in the Zionist religious population that adopts stricter, ultra-Orthodox ways.
Zionist yeshiva	Some of the ultra-Orthodox communities are Zionists, believing Israel should exist as an independent state, even if secular. Others are anti-Zionists, who believe that no political existence for Jews is proper, as Jews need to wait for God to redeem them, and bring about a state abiding to Jewish law. Thus, there are also Zionist and anti-Zionist yeshivot (Jewish educational institutions).
Zohar/The book of Zohar	A central text of the Kabbalah, Jewish mysticism.
Zohar Shapira	A former career soldier in a top commando unit of the IDF who became a peace activist, joining Combatants for Peace.

References

Abu-Lughod, L. and Sa'di, A.H. (eds) (2007), *Nakba: Palestine, 1948, and the Claims of Memory*. New York: Columbia University Press.

Abu-Nimer, M. (1999), *Dialogue, Conflict Resolution and Change: Arab-Jewish Encounters in Israel*. Albany, NY: State University of New York Press.

Adler, A. (1964), *Superiority and Social Interest: A Collection of Later Writings*. Evanston, IL: Northwestern University Press.

Adwan, S., Bar-Tal, D., and Wexler, B.E. (2016), 'Portrayal of the other in Palestinian and Israeli schoolbooks: A comparative study', *Political Psychology*, **37**(2), 201–217.

Aiken, M. (2018), 'Tales we tell', *Journal for and about Social Movements*, **10**(1–2), 170–195.

Alon, N. and Omer, H. (2006), *The Psychology of Demonization: Promoting Acceptance and Reducing Conflict*. Mahwah, NJ: Erlbaum.

Anderson, A.R. and Starnawska, M. (2008), 'Research practices in entrepreneurship: Problems of definition, description and meaning', *International Journal of Entrepreneurship and Innovation*, **9**(4), 221–230.

Assman, A. (2018), 'One land and three narratives: Palestinian sites of memory in Israel', *Memory Studies*, **11**(3), 287–300.

Austin, J., Stevenson, H., and Wei-Skillern, J. (2006), 'Social and commercial entrepreneurship: Same, different, or both?', *Entrepreneurship Theory and Practice*, **30**(1), 1–22.

Bar-On, D. and Adwan, S. (2009), *Learning Each Other's Historical Narratives*. PRIME.

Bar-Tal, D. (1996), 'Development of social categories and stereotypes in early childhood: The case of "the Arab" concept formation, stereotype and attitudes by Jewish children in Israel', *International Journal of Intercultural Relations*, **20**(3–4), 341–370.

Bar-Tal, D. (2000a), 'From intractable conflict through conflict resolution to reconciliation: Psychological analysis', *Political Psychology*, **21**(2), 351–365.

Bar-Tal, D. (2000b), 'Why does fear override hope in societies engulfed in intractable conflict, as it does in the Israeli society?', *Political Psychology*, **22**(3), 601–627.

Bar-Tal, D. (2007), 'Socio-psychological foundations of intractable conflicts', *American Behavioral Scientists*, **50**(11), 1430–1453.

Baron-Epel, O., Garty, N., and Green, M.S. (2007), 'Inequalities in use of health services among Jews and Arabs in Israel', *Health Services Research*, **42**, 1008–1019.

Bekerman, Z. (2018), 'Working towards peace through education: The case of Israeli Jews and Palestinians', *Asian Journal of Peacebuilding*, **6**(1), 75–98.

Ben David, Y. and Rubel-Lifschitz, T. (2018), 'Practice the change you want to see in the world: Transformative practices of social movements in Israel', *Peace and Conflict: Journal of Peace Psychology*, **24**(1), 10–18.

Ben-Ze'ev, E. and Yvroux, C. (2018), 'Palestine, Israel, Gaza, and the West Bank: The muddled mental maps of French and Israeli students', *Journal of Cultural Geography*, **35**(2), 189–209.

Bruner, J. (1986), *Actual Minds, Possible Worlds*. Cambridge, MA: Harvard University Press.

Bruner, J. (1987), 'Life as narrative', *Social Research*, **54**(1), 12–32.

Bruner, J. (1990), *Acts of Meaning*. Cambridge, MA: Harvard University Press.

Bruyat, C. and Julien, P.A. (2001), 'Defining the field of research in entrepreneurship', *Journal of Business Venturing*, **16**(2), 165–180.

Brynen, R. (2000), *A Very Political Economy: Peacebuilding and Foreign Aid in the West Bank and Gaza*. Washington, DC: United States Institute of Peace.

Certo, S.T. and Miller, T. (2008), 'Social entrepreneurship: Key issues and concepts', *Business Horizons*, **51**(4), 267–271.

Christopoulos, D. and Vogl, S. (2015), 'The motivation of social entrepreneurs: The roles, agendas and relations of altruistic economic actors', *Journal of Social Entrepreneurship*, **6**(1), 1–30.

Cope, J. and Watts, G. (2000), 'Learning by doing: An exploration of experience, critical incidents and reflection in entrepreneurial learning', *International Journal of Entrepreneurial Behavior and Research*, **6**(3), 104–124.

Dacin, M.T., Dacin, P.A., and Tracey, P. (2011), 'Social entrepreneurship: A critique and future directions', *Organization Science*, **22**(5), 1203–1213.

Dacin, P.A., Dacin, M.T., and Matear, M. (2010), 'Social entrepreneurship: Why we don't need a new theory and how we move forward from here', *Academy of Management Perspectives*, **24**(3), 37–57.

Downing, S. (2005), 'The social construction of entrepreneurship: Narrative and dramatic processes in the coproduction of organizations and identities', *Entrepreneurship Theory and Practice*, **29**(2), 185–204.

Feniger, Y., Mcdossi, O., and Ayalon, H. (2015), 'Ethno-religious differences in Israeli higher education: Vertical and horizontal dimensions', *European Sociological Review*, **31**(4), 383–396.

Forrer, J. (2010), 'Locating peace through commerce in good global governance', *Journal of Business Ethics*, **89**(4), 449–460.

Frankl, V.E. (1970), *The Will to Meaning*. New York: Noura Books.

Frankl, V.E. (2011), *The Unheard Cry for Meaning: Psychotherapy and Humanism*. New York: Simon and Schuster.

Gabay, R., Hameiri, B., Rubel-Lifschitz, T., and Nadler, A. (2020), 'The tendency for interpersonal victimhood: The personality construct and its consequences', *Personality and Individual Differences*, **165**, 110–134.

Galera, G. and Borzaga, C. (2009), 'Social enterprise: An international overview of its conceptual evolution and legal implementation', *Social Enterprise Journal*, **5**(3), 210–228.

Gartner, W.B. (1988), '"Who is an entrepreneur?" is the wrong question', *American Journal of Small Business*, **12**(4), 11–32.

Gartner, W.B. (1990), 'What are we talking about when we talk about entrepreneurship?', *Journal of Business Venturing*, **5**(1), 15–28.

Germak, A.J. and Robinson, J.A. (2014), 'Exploring the motivation of nascent social entrepreneurs', *Journal of Social Entrepreneurship*, **5**(1), 5–21.

Golan-Agnon, D. (2006), 'Separate but not equal: Discrimination against Palestinian Arab students in Israel', *American Behavioral Scientist*, **49**(8), 1075–1084.

Hallward, M.C. (2011), *Struggling for a Just Peace: Israeli and Palestinian Activism in the Second Intifada*. Gainesville, FL: University Press of Florida.

Halperin, E. (2014), 'Emotion, emotion regulation, and conflict resolution', *Emotion Review*, **6**(1), 68–76.

Halperin, E. (2016), *Emotions in Conflict: Inhibitors and Facilitators of Peace Making*. New York: Routledge.

Hameiri, B., Porat, R., Bar-Tal, D., Bieler, A., and Halperin, E. (2014), 'Paradoxical thinking as a new avenue of intervention to promote peace', *Proceedings of the National Academy of Sciences*, **111**(30), 10996–11001.

Hermann, T.S. (2009), *The Israeli Peace Movement: A Shattered Dream*. Cambridge: Cambridge University Press.

Kacowicz, A.M. (2005), 'Rashomon in the Middle East: Clashing narratives, images, and frames in the Israeli-Palestinian conflict', *Cooperation and Conflict*, **40**(3), 347.

Kahanoff, M. (2016), *Jews and Arabs in Israel Encountering Their Identities: Transformations in Dialogue*. New York: Rowman and Littlefield.

Kimmerling, B. (1983), *Zionism and Territory: The Socioterritorial Dimensions of Zionist Politics*. Berkeley, CA: University of California, Institute of International Studies.

Kimmerling, B. and Migdal, J.S. (2003), *The Palestinian People: A History*. Cambridge, MA: Harvard University Press.

Kriesberg, L. (1993), 'Intractable conflicts', *Peace Review*, **5**(4), 417–421.

Kuriansky, J. (2007), *Beyond Bullets and Bombs: Grassroots Peacebuilding between Israelis and Palestinians*. Santa Barbara, CA: Praeger.

Lehrs, L. (2016), 'Private peace entrepreneurs in conflict resolution processes', *International Negotiation*, **21**(3), 381–408.

Leshem, O.A. (2017), 'What you wish for is not what you expect: Measuring hope for peace during intractable conflicts', *International Journal of Intercultural Relations*, **60**, 60–66.

Leuenberger, C. and Schnell, I. (2020), *The Politics of Maps: Cartographic Constructions of Israel/Palestine*. Oxford: Oxford University Press.

Lieblich, A. (1987), *The Spring of Their Lives*. Tel Aviv: Shocken (in Hebrew).

Lieblich, A., Tuval-Mashiach, R., and Zilber, T. (1998), *Narrative Research: Reading, Analysis, and Interpretation* (Vol. 47). Newbury Park, CA: Sage.

Lieblich, A., Zilber, T., and Tuval-Mashiach, R. (1995), 'Search and find: Generalization and discrimination in life-stories', *Psychologia*, **5**(1), 84–95 (in Hebrew).

Lomsky-Feder, E. (1995), 'The meaning of war through veterans' eyes: Phenomenological analysis of life stories', *International Sociology*, **10**, 463–482.

Lomsky-Feder, E. (2004), 'Life stories, war and veterans: On the social distribution of memories', *Ethos*, **32**(1), 1–28.

Lomsky-Feder, E. and Sasson-Levy, O. (2016), 'The effects of military service on women's lives from the narrative perspective' in H. Carreiras, C. Castro, and S. Frederic (eds), *Researching the Military* (pp. 94–106). New York: Routledge.

Low, M.B. and MacMillan, I.C. (1988), 'Entrepreneurship: Past research and future challenges', *Journal of Management*, **14**(2), 139–161.

Mair, J. and Marti, I. (2006), 'Social entrepreneurship research: A source of explanation, prediction, and delight', *Journal of World Business*, **41**(1), 36–44.

Mair, J. and Noboa, E. (2006), 'Social entrepreneurship: How intentions to create a social venture are formed', in J. Mair, J. Robinson, and K. Hockerts (eds), *Social Entrepreneurship* (pp. 121–135). Basingstoke: Palgrave Macmillan.

Maoz, I. (2000), 'Power relations in intergroup encounters: A case study of Jewish Arab encounters in Israel', *International Journal of Intercultural Relations*, **24**, 259–277.

Maoz, I. (2011), 'Does contact work in protracted asymmetrical conflict? Appraising 20 years of reconciliation-aimed encounters between Israeli Jews and Palestinians', *Journal of Peace Research*, **48**(1), 115–125.

Martin, R.L. and Osberg, S. (2007), 'Social entrepreneurship: The case for definition', *Stanford Social Innovation Review*, **24**(2), 28–39.

McMullen, J.S. and Dimov, D. (2013), 'Time and the entrepreneurial journey: The problems and promise of studying entrepreneurship as a process', *Journal of Management Studies*, **50**(8), 1481–1512.

Melton, P.S. (ed.) (2008), *Sixty Years, Sixty Voices: Israeli and Palestinian Women*. Washington, DC: Peace X Peace.

Morgeson, F.P., Mitchell, T.R., and Liu, D. (2015), 'Event system theory: An event-oriented approach to the organizational sciences', *Academy of Management Review*, **40**(4), 515–537.

Morris, B. (2001), *Righteous Victims: A History of the Zionist–Arab Conflict, 1881–2001*. New York: Vintage.

Ochs, E. and Capps, L. (1996), 'Narrating the self', *Annual Review of Anthropology*, **25**, 19–43.

Or, I.G. and Shohamy, E. (2016), 'Asymmetries and inequalities in the teaching of Arabic and Hebrew in the Israeli educational system', *Journal of Language and Politics*, **15**(1), 25–44.

Owen, R. (2013), *State, Power and Politics in the Making of the Modern Middle East*. New York: Routledge.

Packard, M.D. (2017), 'Where did interpretivism go in the theory of entrepreneurship?', *Journal of Business Venturing*, **32**(5), 536–549.

Rabinowitz, D. (2001), 'The Palestinian citizens of Israel, the concept of trapped minority and the discourse of transnationalism in anthropology', *Ethnic and Racial Studies*, **24**(1), 64–85.

Rabinowitz, D. and Abu-Baker, K. (2005), *Coffins on Our Shoulders: The Experience of the Palestinian Citizens of Israel*. Berkeley, CA: University of California Press.

Rauch, A. and Frese, M. (2007), 'Let's put the person back into entrepreneurship research: A meta-analysis on the relationship between business owners' personality traits, business creation, and success', *European Journal of Work and Organizational Psychology*, **16**(4), 353–385.

Rosenwasser, O. (1995), *Voices from a 'Promised Land': Palestinian and Israeli Peace Activists Speak Their Hearts*. Windham, CT: Curbstone Press.

Rosenzweig, R. (2006). 'Can history be open source? Wikipedia and the future of the past', *Journal of American History*, **93**(1), 117–146.

Roth, S. (2016), 'Professionalisation and precariousness: Perspectives on the sustainability of activism in everyday life', *Interface: A Journal for and about Social Movements*, **8**(2), 29–58.

Saabneh, A.M. (2016), 'Arab-Jewish gap in life expectancy in Israel', *European Journal of Public Health*, **26**(3), 433–438.

Salinas, M.F. and Abu Rabi, H. (2009), *Resolving the Israeli-Palestinian Conflict: Perspectives on the Peace Process*. Amherst, NY: Cambria Press.

Semyonov, M. and Lewin-Epstein, N. (2011), 'Wealth inequality: Ethnic disparities in Israeli society', *Social Forces*, **89**(3), 935–959.

Shane, S. and Venkataraman, S. (2000), 'The promise of entrepreneurship as a field of research', *Academy of Management Review*, **25**(1), 217–226.

Shoshana, A. (2016), 'The language of everyday racism and micro-aggression in the workplace: Palestinian professionals in Israel', *Ethnic and Racial Studies*, **39**(6), 1052–1069.

Spector-Mersel, G. (2008a), *Sabras Don't Age: Life Stories of Senior Officers from 1948's Israeli Generation*. Jerusalem: Hebrew University Magnes Press.

Spector-Mersel, G. (2008b), 'The story of the identity or the identity of the story', *Shviley Mehkar*, **15**, 18–26 (in Hebrew).

Spector-Mersel, G. (2011), 'Mechanisms of selection in claiming narrative identities: A model for interpreting narratives', *Qualitative Inquiry*, **17**(2), 172–185.

Subedi, D.B. (2013), '"Pro-peace entrepreneur" or "conflict profiteer"? Critical perspective on the private sector and peacebuilding in Nepal', *Peace and Change*, **38**(2), 181–206.

Svirsky, M. (2012), *Arab-Jewish Activism in Israel-Palestine*. New York: Routledge.

Thiessen, C. and Darweish, M. (2018), 'Conflict resolution and asymmetric conflict: The contradictions of planned contact interventions in Israel and Palestine', *International Journal of Intercultural Relations*, **66**, 73–84.

Tuval-Mashiach, R. and Spector-Mersel, G. (2010), 'General introduction – narrative research: Definitions and contexts. In R. Tuval-Mashiach and G. Spector-Mersel (eds), *Narrative Research: Theory, Creation and Interpretation* (pp. 7–34). Tel Aviv: Mofet Institute (in Hebrew).

Van de Ven, A.H. and Engleman, R.M. (2004), 'Event-and outcome-driven explanations of entrepreneurship', *Journal of Business Venturing*, **19**(3), 343–358.

Venkataraman, S. (1997), 'The distinctive domain of entrepreneurship research', *Advances in Entrepreneurship, Firm Emergence and Growth*, **3**(1), 119–138.

Venuti, L. (2004), *The Translation Studies Reader*. New York: Routledge.

Vestergren, S.K., Drury, J., and Hammar Chiriac, E. (2019), 'How participation in collective action changes relationships, behaviours, and beliefs: An interview study of the role of inter- and intragroup processes', *Journal of Social and Political Psychology*, **7**(1), 76–99.

Wallach, Y. (2011), 'Trapped in mirror-images: The rhetoric of maps in Israel/ Palestine', *Political Geography*, **30**(7), 358–369.

Weerawardena, J. and Mort, G.S. (2006), 'Investigating social entrepreneurship: A multidimensional model', *Journal of World Business*, **41**(1), 21–35.

Wong, P.T. (2014), 'Viktor Frankl's meaning-seeking model and positive psychology', in A. Batthyany and P. Russo-Netzer (eds), *Meaning in Positive and Existential Psychology* (pp. 149–184). New York: Springer.

Yitshaki, R. and Kropp, F. (2016a), 'Motivations and opportunity recognition of social entrepreneurs', *Journal of Small Business Management*, **54**(2), 546–565.

Yitshaki, R. and Kropp, F. (2016b), 'Entrepreneurial passions and identities in different contexts: A comparison between high-tech and social entrepreneurs', *Entrepreneurship and Regional Development*, **28**(3–4), 206–233.

Zahra, S.A., Gedajlovic, E., Neubaum, D.O., and Shulman, J.M. (2009), 'A typology of social entrepreneurs: Motives, search processes and ethical challenges', *Journal of Business Venturing*, **24**(5), 519–532.

Zilber, T.B., Tuval-Mashiach, R., and Lieblich, A. (2008), 'The embedded narrative: Navigating through multiple contexts', *Qualitative Inquiry*, **14**(6), 1047–1069.

Index

Printed and bound by CPI Group (UK) Ltd, Croydon, CR0 4YY

16/04/2025

14658488-0002